INVISIBLE WOMEN:
A HISTORY OF WOMEN IN THE CHURCH

Sally Hogg

This book is dedicated to my parents: Muriel Hogg, who showed us how much a woman could achieve while 'keeping silent' and Eric Hogg, who supported her endeavours. It is also for my sister Christine, in gratitude for her help and encouragement.

CONTENTS

3

INTRODUCTION:

I grew up in an Open Brethren Church in the middle years of the 20th century.   Each Sunday morning the church met for a breaking of bread (communion) service.   The Brethren believe in 'the Priesthood of all believers' and at this service it was open to anyone to read or expound scripture, pray or announce a hymn.   However 'anyone' was clearly understood to mean any man.   It was the role of women to sit quietly; their prayers had to be silent and if they wished the congregation to hear a passage of scripture or sing a particular hymn then the only way they could do this was by prompting their husband. Those who were unmarried did not even have this option.   Week after week gifted women sat in silence listening to men, not all them equally gifted.   Women could only speak in public to other women or children, and then only if no man was present.   Week after week my sisters and I sat listening to an elderly man drone on about Leviticus; for some reason he felt every Communion service should start with an exposition on Jewish religious sacrifices.   He was the most predictable speaker but there were a couple of others who rivalled him in dullness.   We amused ourselves by reading the Bible.   I usually read Ruth and Esther, which dealt with the adventures of young women.   My younger sister, always more adventurous, read Ecclesiastes.

Women were also required to have their heads covered during services in obedience to Paul's words to the women in Corinth.   (This verse actually referred to women praying or prophesying so should not have applied to women who were not permitted to do either.)   In practice women wore smart hats, an example of following the letter not the spirit.   Women accepted these restrictions with grace.   There was no rebellion, although a few women left to find a church more willing to use their gifts. Some women did make their views known. I can remember my Mother pointing out publicly that people with two hands are able to do far more than people with only one and that the church was handicapping itself by failing to use half its members fully. However, she continued to sit in silence each Sunday, although she was involved in public speaking in other settings. As a child I took this for granted and accepted that it was the way things were and ordained by Scripture. The Brethren believed they had returned to an organisation based on the practices of the early church: they had a lay leadership, no formal Ministers, and no formal inter-church structure, except to support missionaries sent out by the 'Assemblies' (as Brethren churches were generally known). Brethren meetings focussed on the Breaking of Bread or on evangelism, to which they gave a high priority. Brethren were noted for their knowledge of the Bible, which they saw as the ultimate authority. Their ideas on the role of women were based on St Paul and were felt to have the authority of Scripture behind them.

As a teenager I knew there were exceptions, women who were able to teach and preach and take responsibility for leadership. But these women were safely overseas. At that time the Brethren sent out more missionaries than any other denomination and a large percentage of their missionaries were women. Overseas these women faced difficulties and challenges often working in pioneering situations and with large responsibilities. However, when they returned to Britain they could only speak about their experiences to other women. After they retired they too had to keep silent.

My church was not exceptional; only a few denominations at that time allowed women to preach or to be ministers and in this the church was reflecting society. The women, who had rallied round and joined the services or worked in factories during the Second World War, had been banished back to their homes when peace came. Working class women returned to 'women's jobs' involving caring or cleaning. Middle class women who couldn't, or wouldn't, stay at home worked in 'suitable' jobs or in a voluntary capacity. It was unusual for married women to work, but most voluntary organisations depended on women volunteers to carry out tasks at every level except, usually, senior management; the public face of most organisations in the fifties was male. As I grew up I knew that in most fields my gender put my friends and myself at a disadvantage in the job market. To get a senior position women generally had to demonstrate they were not just better than any male candidate for the post but at least twice as good. Instead we were expected to get 'suitable' jobs as secretaries, teachers, nurses or social workers; careers where the majority of workers were women.

In the last half of the 20th century Women's Liberation and other social movements have led to changes in the opportunities given to women and these changes have been reflected in the church. The Church has always been influenced by ideas of its time. Each generation interprets the Bible in the light of its own preoccupations and attitudes. Sometimes this reveals newly discovered or long forgotten truths; but it can lead to a distortion of Christian belief. No one can fail to be influenced by society around them but it is not easy to recognise the basic assumptions about the world we take for granted and which govern our ideas and actions. These assumptions are fed into the minds of everyone, including Christians, by education, the media and the people around us. C.S. Lewis commented on this in an essay on reading old books, especially theology books.

"Every age has its own outlook. It is especially good at seeing certain truths and specially liable to make certain mistakes. We all, therefore, need the books that will correct the characteristic mistakes of our own period. And that means the old books. All contemporary writers share to some extent the contemporary outlook, even those, like myself, who seem most opposed to it. Nothing strikes me more when I read the controversies of past ages than the fact that both sides were usually assuming without question a good deal which we should now absolutely deny. They thought that they were as completely opposed as two sides could be, but in fact they were all the time secretly united – united with each other and against earlier and later ages by a great mass of common assumptions."

For generations religious groups that accepted women in leadership roles were regarded as 'unsound'. Now this situation is reversed in the west, in the eyes of the secular world, and many Christians; it is groups who keep women in a subservient role that are seen as unacceptable.

The Church is slow to change and is nearly always a conservative force in society. It has been said that the Church has the brakes of a Juggernaut and the acceleration of a lawn mower. But even the most conservative accept change over time, and the pace of change in the Church has speeded up in the twentieth century; reflecting the increasing pace of change in a wider society. When I was young I accepted that scripture limited the role of women in the church; although I was less accepting of limitations put on women in secular society; my parents' attitudes and example encouraged me to question them. I was one of many who changed their opinion towards the end of the twentieth century. Bible study and reading works by scholars who have studied to understand what the Bible really said in its original context played an important part in this change of mind.

As I came to believe that women had had a more active role in the early church than I had been taught, I became interested to know how and when this had changed. Christianity's founder accepted women disciples and even sent a woman to tell his disciples the news of his resurrection. How had the faith he founded ended up as a religion which demanded women keep silent? How had the Church of which St Paul wrote "There is neither Jew nor Greek, slave nor free, male nor female, for you are all one in Christ Jesus" become a patriarchal organisation which has sometimes had an inflated view of the value of status and wealth? This book has grown out of my attempt to find answers to these questions in church history; starting in New Testament times and continuing to the present.

Contemporary sources on the earliest Christians are few and are not easy to date; they are often the subject of scholarly arguments. I have regarded the Bible as the oldest and most reliable source available on the early years of Christianity. There are more contemporary sources available for later centuries but they vary in number and quality. In times of instability documents are destroyed, others were lost in the days before printing because no one cared enough to copy them. Documents by, or about, women, were considered unimportant and most have failed to survive. Although there are far more original sources available for later periods few deal with the lives of ordinary

Christian women. When possible I have focussed on the lives of individual women, whose lives exemplified, or contrasted with, the experience of women of their time.

I have tried to consult original sources when possible but I am indebted to many contemporary writers. My debt is greatest to those scholars who in the last twenty years have started to unearth the facts about the 'invisible' women who have lived and sought to serve God, often in difficult circumstances, over the past two thousand years.

1. JESUS, PAUL AND WOMEN

Chesterton wrote a story about an 'invisible' man.   He was not a
figure of fantasy hidden by magic or by a science fiction device but
someone who was so much part of the expected scenery that no one
noticed him.   In history books, until recently, women have been
invisible, their presence taken for granted but rarely mentioned.
History has been mostly 'his story'.   Exceptions have always been
those few women whose status or wealth made it impossible to ignore
them.   A modern example of this tendency to take the presence of
women for granted might be a newspaper report on a City dinner
giving the names of only those considered prominent enough to
deserve a mention.   Unless the Queen was present, all of the
individuals mentioned might be men; yet an equal number of women
would have attended, many in their own right not just as the partners
of male guests.

A similar editing of reality happened in first century Palestine.   In the
New Testament women are only mentioned when they are intrinsic to
the story, in other situations they are treated as invisible.   The
assumption that only men were present at times when women are not
specifically mentioned distorts our understanding of the Gospels.
The part women played in the ministry of Jesus has been consistently
underestimated.

Feminists who are critical of the church and of St Paul find it difficult
to include Jesus in their condemnation.   As we read the Gospels we

see in Jesus a person who did not accept his contemporaries' assumptions about women. He used parables based on women's everyday experiences to illustrate his teachings. He spoke with women, even ones of dubious reputation, and his concern for individuals led him into unconventional situations that offended 'respectable' people. He touched and healed a woman whose illness had made her ceremonially unclean for many years. He saved a woman who had committed adultery from the death prescribed by Jewish Law. It is difficult for the modern reader to understand just how revolutionary Jesus was in the way he spoke to and valued women and how strongly contemporary Jewish teachers would have condemned his behaviour.

Women disciples

When Christ walked the roads of Palestine he was accompanied not only by the Twelve but also by a group of women. Only Luke mentions them in his record of Jesus' life as an itinerant teacher/healer; although both Matthew and Mark confirm their presence, when recording that they were present at the crucifixion. (Luke 8: 1, Matthew 27: 55, Mark 15: 40-41). There is also a mention of Jesus explaining one of his parables 'when he was alone' to 'the twelve and the others around him' (Mark 4:10). These others must have included the women who travelled with him and were part of what would now be called his team.

It is clear that Jesus had female disciples. We are told that Mary, the sister of Martha and Lazarus, 'sat at his feet' (Luke 10:39). In other instances in the Bible this term is used specifically to describe a rabbi/disciple relationship. Her sister Martha is generally pictured as

13

burdened with practical responsibilities, but she also showed that she had been listening and observing. Martha was one of the few who acknowledged that Jesus was the Messiah and Son of God during his lifetime.

There is one clear example of how the Gospel writers shielded their women from public attention. Matthew and Mark both tell of an incident where a woman anointed the Lord's head and feet with expensive perfume. They record Christ's words about her "When she poured this perfume on my body, she did it to prepare me for burial. I tell you the truth, wherever this Gospel is preached throughout the world what she has done will also be told in memory of her". (Matthew 26:6 – 13, Mark 14:3 – 9). Despite Christ's words, Matthew and Mark leave the woman anonymous. It is only John, who identifies her as Mary of Bethany, who demonstrated by her actions that she, unlike the male disciples, had understood the Lord's words about his coming death. (John 12: 1 –8)

Crucifixion and resurrection

One indication of the Gospel writers' concern to give a true record is the account they give of Jesus' death. It shows his disciples, the men who would go on to lead the early church, in a poor light. One of his friends betrayed him to the authorities and another publicly denied knowing him. His male disciples fled in fear when he was arrested. Only the women, and John, followed Jesus to the place of his execution. At the end of that terrible day, when Jesus had been hastily placed in a borrowed tomb, Mary Magdalene and another Mary were still there, sitting opposite the tomb watching and grieving.

It was women who were instrumental in making the resurrection known. As they were going before dawn to the tomb, the guards were going in the opposite direction, to report to the Chief Priest. If it hadn't been for these women the authorities would have had time to react to the events of the night and hush them up (Matthew 28: 11 – 15). Most telling of all, Jesus ignored Jewish tradition, which said a woman could not be a reliable witness, and sent Mary Magdalene as 'an apostle to the apostles' to tell them the astonishing news. As typical Jewish men they did not take her report seriously; although Peter and John did go to check it out for themselves.

Women and Christ's commission

One of the difficulties for people on both sides of the contemporary debate on women's ordination was the fact that there is no record of Christ 'ordaining' his disciples. The nearest equivalents were two occasions after the resurrection. The first was when Christ came to his disciples, who were hiding behind locked doors, and, after reassuring them that he was alive, commissioned them. We do not know for certain if women were present on this occasion but it seems unlikely that the men who followed Jesus would have locked themselves away leaving the women associated with him unprotected. The second occasion was a few weeks later, on the day of Pentecost when the Holy Spirit came down with tongues of fire; transforming a group of frightened men and women, into a force who would 'turn the world upside down'. Christ commissioned all his followers to preach the Gospel not just the men.

Jesus versus Paul?

Recently it has been suggested that the Apostle Paul distorted the pure teaching of Jesus, and created the 'institution' of Christianity. Anger with Paul has been strong among feminists, who see him as the villain of the piece; the originator of all the restrictions the church has put on women.

Jesus' and Paul's words originated in very different circumstances: Jesus was teaching devout Jews about the Kingdom of God, to prepare them for his coming death and resurrection; Paul was looking back on these events and laying out their implications for a mainly gentile audience, with no grounding in the Old Testament. The way they presented their message was also different; they were using different media. Jesus was talking to large crowds in the open air. His hearers were mainly oral learners, who have a great capacity to remember and repeat what they have heard, but only if it is presented in the right way. They need pithy, memorable phrases and stories with a narrative and this is what Jesus gave them. Paul on the other hand was writing letters, which did not need to be memorised, they could be read and re-read. Paul was also a theologian, he had undergone the lengthy training of a Jewish Rabbi, and he writes as a theologian, striving to understand the underlying concepts of his new faith. Inevitably his work has been the foundation of much of the church's theology and practice. But there is no evidence that his contemporaries, who included the Apostles, felt he was changing the Christian message.

The texts that have been cited through the ages to justify keeping women silent come from Paul's letters. Christians who believe in the authority of the Bible have always had to decide which commands are still applicable and which were intended for their original readers and are either no longer relevant or require each generation to find the underlying principle to apply. This dilemma is at the heart of the debate over the Pauline texts that have for so long restricted Christian women.

Women in the Apostolic church

Women played a significant part in the early days of the church. They had a central role in evangelising and in the pastoral care of women. Unlike the Apostles they could go into private households and speak directly to the women there. The large number of women converts in the early church must have been a result of the enthusiasm and dedication of these women. If Paul really intended to teach that women should be passive recipients of Christianity his actions contradicted his words. He acknowledged Phoebe as a deacon; Lydia took a leading part in the church he started at Philippi; he encouraged Priscilla to teach Apollos. St John Chrysostom, speaking in the fourth century, said of Priscilla: "She took charge of Apollos, an eloquent man, taught him the way of God and turned him into a perfect teacher". In the last chapter of Romans Paul greeted those he knew in that City. A third of the friends and fellow workers mentioned are women. He specifically commends four of them for their hard work in the Gospel, an indication of how involved women were in the spread of Christianity in the first century.

Some historians and commentators have tried to explain away any references to women in Paul's letters that do not fit their patriarchal view of the early church. One of the most embarrassing references for them is Junias who Paul describes as an apostle (Romans 16: 7). Junias is a woman's name and for centuries commentators accepted this. St John Chrysostom refers to Junias as woman; Matthew Henry, the puritan divine, writing in the early eighteenth century, mentions that 'some consider they were man and wife'. But Victorian commentators insisted Junias must be a man; since it was clear to them that no woman could be an apostle, and this idea became generally accepted. The New Bible Commentary, published in the middle of the last century, describes both Andronicus and Junias as kinsmen of Paul with no mention of even the possibility that Junias was a woman.

The fact that women could pray and prophecy during worship and could host a church is less surprising when you consider the reality of the early church. Today the word 'church' brings to mind either a building or a national, or international, institution. But in the early centuries of Christianity the word had only one meaning. For Paul, his contemporaries and his immediate successors a 'church' was not a building or an organisation but a group of people. Christianity was an illicit religion so early churches were based in private homes or large households. Meeting in homes meant that the line between private and public places was blurred. Women could take part in worship without scandalising their hearers, since they were in a private house not a public place.

Women played a significant part in the gospel story and in the early days of the church. They had a central role in evangelising other women and in their pastoral care. Unlike the Apostles they could go into the hidden world of women's households and speak directly to them. The large number of women converts in the early church must have been due to the enthusiasm and dedication of these women.

2. THE WORLD WHERE CHRISTIANITY WAS BORN

To appreciate how revolutionary Jesus' attitude was; and to see the early church in its contemporary context, it is necessary to examine the assumptions and beliefs of the people who became the first Christians. The basic assumptions of the people living in the Roman Empire were very different from our own. This chapter looks back at the cultures and experiences that had influenced first century attitudes to women, especially among Jews.

The Romans and the Greeks were the two races who dominated power, politics and philosophical thought in the ancient world when Christianity was born; but they were not the only foreign cultures that influenced the Jewish people. They were part of a series of cultures that had influenced the development of Jewish society and thought, starting with the Egyptians who had enslaved them and later the Canaanites, who lived among and around them.

Women in Assyria, Babylon and Persia

In 597 and 586 BC the inhabitants of Judea, were conquered and taken into captivity by the Babylonians just as 156 years earlier Israel had been taken into captivity by the Assyrians. The Babylonians like the Assyrians had a ruthless method of dealing with subject peoples; they decapitated societies by deporting the nobility, the educated and the skilled. During the almost seventy years of Jewish exile the Babylonians were in turn conquered by the Persians. Cyrus, the Persian who conquered Babylon, followed a policy of encouraging the repatriation of the peoples captured by the Assyrians and Babylonians and allowed many of the Jews to return to Palestine, where they remained under Persian rule.

The Assyrians, Babylonians and Persians had a collective view of people, seeing them as elements in a family or tribe not as individuals. If a man committed a serious crime, especially against the King, his whole family would be killed with him. Legally women were part of a family unit with no rights of their own. In Assyria adultery was a crime against the husband, while male unfaithfulness was accepted as normal. The punishment for ravishing a virgin might be prostituting the offender's wife. They saw this no doubt as 'making the punishment fit the crime'. A man who had damaged the property of another man, his daughter, would have had his own property, his wife, degraded in turn. Women were treated as property not people.

We get a glimpse of a woman in Persian society in the book of Esther. The King, after a week-long party, was drunk enough to demand that his wife should parade herself before his companions so they could admire her beauty. Normally no man but the King would see her – she was attended by eunuchs. Queen Vashti refused and this enraged her husband. When he consulted his advisors about what action to take and they replied "Not only has Queen Vashti done wrong to the king but also to all the officials and all the peoples who are in all the provinces of King Ahasuerus. For this deed of the Queen will be made known to all women, causing them to look with contempt on their husbands. This very day the noble ladies of Persia and Media who have heard of the Queen's behaviour will rebel against the King's officials and there will be no end of contempt and wrath." Queen Vashti's action in not obeying an order that offended against all custom was seen as an attack on the very fabric of society. As a result she lost her position as queen. It is no wonder that her successor, Queen Esther, was very wary of making demands on her husband.

The Jews under Greek rulers

Palestine remained under Persian rule until, in 333 BC, Alexander of Macedon defeated the Persians and established Greek rule in what had been the Persian Empire. Greek Empires, ruled by descendants of Alexander the Great's generals, dominated the Middle East and North Africa for several centuries. The Greeks, confident in the superiority of their own culture, encouraged their subject peoples to adopt Greek attitudes and customs. Greeks saw themselves as superior in every way to 'barbarians', i.e. all other races, and they introduced the Greek way of life to the territories they conquered. Greek rulers did not normally oppose local religious beliefs, instead they assimilated local fertility gods into their own pantheon, identifying them with their own gods and allowing local patterns of worship to continue. This system didn't fit the Jews, whose monotheistic religion was incompatible with the worship of pagan gods.

Women in Greek society

In the Greek culture women were largely confined to the home and had no part in public life. Respectable women in classical Greece had formal rights as citizens but no freedom at all; foreign women in contrast had no rights at all but considerable freedom and were sometimes well educated. Wives and daughters had no more civil rights than slaves and were only educated to manage a household.

Xenophon, writing around 400 BC described his ideal Greek bride "trained from childhood to see and hear as little as possible and ask an absolute minimum of questions". Women in Greece did have some role in religious life especially in cults focused on a goddess. They walked in religious processions and could be prophetesses. The Prophets of Apollo were often women; as were the famous Delphic Oracles. A less palatable role was that of the women attached to temples as temple prostitutes. It is important to remember that the social 'rules' about women and the protection they were given in Greek culture only applied to those with some status and not to the poor or to slaves, who were not protected in any way from the actions of their owner; although his 'property rights' protected them from any ill treatment to which he had not consented.

In Greece the political unit was the city and different cities varied in their customs. Unlike Athenians Spartans encouraged their women to be more active in public, including taking part in sports. The reason for this was their emphasis on eugenics; they wanted strong women in order to produce strong men. In Macedonia women, at least those with wealth and position had more freedom. Macedonian queens were given responsibilities, sometimes ruling in their husband's absence, and Macedonian women could be involved in business.

Legal rules do not always signify as much about the way a society works as might be supposed. When we look at Greek literature we see a more complex situation than their laws imply. Sophocles's play Antigone can be seen as an exploration of the role of women. Antigone, the heroine, chose to obey what she saw as the law of the gods, rather than the law of Creon, the man who had authority over her as her guardian and king. When she has disobeyed his orders and buried the brother who had died fighting against their city, she told him:

"I did not think your edicts strong enough
To overrule the unwritten unalterable laws
Of God and heaven, you being only a man."

Sophocles contrasts Antigone with her more conventional sister Ismene:

"O think, Antigone; we are women; it is not for us
To fight against men; our rulers are stronger than we
And we must obey in this, or in worse than this.
May the dead forgive me I can do no other
But as I am commanded; to do more is madness."

Sophocles appeared to agree with both women. The play makes it clear that he believed Antigone was obeying a higher law and that Creon was at fault. Yet he also portrayed her actions as leading to 'madness' and several deaths, including her own. The subservience imposed on women, did not necessarily always reflect reality; but the assumption was that if a woman acted independently her actions could only have negative consequences, even if she was in the right.

In Asia Minor (now Turkey) the patriarchal Greek system was imposed on a society that had originally been matrilineal in its organisation. Underlying attitudes lingered, especially in religious matters. The temples of goddesses were very powerful in some cities and priestesses were highly placed in their cults. In the first century a high priestess was in charge of the great Temple of Artemis in Ephesus, one of the wonders of the ancient world.

The Jewish people were encouraged, and at times pressured, to adopt Greek customs. Some Jews, especially from the upper classes, conformed but generally Jews resisted elements of Greek culture; especially their religious ideas and their custom of reinforcing the power of rulers by identifying them as gods. However corruption was rife and the high priestly office was sold to the highest bidder. Among pious Jews hostility to the government grew. Eventually Emperor Antiochus IV (175 –164 BC) determined to destroy the Jewish religion, which he saw as the focus of opposition to his rule. He persecuted devout Jews cruelly and transformed the Temple into a pagan shrine to Zeus. The result was the Maccabaean revolt, which established Jewish national independence.

The Power of Rome

Jewish independence was partly achieved with the support of Rome, a rising power, which was beginning to flex its muscles in the east. Israel was ruled by kings descended from the Maccabaeus family. Most of them were despotic rulers; an exception was the only Queen. Salome, the widow of a King, reigned after his death for nine years; she brought peace, both within Judah and with neighbouring countries, and her reign was remembered as a 'golden age'.

In 63 BC Pompey entered Jerusalem, at the invitation of a rival claimant for the Judean throne, and took over the country. Judah was now subject to Rome and they appointed an man who was Jewish by religion, but not race, to rule on their behalf. After his death his son persuaded Rome to make him King. He is known as Herod the Great and he ruled Israel at the time of Jesus' birth. His reign was characterised by an ambitious building programme and his determination to hang on to power at all costs. Despite his marriage to a princess of the previous dynasty, many Jews did not accept Herod

25

and paranoia became his predominant trait.   This was the political situation into which Jesus was born; a country ruled by a despotic and cruel King of dubious legitimacy; a king who ruled as puppet of a Roman Government that counted Israel as part of their vast Empire and stationed an occupying force there.

We call the world in which Christianity was born the Roman world. Rome was the sole superpower, dominating much of the known world. Romans ruled from North Africa to remote Britain by the might of their armies; they built forts, civic buildings, temples and straight roads for their legions.   Rome was interested in a material empire not in a cultural or spiritual one.   Rather than challenge local gods they followed the Greek pattern and identified them with their own pantheon of gods.   In Palestine, however, they worked with the High Priests and accepted the worship of Yahweh as a legal religion. Despite the political power of Rome the dominant cultural influence in much of the Empire was still Greek and Greek culture and language permeated it.   Greek, not Latin, was the lingua franca in the eastern Empire; the New Testament was written in Greek.

Women in Roman Society

The words for 'virtue' in both Greek and Latin are based on the word for 'man'.   For the Greeks and Romans goodness and worth were so bound up with masculinity that they couldn't be separated; to them the idea of a virtuous woman was almost a contradiction in terms.   They did recognise virtue in individual women but honoured them as exceptions to a general rule that women were morally weak.

Roman women of standing had a more public profile than those in Greek society and there are many instances of women running their own businesses. In reading Acts and the Epistles we need to be aware that the situation for women could be different in different cities. It is significant that, of the two women who are most prominent in Acts, Priscilla was from Rome and Lydia lived in Philippi, a Macedonian town and a Roman colony, settled by retired soldiers. The words of Paul that have been used to restrict women were in letters written to Greek cities, Corinth and Ephesus.

Women in Jewish society

Jewish resistance had preserved their monotheistic worship but there was less resistance to attitudes and customs that did not conflict with their faith. Jews absorbed many Greek social assumptions, including those towards women. A Jewish man prayed every day; giving thanks that he had not been born a woman, a Gentile, or a slave. At this time a Jewish woman had little more status than a slave; both were bound to obey a master or husband and neither of them were regarded as reliable enough to give uncorroborated evidence in a court of law. Women rarely inherited property but did have a right of maintenance by a father or husband. Marriages were arranged. At twelve and a half, when she came of age, a girl might have some right of choice, but most parents pre-empted this by a binding betrothal at an earlier age. As a minor a girl was under her father's authority, after marriage she was under her husband's. Although some women might have responsibilities outside the home, their prime responsibility was bearing and raising children. Motherhood was greatly valued in Jewish society and Jewish identity is inherited through the maternal line. Throughout the Bible a woman without children was seen as a woman from whom God's blessing had been withheld.   We do not know how common divorce was in Palestine but legally it was fairly simple for a man to divorce his wife if he wished, but extremely difficult for a woman to initiate a divorce.

Foreign attitudes seem to have influenced the status given to Jewish women in religious life.   Herod's temple had a separate Court of Women; excluding them from the entrance to the inner court of the priests, which Jewish men could approach.   In this it did not follow the Tabernacle, whose structural plan was the original on which all Jewish Temples were based.   Jewish Priests were male and in Exodus it was the males who were required to "appear before the Lord God" (Exodus 23:17), but several passages indicate that women were involved in religious events.   "When all Israel comes to appear before the Lord your God at the place he will choose, you shall read this law before them in their hearing.   Assemble the people – men, women and children, and the aliens living in your towns – so they can listen and learn to fear the Lord your God and follow carefully all the words of this law."   (Deuteronomy 31: 9 – 12)   Jewish religion was inclusive; women, children and even resident aliens, many of whom would have been slaves, were free to join in worship.   Proverbs gives a picture of a woman that indicates women would have had more freedom in Old Testament times.   The virtuous wife, who was valued 'above rubies', was involved in business as well as in caring for her husband, children and household.   (Proverbs 31:10-31).

After the Exile Jews established Synagogues; local buildings where the Law could be read and studied and they could worship God. Synagogues were an inspired innovation.   They gave a local focus for worship and study of the Law; by the first century there were

Synagogues even in Jerusalem itself. The synagogues probably explain why by the first century pagan influences were no longer a major problem in Judaism. Synagogues were the power base of the Pharisees, who were strict adherents of the Law, which they interpreted in minute detail. The Temple was controlled by the Sadducees, the party of the Jewish aristocracy who collaborated with the Roman authorities. There are a number of inscriptions, the earliest dating from a generation before Jesus' birth and others from the following centuries, which refer to a woman having an official role in a Synagogue. The titles applied to women in these inscriptions include Leader, Elder, Priest and Mother of the Synagogue. They are traditionally interpreted as honorary rather than reflecting a real function; although feminist scholars dispute this.

The teachings of the Jewish Rabbis are preserved in the Mishnah, which records the oral teaching of Rabbis before the third century and gives details of their decisions and tenets. The party of the Sadducees died with the destruction of the temple in 70 AD but the Pharisees continued and after the fall of Jerusalem established rules and patterns of religious life for Jewish communities. Although the Mishnah was written around 200 AD it is based on earlier sources and traditions and undoubtedly reflects attitudes that were current in the first century. Rabbinic teaching about women varies; some Rabbis excluded them from religious life but others were less strict. Weekly attendance at Synagogues was not compulsory for women, as it was for men. In theory a woman could read the Torah in the synagogue but in practice this was probably not allowed. One of the sayings in the Mishnah is that 'women did not read the Torah out of respect for the congregation'. A few learned women who had studied the Law are mentioned.

At the other extreme a story is told about Rabbi Eliezer who was asked by a pious woman to teach her the Law. His reply was 'It is better that the words of the Law should be burnt than that they should be given to a woman'. On another occasion the same Rabbi said 'If a man gives his daughter a knowledge of the Law it is as though he has taught her lechery'. Some rabbis even discouraged talking to women; one said "He that talks much with women brings evil upon himself and neglects the study of the Law and at last will inherit Gehenna". Most Rabbis did not think women should be given an opportunity to learn and taught that they should limit their teaching to instructing their children.

This chapter has looked at attitudes and beliefs about women in the ancient world. It was in this patriarchal setting that Jesus lived and taught and which makes his attitude to women so outstanding. It was also the settling in which the first leaders of the church, the writers of the New Testament and later the Early Church Fathers, grew up. It was a world where women were generally restricted in what they could do and to whom they could speak; a world where women had few civil rights and were not regarded as rational beings.

3. WOMEN IN AN UNDERGROUND CHURCH

In this chapter we will be looking at opportunities offered to women by an informally run and illicit religion. There is plenty of evidence for some positions women held in the early church; for others, especially the possibility that women acted as presbyters (elders or priests), the evidence either way is unclear. In view of the prevailing attitudes toward women in the Greco-Roman world, and the general disapproval of them taking any role outside the home, many have thought it is unlikely that women were allowed to take any prominent role in the church. For this reason many commentators have explained away references to women that do not fit their preconceptions.

The Didache

There is one early document that may date back to the period in which the New Testament books were being written or even earlier. The Didache or, to give its full title, 'The teachings of the Lord through the Twelve Apostles to the Gentiles' is an early set of instructions on the Christian life. It is generally dated to the early second century but more recently it has been suggested that it may date, in oral or written form, from as early as 50 AD. One claim is that it arose from the meeting Paul had with Peter, James and the Jerusalem Elders to discuss the implications of the conversion of Gentiles and whether Gentiles should be asked to conform to Jewish religious Laws (Acts 15: 6 – 29). The Didache appears to be a step by step programme for teaching gentile converts, so it would fit this supposition. It also regulates the behaviour of visiting apostles and prophets; making it clear that any who exploit fellow Christians for material gain should be regarded as false teachers. At this time the 'test' for true prophets was a moral rather than a theological one.

There are several aspects of the Didache that touch on the issue of women in the church. One is that it is not gender specific; the literary convention in Jewish writings is to direct teaching to 'my son'; yet the Didache is addressed to 'my child'. It is clear that the convert who is to be mentored according to the pattern laid down may be male or female. Another significant piece of evidence is negative. It has been pointed out that nothing in the Didache restricted the roles women could take in churches. It seems the authors of the Didache felt no need to impose limits on what women could do.

Throughout church history there have been occasions when women have been allowed to extend their responsibilities because necessity has demanded it. If there are too few men to undertake leadership tasks, women may be given an opportunity to take up these responsibilities; this happens especially in rapidly expanding organisations based on the exercise of charismatic gifts. The early church fitted this pattern; it was a fast growing, Spirit led organisation with a preponderance of women. This process can also be seen in other times and places during the history of the church.

In Apostolic times the followers of the Way, (the term they used of themselves) looked to see who was of good character and full of the Spirit and then would lay hands on them to dedicate them to a task. There is evidence that some of the people chosen in this way by the early churches were women.

Women Prophets

Women prophets were common in the apostolic church and this continued for as long as prophecy was valued and encouraged. Prophecy was not generally about foretelling the future but was a form of teaching about the nature of God. Philip, the evangelist mentioned in Acts, had four daughters who were prophets. Paul accepted women prophets; when writing to the rather disorderly Corinthian church he is concerned not to stop them prophesying, but to ensure that when they prophesied they should wear a veil, to denote their respectability. Requiring that women cover their heads is common in a number of religions, including Hinduism. Muslims go further and insist the whole body is covered. Orthodox Jewish women wear a head covering or a wig rather than show their own hair to anyone but their husband. Although the practice of wearing hats to church has died out, some Christian groups still demand that women cover their heads; though they do not necessarily allow them to pray or prophesy.

The Order of Widows

Widows were one of the most vulnerable groups in the ancient world, especially childless widows. In a society where women had little power and were under the authority of male relatives there were few opportunities for an impoverished widow to support herself. We know from the book of Acts that from the very beginning the church provided meals for destitute Christian widows. In the close knit community that grew up in Jerusalem among the followers of Christ the better off were prepared to share with those in need. At this time there does not seem to be any special role for widows. However, by the time 1 Timothy was written the role of widows had been defined: those with close family should depend on the family for support; those who were young enough to remarry were encouraged to do so and excluded from the list of those for whom the church accepted responsibility.   In return for support widows had responsibilities within the church, especially in prayer.

Deacons and Deaconesses

Women deacons date back to New Testament times.   Paul described Phoebe as a deacon (not as a deaconess).   In 1 Timothy there is a list which appears to be of the qualities required in women deacons: although, since in Greek the same word is used for women and wives, it can be interpreted as referring to the wives of male deacons. If this list of qualities is intended to be for deacon's wives it is puzzling that there is no similar instruction for the wives of Elders; the qualities/qualifications of Elders are listed in the same way as those of deacons.   Since we know women deacons existed in New Testament times it seems more likely that "women likewise must be serious, not slanderers, but temperate, faithful in all things" refers not to wives but to women deacons.   'Likewise' in this verse is a direct echo of the earlier instruction about the qualities required in male deacons.

In the early second century Pliny described the interrogation, under torture, of two deaconesses from a local church.   He makes no mention of male leaders, which could mean there were none, or that the male leaders had fled to safety leaving the deaconesses in charge. It is clear that women deacons were an accepted part of the church in the first few centuries. Their main, but possibly not only, functions were with their fellow women. This would fit with the customs in Greco-Roman society where a man would not have access to women, other than their own household. Women's lives centred on their own households and receiving unrelated male visitors was unacceptable.

Consecrated virgins

Paul had encouraged those who felt able to be celibate not to marry. A tradition grew up in the next century of consecrated virgins; unmarried women who dedicated their life to God rather than seeking marriage and a family. The origins of this practice may have been partly practical. The physical vulnerability of young boys, which until recently led to a disproportionate death rate in infancy, has meant that in most societies throughout history more women have survived infancy, if they were allowed to do so. Every society has had to find some way of dealing with 'surplus' women. (This may well have been a reason why ancient Judaism, like Islam, allowed polygamy.) Greco-Roman society had a simple solution to this problem - infanticide. When a Roman baby was born the midwife put it on the floor so the Paterfamilias, the head of the family, most often the baby's grandfather, could decide if he wished to accept the infant into his family. Doubtless most rejected children were girls, though this practice would also have deprived those with an obvious disability of a chance of life. Infanticide of girl babies has been common in many cultures. (When a one child policy was introduced in China many families took steps to ensure that their one child was a son. A whole generation of women was lost and a lack of potential wives is causing problems now. It is estimated there is now a surplus of forty million men in China. In India feticide – aborting females before birth - has become a common practice since it became possible to discover the sex of an unborn child. The high cost of dowries, demanded by the bridegroom's family, which can impoverish a girl's family is driving this but it is leading to a similarly unbalanced society.) When families accepted Christian values they no longer found killing babies acceptable and once Christianity was in a position to influence legislation infanticide was made illegal; although initially exposing children, by leaving them at the roadside to be picked up by someone else or to die, was still allowed. One solution for Christian families was for their daughters to dedicate themselves to God as 'consecrated' virgins. In time a pattern was established for these women to live a quiet life of simplicity and prayer in their homes. They left their home only to attend church, though they could receive female visitors.

Women Priests?

The most controversial issue is whether women were ever ordained as priests in the early church. The traditional view is that this is unthinkable. However, as the issue of women priests has come to the fore in the Anglican and Roman Catholic churches the evidence has been re-evaluated and some writers have come to a different conclusion. As the early church had no central authority and each area could decide on its own practices women presbyters may have been accepted in some areas but not in others. If there were writings that dealt with women priests they have not been preserved; it would be surprising if they had. Only a fraction of written material from the first few centuries of the church has been preserved and every document that has been preserved has had to be copied and recopied many times.   Apart from papyrus fragments, preserved in the dry desert climates of Egypt and the Dead Sea, the oldest copies of books and manuscripts that survive are copies dating from several hundred years after they were written.   Copying a book by hand was a major commitment.   It is not surprising that the copyists did not choose to invest their time in any writings which did not meet their full approval.   We know of several works on the subject of marriage that have not survived, although other works by the same authors were carefully copied.   As the church increasingly became dominated by celibates there was no interest in copying works about women or Christian marriage.

This censorship by neglect is why the information we have about groups and people who were considered heretical is almost all second hand and negative.   The works of their opponents were copied out but their own writings were allowed to decay or were destroyed.   The work of many early writers, orthodox and otherwise, are preserved only in Eusebius, who quotes long passages from earlier authors in his fourth century History of the Church.   His book is a treasure trove of information on the early church but Eusebius was not in favour of women forgetting their 'place'; of the few women he mentions most are either martyrs or were involved with less orthodox groups.

Although there are no documents extant that refer to women in a priestly role there are other types of evidence.   The earliest Christian pictures are in the catacombs, which are corridors and chambers cut out of the rock beneath the outskirts of cities like Rome.   They were used by the early Christians as cemeteries to protect their dead from vandalism and possibly as hiding places in times of persecution.

They include some larger areas as well as the endless corridors of innumerable niches, which served as tombs. In the catacombs in Rome there are paintings of women praying and also a painting of a group of women around a table with one of them apparently breaking bread. The implication of this picture is that a woman was carrying out a function, presiding at a Eucharist, which it is assumed was limited to priests. Some scholars consider that it must just be a picture of a meal rather than a Eucharist. Other advocates of traditional views claim that the woman presiding must be a man, despite a feminine hairstyle.

A few early Christian tombstones describe the deceased as a 'presbytera', a term which, in its masculine form presbyter, is usually translated 'priest'. One inscription from Salona in Dalmatia mentions the Presbytera Flavia Vitalia and dates from 425 CE. Another dating to the end of the fifth century and found in Bruttium concerns the Presbytera Leta. Again these can be explained away, the woman commemorated may have been the wives of priests; even today some societies give women their husband's title. But there may be significance in the fact that all these pieces of evidence for the existence of women priests are literally cast in stone. Stone, unlike papyrus, is difficult to destroy, deliberately or through neglect.

St Thecla

As well as the factual evidence that survives there is a story which throws light on a woman's life as a Christian. The Story of St Thecla is an early 'biography' of a female saint. We do not know when it was written but Tertullian (155 –225AD) mentions it. It is the story of a woman, St Thecla, and is believed to be fiction rather than history; although Cyprian and Eusebius both refer to St Thecla as a real person, so there may have been a basis in fact. The story relates that Thecla was converted after overhearing St Paul preach through a window. She became a Christian and refused the marriage her parents had arranged. She suffered much persecution, partly at the hands of her ex-fiancé, and eventually left home, travelling to other cities where she met Paul, witnessed to the Gospel and healed the sick. Several times she escaped martyrdom miraculously. At one point it says: "Paul replied to her "Go and teach the word of the Lord." This is interesting in that it shows that a hundred years so after Paul it was seen as credible that Paul would tell a woman to go and teach. (Tertullian mentions the story and its author because he objected to this.) The story relates that Thecla continued to teach, preach and heal for many years and lived to a ripe old age.

Christian Gnostics

Not all Christians were orthodox. Some people tried to combine Christian ideas with those of Gnosticism, another popular religious movement of the time. Gnosticism was not a unified movement but a number of sects, Pagan, Jewish and Christian, with common assumptions and attitudes. They all were dualists who believed the physical world was evil. The idea underlying all Gnostic belief was of a secret knowledge (Greek gnosis) known only to an inner circle, and shared with initiates, sometimes by a woman. In contrast the Apostles emphasised that salvation and all truth were freely available to everyone. Gnostic groups believed that man had a divine spark, which had been corrupted by being contained in a physical creation, which they saw as evil and from which they desired to be released. They hoped that their knowledge and ascetic lifestyle would help them to attain unity with the divine.   Again this was not a Christian belief; orthodox Christians wished to be in communion with God but did not aspire to unity with him. There are indications that women had more freedom among some Gnostic groups.   This may have been because they rejected marriage and all physical relationships and concentrated on the life of the mind.   Most Gnostics valued asceticism but a few considered the body so unimportant that they felt they could disregard physical morality.

Until 1945 only a few fragments of Gnostic writings were known to have survived.   Then a number were discovered, along with other classical and Christian writings, in stone jars of papyri at Nag Hammadi in Egypt.   The find included several apocryphal gospels, which were previously unknown or only known by references to them in other ancient books.   Gnostic Gospels mostly date from the second or third centuries and, unlike New Testament Gospels, many include errors that indicate ignorance of Jewish life in the first century.   The writers put their own views into the mouths of Jesus and the Apostles. But they may reflect information that was known at the time but has not survived; one of the Gnostic gospels describes Jesus teaching a group of twelve male disciples and seven women.

Mary Magdalene has a more prominent role than the other disciples in some Gnostic writings.   She is portrayed as having an especially close relationship with Christ, though not a sexual one.   Several apocryphal gospels show Mary Magdalene in dialogue with the Apostles revealing to them secrets Christ had shared with her in a vision.   (The views she attributes to Christ were formulated many decades after her death; so there is no possibility of the dialogues being authentic.) Peter is portrayed as unable to accept the 'truths' she told them. This may just be a third century fiction but it could be a reflection of a real dialogue in the early church between those who accepted women in leadership roles and those who found the idea unacceptable. Peter, whom the New Testament shows was a forceful and opinionated man, might easily have been opposed to a more active role for women.

The Apostles were the source of authority in the first century church so it was common for later writers to strengthen their case by attributing their work to one of them; most apocryphal books, even those written hundreds of years later, bear the names of Apostles. We do not know why Gnostic writers chose to emphasise the role of Mary Magdalene. It may be because of the emphasis among some Gnostic groups on women as spiritual instructors. What does seem clear from the Gnostic writings is that Mary Magdalene was well known to believers even many years after her death. This indicates she may have had a more prominent role in the early church than might be assumed from Acts and the Epistles, where she is not mentioned. Since the discovery of the Gnostic writings in which Mary Magdalene is featured, a few scholars and other writers have tried to work out her role in the early church but lack sufficient evidence. It is quite possible that she had a leadership role; she was certainly recognised as a disciple of Jesus.

In recent years a number of books have claimed that Mary Magdalene was married to Jesus, an idea that had never appears to have been even suggested before the twentieth century. It first appeared in a book by William Phipps, "Was Jesus Married? The Distortion of Sexuality in the Christian Tradition" published in 1970. Phipps argued from the

41

Jewish emphasis on the social responsibility to marry and have children. A year later Charles Davis, a noted Catholic theologian, wrote an article in the Guardian Newspaper, which suggested that Phipps was over-influenced by then current theories on sexual health but supported the possibility that Jesus might have been married. Davis himself had recently left the priesthood in order to marry, so he had a vested interest in making it clear that Jesus had not advocated celibacy.

More recently the idea has been taken up in speculative books, which have added a child, descendants, and a secret society, the Priory of Sion, which they allege protected these descendents over the centuries. The theory has taken on a life of its own; most notably in the bestselling novel "The Da Vinci Code" whose Author's claim that his book is based on fact is often accepted at face value. The idea was not even undermined when a Frenchman admitted he and his friends had invented the 'Priory of Sion' in 1956 and placed the only evidence for its existence, a handwritten list of 'Priors' that included Botticelli, Da Vinci and Victor Hugo, in the Paris library as a surrealist joke. Despite the totally speculative nature of the 'evidence' and the lack of any basis in early documents this idea of Jesus with a wife and descendants caught the public's imagination and is now widely believed.

One Gnostic fragment, the Gospel of Philip, is sometimes cited as confirming a marital relationship between Jesus and Mary. There are three relevant passages; in the first it says "Jesus kissed Mary on..." the next word is missing but it is assumed to be mouth. Kissing then, as now, was a frequent form of greeting; Paul ends two letters with "greet one another with a holy kiss". Another fragment says "There were three who always walked with the Lord, Mary, his Mother, (her) sister and Magdalene, the one who was called his companion." It is suggested that 'companion', which is sometimes translated partner, is a word that means spouse but this theory is undermined by Paul using the same word to describe his friendship with Philemon. The third passage has the disciples accusing Jesus of loving Mary more than he loves them. He admits this but attributes it to her greater spiritual understanding. None of this is constitutes evidence supporting the idea that Mary was Jesus' lover or wife.

Recent books, both those written by feminists and those about the alleged 'holy bloodline' and the conspiracy to hide it, often imply that Gnostics were more positive about women than orthodox Christians. While there was no consistent Gnostic belief system the reverse was often true. In the Gospel of Thomas one of the disciples suggests Mary should leave because women are not worthy of life. The Gnostic Jesus responds by promising to make Mary a man, since, he says, only by becoming men will women enter the Kingdom of Heaven. Mainstream Christians, even those that most restricted women, have still acknowledged their spiritual equality without requiring them to change their gender.

Even the partial records which have come down to us reveal that women had a central role in the early church; not only as the largest group of converts but also in evangelising, and giving spiritual teaching and care to, their families and their fellow women. The growth of the church in the first centuries was due not only to the work of the Apostles and other church leaders but also to these women who are now largely forgotten.

4. "PUNISHMENT ATTACHES TO THE MERE NAME"

This chapter will look at women martyrs who suffered and died for their faith while Christianity remained an illicit religion. Since it is about the interface between Christianity and the Roman authorities it is necessary to start by looking briefly at the political context of early Christianity.

Christianity and the Empire

Rome considered the Way, later called Christianity, illegal but it was their Empire that provided the stability and safe travel, which enabled it to grow. The gospel of Christ spread like wildfire, despite official disapproval and persecution. Women were an intrinsic part of this growth; they spread the gospel among their friends and family and they outnumbered men in the fledgling church. A criticism of Christianity, written by Celus in about 170 AD, called it a religion of slaves, women and little children. A surviving list of garments, confiscated from a church when the entire congregation was arrested, indicates that a majority of them were women.

Rome dominated the Mediterranean area for more than five hundred years and the Empire in Constantinople (Istanbul), which was its heir, lasted almost another millennium. It was not static; the early church developed in a time of constant political change. The first Emperors were Caesars, their family name became a title because Augustus Caesar left the institutions of the republic in place; concentrating on the reality not the appearance of power. Augustus's family soon died out, due to a habit of dying in suspicious circumstances, according to rumour this was often at the hands of relatives. After the death of Nero, the last of the family, there were two ways of becoming Emperor; inheritance, by birth or adoption, or by acclamation by the Army. If an Emperor had been unpopular the Army would put up a candidate to succeed him. Since it is not easy to argue with an Army they usually succeeded; although when different legions acclaimed different generals it became more complicated – in one year there were four Emperors. Roman Emperors often shared power, with a junior Caesar ruling the Western Empire, but the Roman tradition of civil war between rivals for power continued; co-emperors often ended up fighting, each determined to oust the other. Roman Government worked because routine governance of the Empire was the work of the civil service and army. A new person at the top might make changes to the upper echelons but the upheaval would not spread to the lower ranks of centurions and administrators, who ensured that the system continued to run smoothly.

Because the Roman people and Senate did not choose emperors they were often not from Rome and had no personal investment in Rome itself; later Emperor's often chose their own capital in the East. North and west of Rome were frontier areas so it was the east, which had been the home of great empires when Rome was still a village, which were the heart of the Empire and the main source of its prosperity.

It was the Emperors who decided whether Christians were actively persecuted. Christianity was not seen as a serious threat in the early years. There were specific incidents, but no systematic persecution. Paul, and probably Peter, were martyred in Rome under Nero, as were other less prominent Christians. Nero's horrific murders of Christians were designed to distract public opinion from his own shortcomings and did not lead to widespread persecution; but it did set a precedent of executing Christians for no crime other than their faith.

Pliny the Younger

We have a glimpse of early Christians in the correspondence of Pliny the Younger who lived from 61 to 114 AD. The Emperor Trajan appointed him legate for Bithynia, an area of Asia Minor (Turkey). His correspondence with Trajan has survived and throws light on the regime's attitude to Christians. Pliny had to judge those who had been denounced as Christians. As an intelligent man he wanted to find out about the 'crime' they had committed. "In investigations of Christians I have never taken part: hence I do not know what is the crime usually punished or investigated, or what allowances are made…. whether punishment attaches to the mere name apart from secret crimes, or to the secret crimes connected with the name". (He may be referring to a widespread rumour in the ancient world that accused Christians of cannibalism; a misconception probably arising from the words of the Eucharist.) Under threat of execution a number of Christians had recanted and Pliny had asked them about the practices of Christians. "They maintained, however, that the amount of their fault or error had been this, that it was their habit on a fixed day to assemble before daylight and recite by turns a form of words to Christ as a god; and that they bound themselves with an oath, not for any crime, but not to commit theft or robbery or adultery, nor to break their word, and not to deny a deposit when demanded. After this was done, their custom was to depart, and to meet again to take food, but ordinary and harmless food: and even this (they said) they had given up doing after the issue of my edict, by which in accordance with your commands I had forbidden the existence of clubs. On this I considered it the more necessary to find out from two maidservants, who were called deaconesses, and that by torments, how far this was true; but I discovered nothing else than a perverse and extravagant superstition." The Emperor's reply makes it clear that he didn't want his officials to seek out Christians but that those who were brought to their attention, and refused to sacrifice to the deified Emperor, should be executed. He did insist Christians should not be arrested as a result of anonymous accusations; he felt acting on anonymous tips was beneath the dignity of Roman justice. This must have helped to discourage malicious accusations.

Pliny's letters give a unique snapshot of how Christians were seen by the authorities in 111 AD; it is clear that being a Christian was in itself a capital offence. The prosecution did not need to prove any other crime than refusal to worship the Emperor. But many Christians were not prepared to compromise believing that worship belonged to God alone. Pliny confirms the role of deaconesses in the early church. It is not clear whether they were the only leaders Pliny had been able to identify or whether he chose to interrogate them because their inferior status allowed him to use torture. We know that later in the century church leaders sometimes went into hiding when a persecution began, so the deaconesses might have been left in charge.

Pliny's letters also show that in less than a century Christianity in Bithynia had grown sufficiently to have seriously affected the level of business at pagan temples, and the livelihood of farmers who supplied the fodder to feed the animals who were sacrificed in great numbers in many temples. The loss of this lucrative market no doubt affected farmers' profits and led to complaints against Christians. Local complaints could lead to active local persecution, just as accusations by personal enemies might lead to individuals being prosecuted. For many believers the alternative to making a sacrifice to the deified Emperor was the arena; a place where the deaths of criminals, gladiators and wild animals provided entertainment for bloodthirsty crowds. The old Roman tradition of gladiatorial fights at funeral 'games' had degenerated in imperial times, and the population had become addicted to the spectacle of death as entertainment. Innumerable exotic animals, many imported at great expense from the edges of the Empire, met their death in the arena. So did many humans: gladiators, prisoners of war, criminals, and political offenders like Christians, they all died to entertain the Roman public. Roman Emperors knew they needed to provide both 'bread and circuses' to keep the population of Rome acquiescent. Even early Christian Emperors feared to interfere with this entertainment but in the Byzantine period chariot racing became the focus of public excitement and rivalry instead.

Christian martyrs

It is not clear just how many Christians were executed for their faith during the first three centuries but martyrdom was always a possibility and women were not exempt. Martyr is the Greek word for witness and those who faced death for their faith were described as witnesses. It is clear from reports of individual martyrs that those in charge aimed at long drawn out and painful deaths to increase the entertainment value of the spectacle. The treatment of slaves seems to have been especially cruel but their Christian owners also faced both wild beasts and death for their faith. A letter describing the death of martyrs during a persecution in 177 AD has survived; preserved by Eusebius. Christians in Lyons were tortured to death, on the instructions of Marcus Aurelius. One slave woman was subject to particular ferocity and cruelty before her death.

"The blessed Blandina, last of all, having, like a highborn mother, exhorted her children and sent them forth victorious to the King, travelled herself along the same path of conflicts as they did, and hastened to them rejoicing and exulting at her departure, like one bidden to a marriage supper, rather than cast to the wild beasts. And after the scourging, after the wild beasts, after the frying pan, she was at last thrown into a basket and presented to a bull. For a time the animal tossed her, but she had now lost all perception of what was happening, thanks to the hope she cherished, the grasp of the objects of her faith and her converse with Christ. Then she too was sacrificed and even the heathen themselves acknowledged that never in their experience had a woman endured so many and terrible sufferings".

Blandina seems to have had an important role in the church in Lyons but we are not told what it was.

Fifty years later two women, Perpetua and Felicia, were among a group martyred in Carthage. They seem to have been recent converts under instruction. Perpetua's diary of her imprisonment has been preserved. The fact that Perpetua came from a 'good' family and was a new mother did not save her. She details her father's efforts to persuade her to recant and her own determination not to deny her Lord. She writes of the practical difficulties of being a nursing mother with a new baby while in prison awaiting execution. Felicia, her companion and slave, was heavily pregnant; she and her fellow prisoners prayed that she would be delivered early so she could die with her friends and fellow Christians; rather than being imprisoned until the baby was born and then killed in the company of criminals. This prayer was answered and she died with them, leaving her baby to be adopted by a Christian 'sister'.   Perpetua and Felicia did not have an easy death, being exposed to wild animals before being executed by the sword.   The courage and steadfastness of these Christians was an inspiration to their fellows and a testimony to onlookers.   It is not surprising that later the church gave them the title of 'saints'.   This usage gave the word a more specific meaning than the one in the New Testament; in Paul's letters he describes all Christian believers as 'saints'.   Those who were arrested and admitted their faith but were not killed were known as 'confessors'.   They were consulted on issues of faith and their pronouncements had great authority.

Later persecutions

Under some later Emperors Christians were persecuted more systematically; as Christianity became more widespread it was seen as more of a threat to the status quo and the old religion.   The Emperor had despotic powers but was also the figurehead of a mighty army and a huge civil service.   Identifying him as a god increased his authority outside Rome and made rebellion less likely; so anything undermining this was seen as dangerous to public order.   It was the emperors who governed efficiently who were most likely to persecute the Christians since they saw them as a threat to good government.   There was active persecution under Marcus Aurelius, still admired for his philosophical 'meditations', while his incompetent son, Commodus, actually protected Christians, possibly at the request of his concubine Marcia, who was rumoured to be a Christian.

There were alternatives for those who could not face a terrible death. Cyprian of Carthage and another bishop went into hiding during a time of persecution, managing their flocks by secret correspondence. However, they lost moral authority because of their flight. Many Christians gave confessors, Christians who had been imprisoned for their faith but not executed, greater authority than bishops. This would have been a serious concern to Cyprian whose writings emphasise the authority of bishops. Less than ten years later Cyprian chose not to go into hiding during a new persecution and was martyred. A few individual Christians showed undue enthusiasm for martyrdom. This led to the Church announcing that anyone courting martyrdom should be regarded as a suicide rather than a martyr.

There were some reigns during which Christianity was tolerated, but these were followed by a backlash and further persecution. In the mid third century the church was allowed to own property and could acquire church buildings instead of meeting in homes as it had always done. When Diocletian became Emperor in 284 and set about reorganizing the Empire; he revived the cult of Emperor worship and expected his court to treat him as semi-divine. As part of this process he systematically persecuted Christians, focusing on Church leaders.

In 313 the Co-Emperors Constantine and Licinius introduced a policy of religious tolerance, ending thirty years of persecution. The Edict of Milan granted freedom of religion for all, both Christians and pagans. A new era started, being a Christian became socially acceptable and belief was no longer hazardous or harmful to a man's status.

Martyrs and the church

Tertullian said that "in the blood of the martyrs is the seed of the church". There is no doubt that during these years of opposition and persecution the church grew by leaps and bounds. The catacombs indicate how many Christians there were in Rome, innumerable bodies were placed in niches stacked high in their long passages. Converts knew they would sacrifice much, possibly even their lives, for their faith; yet they still accepted the Christian message. Women outnumbered men in the early church, especially among the upper classes, so there were many female martyrs. Throughout history fervent forms of Christianity have appealed most strongly not to the rich, successful and complacent but to underdogs; the powerless and those who are hurting. It was not the dominant Greco-Roman men who responded to the Gospel but their wives, daughters and slaves. In the early church slaves were accepted; slaves or freedmen, many of whom were well educated, could become church leaders, even bishops. There are indications that wives of prominent men, even members of the imperial family, were interested in Christianity. The niece of Emperor Domitian was sent into exile, probably for being a Christian since the accusation against her was atheism. At the start of his persecution Decius insisted on his own wife and daughter sacrificing to the gods, which implies they had been involved with Christians. The mother of the Emperor Alexander Severus sent a military escort to bring Origen, a noted Christian teacher, to Antioch so she could question him and test his understanding of divine things.

Male converts from the educated classes were often second generation believers, brought to faith by female relatives. Wives, mothers and sisters turned to Christ and there are many stories of how they influenced the men of their family to follow. The fact that it was initially the women who followed Christ was implied by the Emperor Julian, who is known as 'the Apostate' because of his efforts to turn back the tide of Christianity. He complained that Christian women were giving their money to succour the poor and in a speech told the citizens of Antioch "Every one of you allowed his wife to carry everything out of his house to the Galileans".

At a time when having faith in Christ was a capital offence, women of all classes: slaves, ordinary women, even well born and wealthy women, became Christians. During this period faith was not easy; when women 'gossiped the gospel' to their friends or taught their children about Christ they might be risking their lives. Centuries later missionaries coined the term 'rice Christians' to describe those who they feared had turned to Christianity for material benefits. In these early centuries there were no rice Christians, no one benefited materially or furthered their career through conversion to Christ.

5. THEOLOGIANS, PHILOSPHERS AND WOMEN

Early Christians used their minds, as well as their hearts and spirits, to comprehend their new faith.   Like humans throughout history, they sought to adapt their new beliefs to fit their underlying assumptions about the world.   Early Christian scholars all had a classical education and this formed their mindset.   They brought to their Christian studies views on women, which were firmly grounded in Greek thought.

Theology is the study of the nature of God.   As the early Christians preached and taught, a Christian theology began to emerge.   The new, revolutionary religious ideas were exciting and provoked debate; theology developed as a response to challenges to the church's message.   In order to defend the truth Christian scholars had to clarify and define it.

Combating false teachers.

The Apostles did not try to define and systematize their knowledge. The Didache gives a practical test, not a theological one, for false prophets, who could be recognized not by their views but by their interest in benefiting materially from their teaching.   (A test that is still useful in judging religious leaders.)   The test for error that Peter and John used to identify false teachers was simple - they could be recognized by their attitude to Christ.   "Every spirit that acknowledges that Jesus Christ has come in the flesh is from God". (1 John 4: 2)   This test recognised that the incarnation was the belief that people, especially educated people, found most difficult to accept. For people who had been taught that all matter was evil and could not touch the spiritual realm, the incarnation, God becoming man, was incomprehensible and unthinkable. Those who were attracted by Christianity but found the incarnation too much to swallow sought alternatives. Some, influenced by a Gnostic belief that all matter is inherently evil, said Christ was a spirit who appeared in the form of a man, and so had not really died; others said that he was a man but not God. The next few centuries were a ferment of ideas and uninhibited debate among Christians and the most controversial issue was the nature of Christ.

Christianity and pagan philosophers

In the second century a number of Greco-Roman scholars converted to Christianity. They wanted to understand how their new faith interacted with the philosophical ideals of their age. Their aim was to make Christianity intellectually respectable and more appealing to educated people and to disprove the libellous stories being circulated. Christians were regarded as atheists; rumour also associated them with cannibalism and sexual orgies. One Roman lawyer in around 200 wrote particularly libellous version of these rumours and sought to lend substance to his allegations by ending "If this does not happen in fact, it does so in their minds, since that is their desire."

Plato's views on women

The ideas of Greco-Roman philosophy, especially those of Plato, dominated intellectual life in Roman world. He was greatly admired and philosophers of the time studied and developed his thought.

Intelligent Christians wanted to reconcile his ideas with their beliefs. Plato's references to women were either negative or ambiguous. In the Symposium, a debate on love, one speaker suggests that only inferior men love women as well as boys ('Boys' here refers to adolescents not children; Plato makes it clear that romantic or sexual love with children is morally repugnant) and that men who love women are loving bodies not souls, "they chose the most foolish persons they can". In the text no one contradicts this assertion. In another Socratic dialogue, Timaeus, Plato describes his ideas of the afterlife.

"He who lived well during his appointed time was to return and dwell in his appointed star, and there he would have a blessed and congenial existence. But if he failed in attaining this, at the second birth he would pass into a woman, and if, when in that state of being, he did not desist from evil, he would continually be changed into some brute."

On the ladder of reincarnation he pictured women as between men and beasts. Underlying all this is Plato's absolute conviction that women are intrinsically inferior to men.

Influenced by Plato and the Stoics Christian thought became impregnated with the idea of subduing the body to nurture the spirit. Aspects of this view linger two thousand years later. Few realise that a common view of the afterlife, of survival as a spirit in a vague and disembodied eternity, is based more on Plato than the Bible, which places it in a renewed earth, redeemed from the Fall. The idea of Heaven as a place where people sit on clouds and sing or play the harp owes more to Plato than Scripture.

Aristotle's view of women

Another Greek philosopher who was influential, and would be even more so later, was Aristotle. He was a natural scientist as well as a philosopher; but some of his views were based on his underlying assumptions rather than observable facts. He taught that women only provided the material from which a new life was created, the form which a child took was entirely supplied by the father. He saw the birth of a female as the result of a sperm failing in its attempt to re-create itself; although he admitted that it was necessary for enough of these 'incomplete men' to be born to perpetuate the race.

Aristotle believed the social hierarchies he observed reflected intrinsic worth. Thus women, who were treated as chattels, must be inferior. So were slaves; even those born free and enslaved through no fault of their own. He did recognise there were a few who were enslaved but not 'slavish' by nature but he saw them as exceptions. The concept of institutionalisation, the idea that people who are forced to adapt to an institution like slavery have their behaviour and attitudes moulded by it, never occurred to Aristotle or his followers. Nor did it occur to them that women were less able to reason because they were denied education. Greeks were snobs; in their eyes only freeborn Greek men were capable of rational thought and worthy of exerting power over others.

The new Christian intellectuals brought these pagan ideas and attitudes to women to their theological studies. They tried to harmonise Christianity with philosophy without losing its unique message. As Christian apologists they sought to make the faith acceptable to intelligent outsiders. This drive for intellectual and social respectability involved playing down the role taken by women in the church; since the learned all agreed that they were incapable of anything but 'womanly' tasks.

Clement of Alexandria

Clement (died c 215) was a noted teacher and writer. He wrote a treatise about teaching and in it he accepted that women should be taught with men. One chapter was entitled 'Men and women alike under the instructors charge'. In it he wrote: "Let us then, embracing more and more this good obedience, give ourselves to the Lord; clinging to what is surest, the cable of faith in him, and understanding that the virtue of man and woman is the same. For if the God of both is one, the master of both is also one; one church, one temperance, one modesty; their food is common, marriage an equal yoke; respiration, sight, hearing, knowledge, hope, obedience, love all alike. And those whose life is common, have common graces and a common salvation; common to them are love and training". It was probably due to the influence of Clement that some later teachers accepted women students.

Tertullian

Tertullian (c155 – c225) was a brilliant writer and Christian apologist who demanded that Christians separate themselves from pagan corruption. He was a lawyer trained in rhetoric and he conceived the task of a Christian thinker as a conflict with diabolical forces, which must be won. Henry Chadwick writes "Because he understood his intellectual role in this way he had no hesitation about using arguments that were fallacious if only they would gain him the victory over his immediate adversary. If he could outmanoeuvre the devil by dialectical subtlety, so much the better." Some of Tertullian's comments on women shock modern audiences by their apparent misogyny but his strongest criticisms of women appear when he is writing for an audience of women not when he was writing about women for an audience of men. He suggested that it was man not woman who was created in God's image and claimed "You women destroy so easily God's image, man". He also accused women of being "The devils gateway" leading men into temptation as Eve had led Adam. Unlike Paul he suggested Eve was primarily to blame for the advent of sin into the world. However, he could also take the opposite view when it suited his argument.

Tertullian's teaching on women falls very harshly in modern ears but there is evidence it did not reflect his total view of women. He ended up leaving the mainstream Church to join the Montanists; a charismatic sect whose beliefs were partly based on the teachings of two women prophets. Tertullian was attracted by the Montanist's strict moral views and did not condemn their prophets; as he had condemned another woman prophet whom he considered unsound. Unlike many of the later Church Fathers Tertullian was married and a letter written to his wife has been preserved.

"Where can I find the word to describe adequately the happiness of that marriage which the church cements, which the oblation confirms and the blessing seals? The angels proclaim it and the heavenly Father ratifies it…What kind of yoke is that of two Christians united in one hope, one desire, one discipline and one service? Both are children of the same Father, servants of the same Master; nothing separates them, either in the spirit or in the flesh…They are both equal

59

in the church of God, equal at the banquet of God, equal in trials, persecutions, consolations".

This hardly fits with his teachings about women. Tertullian's views seem to be a mass of contradictions but this may be mainly because of his enjoyment of controversy and willingness to use any argument, even if fallacious, to win a debate. The letter to his wife, which was not written to win an argument, is likely to express genuine feeling.

Origen

Origen (c185 – c253), a contemporary of Tertullian, who was possibly the most admired Biblical scholar of his age, was prepared to accept women as students. This may have been due to the influence of Clement of Alexandria. Despite this willingness to teach women he wrote; "For it is improper for a woman to speak in assembly, no matter what she says. Even if she says admirable things or even saintly things that is of little consequence since they are from the mouth of a woman." Origen lived an austere and celibate life. Eusebius reports that he castrated himself to ensure his chastity and so he could teach women without scandal. Eusebius was writing a century later so this may not have been true, though some authors accept it as fact.

Christian writers, educated to identify women with Flesh not Spirit, began to teach that it was man who was made in God's image; woman was created in man's image and so partook of the image of God only indirectly. Origen wrote "What is seen with the eyes of the creator is masculine and not feminine, for God does not stoop to look upon what is feminine and of the flesh." Here Origen was commenting on Exodus 23: 17 where the text directs that three times a year all

Hebrew men should appear before God; he reads into it a judgement on womankind that is not present in the original. The feminine, in his eyes, was material not spiritual and therefore so inferior that God, who was a Spirit, did not even want to look at it. He also saw women as a temptation to men and a threat to their chastity but he did accept that men were ultimately responsible for their own weakness.

Other Early theologians

Some other Christian writers saw lustful thoughts and actions as the fault of the woman who inspired them, rather than the men who entertained them. Similar attitudes can be seen today in police and lawyers when they suggest a woman has contributed to her own violent rape by her dress, behaviour or past sexual experience.

These early theologians looked for reasons to justify their belief that woman was an inferior species who should be under man's authority. They believed it was man, not mankind, who was the crowning work of creation. Men were created in the image of God but women were created in the image of men, reflecting God's image at second hand.

This emphasis on women as preoccupied with flesh and occasioning sin in men, led some clergy to think that the only 'good' women were those who sought out a life of perpetual virginity and made themselves physically unattractive. From the second century Christian women, especially those with a position in the church, must have faced a continual struggle against denigration, not just of them personally but of their whole sex. It must have been similar to the situation that can still face black people in our society. I have worked with black women who said that at times they were forced to listen to sweeping negative generalisations about black people from colleagues, only to have the speaker add "I don't mean you of course, you're different". After the third century women working in the church probably had to listen to similar remarks denigrating their whole gender.

As chastity became increasingly valued the number of Church leaders and theologians who were married steadily diminished; so it is not surprising that women began to be identified as a source of temptation and therefore of sin. For fifteen hundred years, until the Reformation, celibate men were responsible for theological writing and for training future church leaders. In the Roman Catholic Church they still are.

St Augustine

Augustine (354 – 430) does not seem to have the streak of misogyny shown by some other writers and he valued the women in his family but he had a strong sexual drive and felt he could only achieve chastity, which he believed was the mark of a spiritual Christian, by keeping apart from all women. Like his contemporaries he had a negative view of sexuality; influenced no doubt not only by philosophy but also by the teachings of the Manicheans, a Gnostic cult he had followed for years before becoming a Christian. Augustine's teaching was largely based on the views of his time but his intelligence, clarity of expression and moral stature gave his words an authority that outlasted his own age. Augustine saw sexuality and procreation as part of God's original plan for humanity. He believed that the Fall led to a division between the will and sexual desire and saw this distortion of the will as its main legacy. This view emphasised the close connection between sex, and therefore women, and sin. Augustine taught that when Eve was created to be a "helper" to Adam it was to bear his children; "If one rejects giving birth to children as the reason why woman was created, I do not see for which other help the woman was made for the man." Augustine does not seem to have considered the implications of the fact that the word for "helper" used to describe Eve is also used to describe God in the Psalms. Augustine was not the first of the early church fathers to devalue women's abilities and contribution to the church but he was certainly the most influential in the long term. The views Augustine expressed on sexuality and on women were based on earlier teachings but it was Augustine's theological writing that most strongly influenced the Western Church for centuries, partly because, unlike most of the earlier Church Fathers, he wrote in Latin not Greek. In time his views on sexuality became an intrinsic part of the teachings of the Catholic Church. When Popes in the twentieth and twenty first centuries denounce birth control as sinful it is because of Augustine's teaching, reiterated over the centuries, that sex for procreation is acceptable but sex designed to strengthen marriage through mutual pleasure is sin.

'Manly' women

The church recognised godly women but saw them as honorary men surpassing their sex. Eusebius wrote of the persecution under Maxentius: "As for the women, schooled by the divine word, they showed themselves as manly as men." When Augustine preached on the anniversary of the martyrdom of Perpetua and Felicitas he lauded their courage and endurance by saying they acted like men. Women who showed courage or ability were seen as exceptions, the honour they earned not reflecting on others of their gender.

There is no doubt that some of the early church writers were unwilling to accept women as 'one with them in Christ Jesus' and wished to restrict them to acts of worship or service that were under close male supervision. Priesthoods have always placed themselves between God and the laity but from the third century onward the clergy seem particularly anxious to control women and prevent them taking any active role except under careful supervision. It is fair to say that some writers showed real acrimony in their attitude to women. It seems likely that they were reacting to women in the church having more independence and more prominence than they believed was socially or theologically acceptable. Many theologians from the second century onwards showed a streak of misogyny and a few of them used their position to undermine the position of women within Christianity. Attitudes to women among their contemporaries must have made the prominent roles that some women had in the early church an embarrassment; something a maturing church wished to put behind them.

6. "BY CHASTITY MEN AND WOMEN CAN BECOME AS THE ANGELS"

In this chapter we will be looking at the cult of virginity. An extraordinary change in attitudes to marriage and procreation took place from the second century. Christians began to put increasing value on chastity as a sign of piety and to downgrade the value of marriage. As a hierarchy of clergy developed the church began to regard celibacy as the ideal for clergy, especially bishops. The early church expected the second coming of Christ at any time. There was no point in committing themselves to this world if it would soon be gone. Living with a continual threat of persecution and possible death formed the mindset of early Christians. They had to make costly decisions and face hard questions; their faith was never easy. In this atmosphere the virtues of self-denial and chastity became paramount for many Christians and they came to admire above all those who were prepared to adopt an ascetic and sacrificial lifestyle. They admired not only virgins but also those who lived a chaste life after previous sexual experience.

Celibacy and the apostles

Most people in the New Testament church, men and women, were, or had been married. We are not told the marital status of the Apostles, except for Peter and Philip, but as devout Jews they would have married, probably in their late teens. Paul may also have been married, since he says he fulfilled all the duties of a devout Jew and this included a duty to marry and have children.   At the time of his missionary journeys he was unmarried.   He may have been a widower but another possibility is that when he became a Christian his wife's family took her away and arranged a divorce.   It was not easy for a woman to get a divorce but it could be done if a male relative took the initiative.   If Paul did have a wife and her family appealed to the religious authorities in Jerusalem they would have been pleased to rule against him and grant a divorce; they must have been very angry when he suddenly changed from being the worst enemy of the followers of Jesus to being one of Christ's most passionate advocates.   Arranged marriages are still common in some parts of the world and in societies where this is normal it is not unusual for relatives to intervene in a marriage.   Even today many Muslim converts to Christianity lose their wife and children in this way.

Paul chose to remain single throughout his ministry, devoting all his attention, strength and passion to the cause of the Gospel but Peter took his wife with him on his missionary journeys. She was probably martyred for her faith before he was.   Eusebius quotes Clement reporting how Peter had encouraged her as she was led off to a martyr's death, some time before his own execution.   This apostolic example was overlooked as attitudes changed and it was Paul's singleness that was regarded as an example for Christians to follow.

St Thecla

Looking at the books valued by earlier Christians we can see this attitude developing.   The story of St Thecla, written before 225, is revealing in its attitudes to women and virginity.   It is fictional but is interesting as an account of a Christian woman teaching, preaching and healing the sick. The part of the story that is relevant to this chapter is the emphasis on Thecla's determined virginity, which is threatened on a number of occasions during her adventures. In the final scene Thecla, by then extremely old, was living in a cave and still working - teaching and healing. Local doctors saw her healing powers as a threat to their business. They decided that the goddess Diana gave her power because of her virginity, and sent a group of young men to rape this elderly lady so she would no longer have Diana's favour. The story relates that the rock wall of her cave opened up to let her through and then closed behind her, thwarting her assailants.

Choosing austerity

The self-sacrificial mindset fostered by persecution did not end with Constantine's edict of toleration. In the fourth century some Christians continued to seek out hard choices and to confirm their devotion by adopting an austere and sacrificial lifestyle. There were other forces that reinforced this emphasis on austerity. Christianity spread fast, especially in the cities of the Eastern part of the Empire. Yet Christians still received classic education based on Greek and Latin literature and art and their way of life differed little from their pagan neighbours. Christianity was fashionable and the serious minded looked for a way to identify, and demonstrate, their own serious commitment; the ascetic life provided that way. Individuals dedicated themselves to a life of ascetism and chastity and communities developed devoted not only to God but also to those ideals.

The Desert Fathers (and Mothers)

Christians had long admired austerity but in the fourth century a man called Anthony introduced a new rigor to Christian asceticism. He renounced his property and retreated to live a life of extreme poverty and hardship as a hermit in the barren Egyptian desert. St Anthony sought solitude so as to live a life of spiritual warfare and prayer. Later those who wanted his spiritual guidance or wished to emulate him sought him out. Within a few years of his death Athanasius, Bishop of Alexandria, wrote his 'Life of Anthony' and through this book a man who had lived in isolation as a hermit, influenced the entire Christian world. From the example of St Anthony, and a few others, grew the practice of Christians who wished to be especially devout living as hermits either in total isolation, or in groups of individual cells.

Women had less need to retreat from civilization in order to live a dedicated life; they generally already lived quiet and private lives. A number of women did become hermits, stories about them and their sayings have been preserved along with stories and sayings of the monks. From the stories it appears many of those who went into the desert had been prostitutes or actresses, both careers that kept a person in the public eye and offered few opportunities for serving God. A number of these female hermits protected themselves by living as men; in several stories only death revealed that the 'holy man' was a woman.

One woman who lived in the desert but was not trying to live down a dubious past was Syncletica. She came from a well-off Macedonian family who had settled in Alexandria. The death of her parents and brothers left her in charge of her blind sister. She gave away her possessions cut off her hair and lived in a tomb outside the City with her sister. Her Life, which was attributed to, but almost certainly not written by, Athanasius, is mainly an account of her discourses. She is not associated with any miracles and did not make a display of her ascetic lifestyle as she believed that "Virtue disclosed is virtue destroyed." Like St Anthony Syncletica attracted others who wished to serve God in the same way and other women settled in the same area so she became the leader of a community. She did not overvalue chastity, seeing obedience as a higher virtue. "Chastity is in danger of pride, obedience has the promise of humility." Judging from her discourses she was both intelligent and wise; she avoided the extremes of ascetic living which she felt could distract from concentrating on God. Living alone in the desert was mainly a masculine lifestyle; but it was women who started living in communities in order to follow a life of prayer and work and it was these groups of women who were the real forerunners of the monastic movement.

Chastity in pagan thought

To understand why chastity became so important we need to look at the context. Celibacy was unusual but not unknown in Judaism; the Essenes, a dissident Jewish sect, practiced it. Josephus, the first century Jewish historian, admired them for it. A tradition of a celibate priesthood was more common in Paganism. The Vestal Virgins were seen as both embodying and protecting the city of Rome. In some pagan temples celibacy was not a lifestyle but a life sentence, males could only serve the goddess after undergoing voluntary castration.

Greek Philosophy valued the spiritual above the physical and philosophy 'schools' at the beginning of the first millennium lauded austerity. Stoic and other philosophers greatly admired self-discipline and self-control. Pagan sages were admired for their continence and austerity. Forced by circumstance into poverty Diogenes, made his lack of possessions and family ties into a philosophy. He lived a wandering life, begging and sleeping rough, but he became such a celebrity that he was visited by Alexander the Great. Another influence was Gnostic thinkers, who saw the influence of the material world as totally evil and regarded having children, which by creating a new life increased the total amount of matter in the world, as a hindrance to a person's spiritual development.

Although Christians did not buy into these belief systems they were inevitably influenced by the ideas current among their contemporaries. Their ascetic life style was one of the few qualities that the Roman world admired in Christians who they otherwise regarded with contempt. Galen, the renowned second century physician, who wrote disparagingly of Christians who took things on faith, also wrote: "Their contempt of death is patent to us every day, and likewise their restraint in cohabitation. For they include not only men but also women who refrain from cohabiting all their lives; and they also number individuals who in discipline and self control, have attained a pitch not inferior to that of genuine philosophers."

Garry Wills, in his biography of St Augustine, suggests that his determination to lead an ascetic life after his conversion was less due to his new faith than to the pagan philosophical values he had long espoused. "There was a competitive note to this ascetical break with "lower" life. Though it was possible to be a Christian but not an ascetic that did not fit late-antique views of what was proper for a philosophical adherent to any serious moral program." His faith gave Augustine the ability to live a life of continence, (he had previously tried to and failed), but his faith was not its inspiration. It was his grounding in pagan philosophy that prevented him seeing an alternative to celibacy as he started out on life as a Christian.

Self sacrifice a means or an end?

In this moral climate admiration for virginity began to take on an emphasis that had little connection with the teachings of Jesus, or Paul. Paul had led a difficult and sacrificial life, suffering hardship, shipwreck, torture, imprisonment and finally death, but he never sought difficulties or hardship; he merely ignored the risks he ran in his dedication to serving Christ and the church. For some later Christians the hardship and suffering were self inflicted; a way of demonstrating their dedication to their faith. A life of self-sacrifice in the fourth century involved not only sexual denial; ascetics also renounced other 'worldly pleasures'. These included not only comfortable clothes and appetizing or, in some cases adequate, food, but also bathing. To modern minds this latter idea seems almost incomprehensible but it is more explicable in the Roman context. In the Empire public bathhouses were an important feature; they were not just for washing, they were centres of social and business life. In Roman life a bath was not just a matter of getting clean, it was one of life's major pleasures. Some bathhouses doubled as brothels, which must have added to Christian disapproval.

71

Christians and the duty to marry

Christians in the fourth century admired those, married or unmarried, who lived a chaste life.   This attitude may not have been as widespread as it appears.   Celibate men wrote most of the books that have come down to us.   Chastity may have been regarded as the ideal but most ordinary Christians married and had children.   However, Christian teaching introduced a fundamental change in how marriage was regarded.   St John Chrysostom taught that people's bodies belonged to themselves and to God, not to their family or city. Previously both Jews and Gentiles had taught that marriage and children were a duty everyone owed to their family and society. Rome had even enforced this with legislation.   Now people were being taught that marriage was no longer a public duty but only necessary to help people to deal with their sexual urges.   Pious teenagers were torn between pressure from their parents, who wished for grandchildren, and their own religious aspirations.   Stories of the lives of many third and fourth century saints included scenes where they were pressured to marry and resisted this pressure unto death. Continence within marriage was also admired and some couples after marriage decided, either before or after the arrival of children, to abjure sexual relations.   In the instances that have come down to us of younger couples deciding to live chastely, the initiative often seems to have come from the wife, who persuaded her husband to agree. Married men who became bishops seem to have been expected to live continently with their wives, or even live apart in Christian communities.

Christian ascetics

Asceticism started as a life of self-denial; prayer and fasting were the important factors. However, in time it was chastity that became the central ideal. In legends of saints their defence of their virginity often comes over as more important than the faith that motivated them. These stories are often fictional; they may record the names of genuine martyrs but their content reflects not their real lives but later preoccupations of the Church.

This cult of virginity had theological as well as practical results for the Church. Theologically it led to the dogma of the perpetual virginity of Mary, the Mother of Jesus. The identification of righteousness with chastity made it impossible for them to accept that the woman chosen to be the "God-bearer" might have lived a normal married life with Joseph. Therefore they elected to ignore the contemporary evidence of the Gospels, which record that Jesus had a number of brothers and sisters, and declared Mary a perpetual virgin whose marriage was never consummated.

St Jerome

The theologian whose views on chastity were most extreme was St Jerome. This can be seen in his writings 'Against Helvidius'. Helvidius had written a pamphlet which dared to suggest that Mary was not a perpetual virgin but that, after the birth of Christ, she had lived with Joseph and had further children; a view that a straight reading of scripture appears to support. Jerome was enraged and wrote a detailed exposition on why the Gospels could not possibly mean what they appeared to say. He is not content to defend the virginity of Mary but moves on to consider Joseph. A frequent explanation of Jesus' brothers and sisters is that Joseph was a widower with children. Jerome fiercely rejected this. "I claim still more that Joseph himself on account of Mary was a virgin...for if as a holy man he does not come under the imputation of fornication ...The conclusion is that he, who was thought worthy to be called father of our Lord, remained a virgin." Jerome makes a weak attempt to present a more balanced view but cannot quite manage it, "I do not deny that holy women are found both among widows and those that have husbands; but they are such as, even in the close band of marriage, imitate virgin chastity". Jerome appears to feel that by chastity men and women can become as the angels; "it is this angelic purity which secures to virginity its highest reward".

Jerome regarded chastity as possibly the most important Christian virtue. Jerome introduced his preoccupation with chastity into his interpretation of the parable, which Jesus used to illustrated how people hear and understand, or fail to hear and understand, his message. He stated that those in the parable who bore fruit thirty fold were married Christians, those who bore fruit sixty fold were widowed or living in a chaste relationship with their spouse, and those who bore fruit a hundredfold were virgins.

Jerome accepted that in the Old Testament mankind had been told by God to marry and have children but suggested that Paul had changed that. "But once in tones of thunder the words were heard "The time is shortened that henceforth those that have wives may be as though they had none" " . Jerome's dramatic words conjure a picture of Paul's words coming down from Mount Sinai, like new Commandments to supersede the old. He ignores the context and the fact that Paul explicitly says he is not giving a command from the Lord but his own judgement and that his words are a response to the circumstances of his day.

"Now about virgins: I have no command from the Lord but I give a judgement as one who by the Lord's mercy is trustworthy. Because of the present crisis, I think that it is good for you to remain as you are. Are you married? Do not seek a divorce. Are you unmarried? Do not look for a wife. But if you do marry, you have not sinned; and if a virgin marries, she has not sinned. But those who marry will face many troubles in this life and I want to spare you this. What I mean, brothers, is that the time is short. From now on those who have wives should live as if they had none; those who mourn as if they did not; those who are happy, as if they were not; those who buy something, as if it were not theirs to keep; those who use the things of the world, as if not engrossed in them. For this world in its present form is passing away." (1 Corinthians 7: 25 – 31)

Jerome was probably not the first, and was certainly not the last, to take a verse from Paul completely out of context and use it to support his own views. Even his contemporaries felt that Jerome had overstated his case and some of his friends tried to suppress 'Against Helvidius' for fear it would damage his reputation.

Jerome saw women as very powerful, capable of feeling, and inspiring, uncontrollable emotions. "It is not the harlot or adulteress who is spoken of; but woman's love in general is accused of ever being insatiable; put it out, it bursts into flame; give it plenty it is again in need; it enervates a man's mind and engrosses all thought except for the passion which it feeds."

Clearly Jerome saw women as threatening and dangerous not because of anything they did but because of what they were. He did not, however, allow this to interfere with his chaste but close relationships with several Roman matrons.

Not all writers of the time agreed with Jerome. We know of one, a priest called Jovinian, whose views were very different. He wrote "Virgins, widows and married women who have been once passed through the layer of Christ, if they are on a par in other respects, are of equal merit." Jerome was incensed by this view and wrote a book to refute it. Unfortunately we only know of Jovinian's work through Jerome's words; this quote is almost the only direct evidence of Jovinian's views. We don't know how common views like Jovinian's were, or whether other authors wrote in similar vein. Clement of Alexandria wrote positively of marriage but his treatise on marriage has not survived. Until the Reformation we have no record of theologians writing positively about marriage. The monks, whose laborious copying preserved ancient books, were not interested in copying any that might undermine or devalue their celibate way of life.

Side effects of venerating virginity

Valuing purity led to an increasing emphasis on sexual sins, which had not been characteristic of the Apostolic church. Jesus, while making it clear he upheld Jewish moral laws, was less concerned with sins of the flesh than those of the spirit. He is gentle in dealing with women who had committed sexual sins. There is only one group of sinners whom Jesus condemned strongly – religious hypocrites; those who followed the letter of the law but neglected the spirit; those who placed obstacles between the people and God and who valued outward respectability over inward goodness. Christ warned his followers "do not judge, or you too will be judged". The Apostles, including Paul, knew that self-righteousness and lack of charity were worse than the physical sins of pagans.

Some of the early Church fathers understood this; they were not all obsessed with the sins of the flesh. St Augustine was much more concerned to preach against greed, violence and deception, which he saw as calculating, satanic sins. He was more tolerant of sins of the flesh, which he felt Satan, having no body, could not commit. In general, however, the church throughout its history has preferred to forget that the sins condemned most strongly in Scripture are not the sins of the flesh but hypocrisy, denial of social justice, lack of love and cruelty.

During the fourth century the church began to call Mary by the title Theotokos, the Godbearer. Interestingly the title was officially approved in Ephesus, the great centre of the cults of mother goddesses. Constantine started a practice of Christianising pagan religious places and festivals; many ancient churches are built on the site of ancient temples and Jesus' birth is celebrated at the time of a pagan midwinter festival. Maybe the introduction of this title for Mary was a way to Christianise mother goddess cults. Certainly there have been times and places where the worship of the Virgin has become a cult and where her Son has been treated as almost incidental to adoration of his Mother.

It is only possible to speculate about the ways that this changed attitude to sex and marriage reflected changed attitudes to women in general. One result would have been fewer preachers who affirmed women in their role as wives, mothers and homemakers. These roles have been essential to the identity of the majority of women in every society and were highly valued in Jewish and most pagan societies. Now married women had to accept that, in the eyes of many clergy, they were inferior, unable to aspire to the piety and holiness of their celibate sisters.

Celibacy and monasticism

One obvious practical effect of the idealization of virginity was an increasing emphasis on clerical celibacy; although this did not become compulsory in the western church until 1138 and has never been compulsory for ordinary priests in Orthodox Churches. This emphasis on celibacy for those holding office in the church was applied more stringently to women. The Council of Chalcedon in 451 AD ruled on the subject of women deacons "If after receiving ordination and spending some time in the ministry she despises God's grace and gets married, such a person is to be anathematised along with her spouse". The same Council declared that dedicated virgins who later married were to be excommunicated. Incidentally this Canon reveals that some women were officially ordained in the fifth century, though it is referring to deacons not priests.

As more preachers and scholars lived a celibate life fewer would have had any understanding of the real difficulties and pressures women faced. Instead women were seen as temptresses, threats to men's peace of mind and the welfare of their souls. Even today, during recent scandals in the Roman Catholic Church, it has been noticeable that celibate priests identify and sympathise with erring colleagues, rather than children, or women, they have abused.   Sympathy for those struggling with the pressures of celibacy has contributed to the Church hushing up scandals at the expense of the victims; sometimes refusing to recognise abuse and allowing it to continue unchecked.

As the clergy became more powerful not only women but the laity in general began to be marginalized in the life of the church. One result of this idealisation of the celibate life was the growth of monasteries. These were to have a vital role in Europe during the years after the end of the Western Empire, years once called the dark ages.   They preserved not only the faith but also literacy and learning. Until the Renaissance it was monks and nuns who produced, or commissioned, almost all art, architecture, formal music, science and history.   They also provided the only hospitals and care for the poor; charity was funnelled through the church.

Even in the lands conquered by Islam Christian communities and Christian monasteries survived. The Koran gave the choice of conversion or death for pagans; but it allowed Christians and Jews who refused to convert special status, provided they submitted to the authorities and paid a special poll tax. For both climate and political reasons Eastern monasteries had an important role in preserving ancient manuscripts. Without the manuscripts they preserved, much less would be known about the ancient world and the early church.

7. THE AUTHORITY OF THE CLERGY

The apostolic church had a loose structure; its authority was informal and personal. This chapter looks at how a hierarchy developed and the ways that an increasingly influential and powerful clergy sought to control the laity, especially women.

The Apostolic church

The first century church seems to have had little formal organisation; although the Apostles had authority because they had been taught directly by Christ; those taught directly by the Apostles also seem to have been regarded with great respect. Very early on there was a distinction between deacons, who had practical responsibilities, and the Apostles who had spiritual leadership but there are no job descriptions for either role or attempts to limit their responsibilities. In his letters Paul mentions both elders, (presbyters or priests) and overseers (bishops) but does not suggest that one group had more authority than the other; in fact at times he seems to use the two terms interchangeably. (Acts 19: 17 & 27.) Early churches were all independent, but until its fall in70 AD Jerusalem was regarded as the mother church; Paul went there to consult the apostles and elders over the vexed question of whether Gentile converts needed to follow Jewish religious Laws. (Acts 15: 2) James, the brother of Jesus, who was the leader of the Christian strand of Judaism based in Jerusalem, and Peter were acknowledged as leaders. But Paul was prepared to challenge Peter when he thought he was wrong (Galatians 2: 11).

St Ignatius

After the deaths of the Apostles and those directly taught by them, bishops became a source of authority. They began to have a role distinct from, and senior to, presbyters. This process can be seen developing in the letters of St Ignatius (c35 – 107). He was the bishop of Antioch, the church that had commissioned Paul for his missionary journeys, and traditionally was appointed bishop only a few years after Paul's death. We know nothing of his background except that he was probably a slave. (He clearly identifies himself as a slave but some believe he was using it as a metaphor.) He was so esteemed in Asia Minor that the Elders of local churches travelled, some long distances, to meet him as he journeyed to Rome. The occasion of his journey was his arrest, conviction and death sentence for the crime of 'atheism', and the subsequent decision of the Antioch civil authorities to send him to Rome as part of their contribution to the Roman Games. Although Rome was a huge city it did not produce enough criminals to supply its appetite for watching people die in the arena, so provincial towns had to send Rome their yearly quota of convicted criminals. During his journey Ignatius wrote letters which have been preserved. Most of our knowledge of Ignatius comes from these letters. Ignatius's letters have been re-copied and valued partly because of their warmth; he comes over in them as a gentle man who truly loved his Lord and his fellow Christians. But the letters also survived because Ignatius's preoccupations became important to the church in the following centuries. One was his veneration of martyrdom. Another was his anxiety about false teaching and division among Christians; his solution was to seek unity through obedience to bishops. "Follow your bishop, every one of you, as obediently as Jesus Christ followed the Father. Obey your clergy too, as you would the Apostles; give your deacons the same reverence that you would to a command from God. Make sure that no step affecting the church is ever taken by anyone without the Bishop's sanction. The sole Eucharist you should consider valid is one that is celebrated by the bishop himself, or by some person authorized by him. Where the bishop is to be seen, there let all his people be; just as wherever Jesus Christ is present, we have the worldwide church." It is interesting just how strongly Ignatius feels he needs to uphold the authority of bishops, this is only one example of a number of similar passages in his letters. However, unlike Cyprian, who wrote over a century later, Ignatius does not seem to have a priestly view of the bishop's office. He sees the bishops as a source of authority that could protect against division and false teaching; he does not surround them with a mystic aura of priesthood. It is also interesting that he insists those presiding at the Eucharist must be authorised by the bishop but does not suggest that there is any other limitation on who could undertake this task. Presumably if a bishop felt it was right he could authorise a woman to preside.

Bishops were the final religious authority for Christians in each city or town. Bishops seem to have consulted each other but after consultation each was free to act according to his conscience. When the bishop in Alexandria condemned Origen for some of his views, Origen moved to Palestine and worked there for the rest of his life. The bishop there was prepared to ignore the decision of his fellow bishop and of the bishop of Rome, who had sided with the Alexandrian Bishop. Despite this lack of central leadership there was a sense of unity in the churches.   St Ignatius, in the letter quoted above, was the first to describe it as the catholic, or universal, church. His definition was "Where Jesus Christ is, there is the catholic church".

From the second century church leadership became more formal and in time the new clergy, as well as asserting their authority over the church, developed the idea that their role had a priestly character. They were not the only recognised authority; confessors, imprisoned Christians who had confessed their belief in Christ and survived, were sometimes seen as more authoritative than bishops, even by the bishops themselves.

Cyprian

Cyprian (c200 – 258), was Bishop of Carthage in the third century, he was appointed Bishop only a couple of years after his conversion so was probably not well grounded in the Scriptures and Christian teaching. He took the debate about the authority of bishops to a new level.   He had a very high view of the role of the clergy and saw bishops as inheriting apostolic authority.   Unlike Ignatius, Cyprian saw clergy not just as church leaders but as priests.   He also asserted the primacy of the Bishops of Rome, as successors to St Peter, but thought that the Bishop of Rome could no more dictate to other bishops than Peter had been able to dictate to the other Apostles. Stephen, the Bishop of Rome disputed this and denounced Cyprian as Antichrist.   This is the first known occasion in which a Bishop of Rome cited Christ's words "You are Peter, and on this rock I will build my church" (Matthew 16:18-19.) in support of his claim to authority over other bishops.

Cyprian was also the first to take the view that salvation was only available through the mainstream church and that baptism by heretics or schismatics was invalid; only within the Church were there true sacraments.   In his own words "No one can have God for his Father who has not the Church for his mother."   Stephen, the Bishop of Rome, also disagreed with Cyprian on this issue, so this view did not become part of the Roman tradition.   Cyprian's view that only 'his' church was the true church, has found many echoes in later church history.

Women's ministry and the disappearance of prophecy

This emphasis on the authority of bishops, had considerable implications for women.   As the informal charismatic church of the first century became more formal, and charismatic gifts and the guidance of the Holy Spirit became less central, women were more restricted.   From the second century women prophets were discouraged and after that time they were mainly associated with less orthodox groups.   It is not clear whether this was because by then only congregations outside the mainstream would accept women prophets, or whether accepting a woman prophet was in itself regarded as evidence of unorthodoxy.   This was part of a general turning away from 'charismatic' gifts from the second century onwards.   From that time on the mainstream church seems to have felt uncomfortable with phenomena such as prophecy and speaking in tongues.   It was not until the twentieth century that these practices were again accepted publicly in major denominations.

As the church became more established, more formal and less charismatic (i.e. less focussed on the 'charisma' or gifts of the Holy Spirit) they no longer sought out those they felt were full of the Spirit and appointed them as leaders.   Instead the bishops would accept people they considered suitable and 'ordain' them; laying hands on them at ordination and praying for the Holy Spirit to enter into them. It is not clear when this change in practice happened, although it certainly predates Constantine, but it would have had very significant consequences for women.   The Holy Spirit is unaccountable, and chooses for reasons of his own, often irrespective of gender or status. Humans choose those they consider appropriate and churches generally sought people who had the administrative or scholarly abilities that in their opinion were needed.   Once men were choosing church leaders, a suitable candidate for office was unlikely to be a woman or a slave, two groups that were strongly represented in the early church. This process can be seen in the church at other times, as a movement becomes mainstream women are excluded from leadership responsibilities.

By the third and fourth centuries practical or worldly considerations were certainly influencing church appointments.   In 248 Cyprian was appointed bishop only a couple of years after his conversion from paganism.   St Ambrose, who was Roman Governor of Liguria, (Northern Italy) was appointed as Bishop of Milan in 371 A.D. without having previously served as a priest and before he was even baptised.   Clearly by this time the church authorities were less concerned about spiritual maturity than academic or administrative ability; they may also have been influenced by social status.

The Montanists

One example of a group where women prophets were important was the one started by Montanus in the late second century. Montanists emphasised the 'charismatic' gifts, which had lost their central role in worship by then, and they valued prophets above bishops. This would not have pleased bishops who were actively asserting their authority throughout the second century. The clergy were not prepared to accept the authority of prophets, true or false, whom they could not control and who were accountable only to God. Montanus shared leadership of the group he founded with two women prophets, Priscilla and Maximilla. It appears their theology was orthodox and they were ascetic in their practices, but they were strongly criticised by local bishops and by those aiming at making Christianity, which was still illegal, more socially acceptable. The Montanists, like many sects since, thought that only they had the truth and that everyone else was wrong and this may have contributed to their rejection by the mainstream church.

One notable convert to Montanism was Tertullian. In view of the 'anti-women' attitudes in his writings it is interesting that he was willing to support and eventually join a group who accepted and valued women prophets. Tertullian gives a glimpse of a Montanist woman who had visions in his work 'On the Soul'. He describes "a sister whose lot it has been to be favoured with gifts of revelation, which she experiences in the spirit by ecstatic vision amidst the sacred rites of the Lord's Day in the church." She would tell the church leaders, about her visions after the service so that they could be "Examined with the most scrupulous care, in order that their truth may be probed". He quotes one of her visions in support of his thesis about the soul. Maximilla seems to have outlived Montanus and the other Montanist leaders, who may have been martyred. Alone, she was subject to considerable pressure by local bishops to give up leadership. Eusebius tells us "The Holy bishops attempted to silence the spirit that was in Maximilla" and quotes a report of her saying "I am driven away like a wolf from the sheep. I am not a wolf; I am word and spirit and power".

Gnostic groups continued to be more accepting of women as prophets and leaders, even after more orthodox churches relegated them to minor roles. An example is the Valentinians. Valentinus was a Platonist living in second century Rome. Like other Gnostics he believed the physical world was evil and so was unable to accept the incarnation, for him the idea of God becoming man was impossibility. Peter Brown points out "By claiming the redeemed had overcome sexual desire Gnostics were able to accept women as equal partners in the intense group life of a Christian intelligencia." In a treatise he wrote, 'On Heretics', Tertullian was very critical of the Valentinians' leadership practices, which he regarded as irretrievably lax. In a long paragraph detailing their various failings he includes these comments on women; "The very women of these heretics, how pert they are! For they are bold enough to teach, to dispute, to enact exorcisms, to undertake cures – it may be even to baptise." It is not clear whether Tertullian would have accepted any of these activities from women if they had been enacted in the mainstream church and with the approval of male leaders but it seems unlikely. From his description of the 'sister' who had visions she does not seem to have spoken them out during the service but to have reported them afterwards to church leaders so they could judge whether her vision should be made public.

The Didascalia and controlling laity

As women prophets were being sidelined, the role of 'widows' attached to the church was being developed. An order of Widows developed which no longer seemed to be connected with the church offering support to widows in need and membership seems no longer to be limited to actual widows. Age was an important qualification for the order of widows, as it was for women deacons; although sources vary on whether women were qualified at 40, 50 or 60. In the Didascalia Apostolorum, a document written in third century Syria, the authors were anxious to regulate the behaviour of women and limit their responsibilities in churches,

"It is neither right nor necessary therefore that women should be teachers, and especially concerning the name of Christ and the redemption of His passion. For you have not been appointed to this, O women, and especially widows, that you should teach, but that you should pray and entreat the Lord God. For He the Lord God, Jesus Christ our teacher, sent us the Twelve to instruct the People and the Gentiles and there were with us women disciples, Mary Magdalene and Mary the daughter of James and the other Mary; but He did not send them to instruct the people with us. For if it were required that women should teach, our Master Himself would have commended these to give instruction with us."

The Didascalia also counselled against women baptising; using the odd argument that if it were lawful for women to baptise Jesus would have been baptised by his mother, instead of John the Baptist. The Didascalia encourages the appointment of deaconesses and describes their functions including: preparing a woman for baptism and teaching her after the ceremony, visiting and ministering to the sick and visiting women in pagan households where a man visiting would not be acceptable. It includes the instruction "let a woman rather be devoted to the ministry of women and a male deacon to the ministry of men."

It is interesting that in the third century there was a clear recognition that Jesus had women disciples. There is no reason to think that the reported Apostolic limitation on women is authentic. The writers sought to give their teaching authority by attributing it to the Apostles but their agenda is clearly that of the third century. A distinction was growing up between ordinary Christians and the clergy, who were anxious to emphasise their authority over the laity, including widows. "Widows ought then to be modest, and obedient to the bishops and deacons, and to reverence, respect and fear the bishop as Go". In the first century writers were clear that only God, no man whatever his office, should be reverenced as God.

It is interesting to contrast the Didascalia Apostolorum with the Didache, written a century or so earlier. The titles of both claim they are the teaching of the Apostles. The Didache could have been written early enough to represent their teaching, but the Didascalia was written in third century Syria. However the text of the Didache has no reference to the Apostles whereas the Didascalia frequently asserts its authority by referring to the Twelve as its writers. The aims of the Didache are spiritual, to encourage converts and teach them the faith. The writers of the Didascalia appear more concerned to reinforce the authority of bishops and clergy and buttressed their arguments with the authority of the long dead apostles.

The Didascalia does provide interesting negative evidence. The fact that the writers felt it necessary to be so emphatic in forbidding women to teach and baptise implies that in some churches they were doing these things. Otherwise they would not have needed to assert so strongly the reasons this was, in their opinion, wrong. It is possible their instruction that women deacons should only work with other women may indicate that this was not the practice in all churches.

This chapter has looked at the way an ecclesiastical hierarchy developed after the death of the Apostles. Presbyters and episcopa (Priests and bishops) began to assert their authority over the laity. The clergy were particularly concerned to assert their authority over women, to ensure they did not take roles which they believed should be restricted to male clergy, and to exercise control over them in the roles in which they were accepted.

8. CHURCH AND STATE

It was Emperors who decided whether Christians should be persecuted and it was an Emperor, Constantine, who ended the persecution. He made Christianity legal, encouraged the church and gave its clergy advantages over their pagan rivals. This chapter will look at this pivotal event and some of its consequences for women in the church. Following Constantine's decision new attitudes and practices emerged and developed over the following centuries.

Constantine

Constantine defeated his rivals and made himself sole Emperor in the west in 312 when he invaded Italy and won a battle outside Rome against his last rival. The odds were against Constantine, who was far from his base and had a smaller army; so his victory was regarded as a sign of divine favour. No one is certain when or how Constantine came to favour Christianity. Like other prominent converts he was no doubt influenced by his Mother, St Helena, who was a Christian. During his reign she was active in developing the newly legal faith. She is best known now for her visit to Palestine, where she identified the sites of events in the life of Christ and is said to have found the true cross. Constantine may also have seen Christians as a strong cohesive group whose support would strengthen his position. Christianity had spread throughout the Empire and it is likely that in some areas Christians outnumbered pagans. Before turning to Christianity Constantine may have already been a monotheist, worshipping the Unconquered Sun, a belief system that combined the cult of Apollo with that of Mithras. The commemorative arch that was built by the Roman Senate to celebrate his 312 victory is dedicated to the Unconquered Sun.

Christians were encouraged to attribute Constantine's victory to Christ. At some point they started to see Constantine as a fellow Christian, not just a sympathiser, but he was not baptised until the last few weeks of his life, when he knew he was dying. This does not mean he had not adopted the Christian faith earlier. The early church took baptism very seriously indeed and believed that, though the worst sins before baptism could be forgiven, once baptised a person must live a pure life. Constantine, like so many rulers, kept a ruthless grip on power; he executed his wife, son and several in-laws. He must have felt the life of a baptised Christian was not something he could afford if he was to hold on to power. At the end of his life, when he knew he had not got long to live and would not gain any political advantage from an appearance of Christianity, he chose to be baptised.

Within a few years of Constantine's victory in the west his co-emperor Licinius, who still ruled the eastern Empire, began to plot against him and turned against Christians, driving them out of his palace. In the Roman Empire a Caesar's palace was the centre of Government; so Licinius's action amounted to firing all Christian civil servants. He insisted that: 'soldiers in the cities' (the police) should be deprived of rank unless they sacrificed to pagan gods; bishops should not communicate with each other; men and women should not worship together; and women should be taught only by women. His measures may have been designed only to impede the church but the measures against women probably indicate that he objected to the freedom given to Christian women.　　After Licinius's defeat Constantine was sole Emperor in both east and west and it is from this date, 324, is reckoned the beginning of the "Christian Empire".

Christianity's changing status

Constantine gave the church official buildings for religious use and built a number of new buildings for Christian worship.　Although a few churches had acquired buildings, in times when Christianity was tolerated, these must have been utilitarian.　Christians in the early church focussed on people not buildings but Constantine built beautiful basilicas for Christian worship several of which are still extant, although long since rebuilt.　The most famous is Hagia Sophia in Istanbul, later a converted to a mosque and now a museum.　In these basilicas worship became for the first time an aesthetic as well as a spiritual experience.　As churches became public buildings women lost the relative freedom they had had in house churches which could be seen as private rather than public spaces.

Constantine also changed the law to allow Christian communities to receive bequests; Christians could now leave money in their will to the church.　The church of the fourth century was still relatively poor and most of its income was used for charitable purposes.　Now some Christians became more equal than others, not because of their learning or piety but because of their position in the world.　Most of the women who were prominent in the fourth century church and renowned for their piety were wealthy.　They were pious but it was probably their generosity that ensured their lasting fame. Constantine reinforced the authority of the Clergy by giving them legal privileges. He gave Episcopal tribunals civil jurisdiction and gave bishops equal status to governors. Bishops had been increasing their spiritual authority over their congregations during the previous century, now they also wielded secular power.

Imperial Authority in church affairs

Emperors felt the need to control religion to ensure a peaceful and cohesive Empire. For Constantine and his successors, unity in the Christian church was vital since disunity would bring public disorder. Emperors had a strong interest in resolving theological disputes before they spread out into the streets and caused a riot. The clergy had already become increasingly concerned to discourage and control believers whose views or practices were different. Now Christians encouraged Emperors to intervene by appealing to them to arbitrate in their disagreements. As well as arbitrating in minor disagreements the Emperors convened Church Councils, assembling as many bishops as possible to resolve contentious issues. In less than a century Christianity went from an illegal faith, punishable by death, to a state religion; although the decrees against the old beliefs were not applied rigorously.

Changed status, changed attitudes

The consequences of imperial recognition of Christianity were not just political; the church had to adapt some of its beliefs and practices to fit its new status. One change was to formally approve of Christians being soldiers, since a religion accepted by the State couldn't undermine that State's right to enforce its decrees. J N Hillgarth suggests that by the fifth and sixth centuries this acceptance of the military may have gone further.

"The church acquired a military and legal stamp in these centuries – when its hierarchy was modelled after the militarised hierarchy of the late Roman Empire and its God after that Empire's despotic ruler and his lesser imitators the barbarian kings, - that is not yet effaced."

There was no place for women in a military hierarchy, so women were increasingly sidelined.

Religious art indicates a radical change in attitude. In the Catacombs, the main repository of second and third century Christian art, the most popular representation of Christ was as the good Shepherd; a symbol of the loving Saviour who was prepared to lay down his life for his people. In the great basilicas built in succeeding centuries the central image was of Christ as ruler of the world. This emphasis on Christ, as ruler and judge, rather than saviour, distanced him from individual believers and must have contributed to the growth of cults building up around the Virgin and other saints. They were increasingly seen as intermediaries who could be approached to intercede for the ordinary believer in need of healing or protection. The New Testament clearly states that Christ is the only intermediary between God and man but by the sixth century there was less and less emphasis on studying the Bible itself. More and more laity, and even clergy, no longer studied the Bible but focussed on secondary sources, the books and commentaries of the 'Church Fathers'.

Changes for women in the church

The position of women in the church did not change abruptly but the limitations and controls put on them continued to increase. The development of an authoritarian church accelerated in the fourth century. The structure became more formal and church members were not encouraged to challenge ecclesiastical authority. It is likely that the last house churches were replaced by churches based in public buildings. Churches were now public spaces and so no longer part of the private sphere, in which women had had some freedom. Society still regarded a woman putting herself forward in public as unacceptable. Ensuring that women were confined to a subordinate role was important to clergy who were enjoying their new status and authority.

Women who taught and baptised continued to have a place in some churches but the practice was increasingly discouraged. How common it was for a woman to be ordained and exactly what her duties would have been remains unclear, but it is likely her ministry was restricted to women. The written evidence remains largely negative; there is no need to forbid things that are not happening so the strong condemnations of, and bans on, various activities by women imply that these activities must have been happening in at least some areas. Written evidence for women carrying out priestly functions appears in the canons of the Council of Laodicea (352 AD). The Council was concerned to establish a hierarchy of clergy and this is the subject of many of their decisions. One of these, Canon XI, stated "Presbytides, as they are called, or female presidents are not to be appointed in the church". This is clear evidence that 'Presbytides' did exist in some places; otherwise the Council would not have been concerned to forbid the practice. There is also confirmation in a letter of Pope Gelasius I, written at the end of the fifth century, in which he complains that women were officiating at sacred altars and taking part in ecclesiastical affairs that should be the business only of men.

The appointment of women as deacons certainly survived the legalisation of Christianity by many years, but increasing efforts were made to limit what they could do. The Council of Chalcedon, meeting in 451 AD, included two directives on women. The first said that "No woman under 40 years of age is to be ordained a Deacon and then only after close scrutiny." This was in fact a reduction of an earlier age qualification, which had been sixty. The second stated that women are not permitted to speak out in church. The canons of the Council of Chalcedon confirm that women were not only appointed but were formally ordained as deacons.

Worldly considerations influenced what was considered acceptable behaviour in women. It cannot be a coincidence that almost all the prominent Christian women, in the fourth and fifth centuries, were wealthy in their own right. Their devotion to God and willingness to live a sacrificial life cannot be doubted but nor can the influence of the generosity with which they supported churches and individuals and gave to charitable work for the poor and needy. This generosity must have influenced the way they were regarded and what was expected of them. Wealthy women were not always bound by all the restrictions that bound others and were given opportunities not open to ordinary women. We know that Olympias was made a deacon when aged only

30, well under the usual age qualification. Rules may also have been stretched to give other wealthy women more scope. Certainly women who founded Christian communities were able to set the rules by which those communities lived.

This chapter has considered the changes for the church that followed imperial recognition. The reign of Constantine was a pivotal point; the time when a marginal, often persecuted religion became mainstream. Within a few years Christians had become part of the establishment with all the worldly advantages and spiritual disadvantages such status can bring. This accelerated the process of adapting their beliefs and practices to the society in which they lived; the outsiders had become insiders and began to act accordingly. It became important that women did not act within the Christian community in ways that would be disapproved of in secular society. It seems clear that women who wished to be active with the church found fewer and fewer options open to them.

9. "WHO SO SURPASSED HER SEX"

This chapter will look at women's lives during the fourth and fifth centuries, especially the lives of a few prominent women, who lived and worked within the Christian community. Their stories demonstrate both the opportunities and the restrictions women found within the church. Christianity had spread fast in the Eastern Empire. In Rome the upper classes were more reluctant to embrace Christianity, which they associated with the poor and slaves. In the late fourth century aristocratic Romans made determined efforts to protect 'Old Roman values', including their pagan religion.

Women as wives and mothers

As always marriage and motherhood were the lot of most women but wives and mothers are the group about whom least is known. Sermons on marriage have been preserved but we have few records of the experiences of ordinary women. Robert Markus suggests marriage was undergoing changes in the fourth and fifth centuries:

"The inequality of the partners was already becoming attenuated during the early centuries of our era, and there are widespread symptoms to suggest the emergence of a notion of the married couple as a partnership of equals. The relationship of marriage was becoming impregnated by the ideals of mutual affection and respect, and considered as the exclusive area for the partners' sexual activities. If we can trust the figures which suggest that Christians tended to marry at a notably higher age than their pagan contemporaries,

Christianity would appear to have reinforced these shifts towards marriage as a more personal and free partnership of equals."

Marriage was developing into a more positive form, to modern eyes, but at the same time it was losing its previously unrivalled position as the most valued career choice for a woman.

Consecrated virgins and widows

The practice of virgins dedicating themselves to Christ was encouraged by the church. These 'consecrated virgins' were regarded as supernaturally protecting their household by their dedication to God and by their prayers. This apparent mystical power of virgins extended from their families to the community. These women sat separately in church and were seen as bringing credit to their churches and bishop. From the fourth century some of these consecrated virgins and widows lived communally with other women of like mind. Consecrated upper class widows and spinsters had a strong influence in some areas.

By the fourth century the role of consecrated virgins, even outside communities, was formalised. The Council of Elvira in 305 decreed that a consecrated virgin who broke her vows should be excommunicated; although, if she was seduced only once and repented for the rest of her life, she could be given communion "at the last". The rationale for insisting virgins be true to their vow was that consecrated women were described as 'brides of Christ' The implication of this was that any sexual relationship, even within marriage, was adultery. This decree was repeated in the Canons of the Council of Chalcedon in 451. St Paul's concept of individuals remaining single to devote themselves to the spread of the Gospel was now a formal arrangement; sometimes not even a voluntary one. Daughters were social or financial assets to be disposed of to their family's best advantage. A family might decide to devote their daughter to God just as they might decide to marry her to a man of their choice; either way she was expected to abide by their decision. Some families changed their minds and decided on an advantageous marriage for a daughter previously dedicated to God. The rules about virgins who broke their vows may have been addressing this issue as much as trying to ensure the woman herself remained true to her calling.

A few pious women founded monasteries, where other women could join, not a household, but a community. The long tradition of religious communities started from these groups of women choosing to live together and follow a life of prayer, study and charitable work. It is not known how worship was organised in these women's communities; it is likely they joined with a local church or a male community. The complaints of Pope Gelasius, mentioned earlier, indicate that some women's communities conducted their own services.

Women as patrons

One role women were always encouraged to take was that of patron; supporting an individual or church financially. By the fourth century noted preachers and writers received support, moral and financial, from wealthy women. They often tutored these women in their studies of the scriptures, and encouraged them in a self-denying and celibate lifestyle. Melinia the Elder (c341 – 410) was left a young wealthy widow and fled from her family to avoid remarriage. She left her son with a guardian in Rome and proceeded to live an independent and ascetic life. After travelling in the Middle East she settled in Jerusalem where she founded a community; her generosity gave her an important position in religious circles. She devoted herself to a study of theology and acted as spiritual guide to other Christians, some of them men. One admirer called her "this female man of God".

Women as Ascetics

A number of godly women in the fourth and fifth centuries were eulogised informally in long letters about their lives which were circulated among their relatives and friends. Jerome, for example, wrote biographical accounts of his closest female friends, Paula and Marcella, and of Fabiola, the woman who founded the first Christian hospital. These wealthy women rejected a life of luxury in the upper echelons of Roman society and in consequence no doubt lost status among their social peers while gaining honour in the Christian community. They were prepared to live ascetic lives without basic comforts like mattresses, adequate food, new clothes and personal cleanliness.

Paula (347 – 404) was a wealthy Roman widow, who became a disciple of Jerome. Her friends did not see Jerome's influence on Paula in a positive light. Palladius in his Lausiac History wrote:

"Among them was the Roman matron Paula, who was mother of Toxotius. A certain Jerome from Dalmatia stood in her way, for she was well able to surpass everyone, being a genius of a woman. He thwarted her with his jealousy and prevailed on her to work to his own end and purpose."

When Jerome left Rome, Paula followed him to Palestine with one of her daughters, leaving her younger children behind in Rome; Jerome paints a sad picture of the pain the parting caused the children and Paula.   After travelling to visit prominent Christian teachers she settled in Bethlehem near Jerome, and there lived an ascetic life dedicated to Bible study.   Paula did not believe in moderation in her self-denial.   Jerome wrote that she was "Not mindful of home, of children, of servants, of possessions, of anything that pertains to the world".   Paula and her daughter had an understanding of Hebrew that Jerome considered superior to his own.   He dedicated his translation of the Bible into Latin to them and it is likely that their work contributed much to this translation, which remained the standard Biblical text for Roman Catholics until the twentieth century.   In Bethlehem Paula founded three monasteries for women and one for men, headed by Jerome.   Paula gave her wealth to charity for the benefit of the poor, the needy and the sick.   Jerome wrote of her "What poor man as he lay dying was not wrapped in blankets given by Paula?   What bedridden person was not supported with money from her purse?"   Paula was as immoderate in her giving as in her fasting. When she died she left her daughter nothing but debts, and the responsibility for supporting her fellow nuns.

Women as scholars

Melania and Paula devoted themselves to their studies but the pre-eminent fourth century woman scholar was probably Marcella (325 – 410).   Marcella was a well to do Roman who was widowed after seven months of marriage.   She was one of several wealthy and pious women in Rome who assembled groups of devout women to study the

Bible in their homes. Marcella's group asked Jerome to be their mentor; he encouraged them to live ascetic lives and to study the Scriptures in Hebrew and Greek. Jerome called Marcella, his "task mistress" because of her intellectual rigour and frequent requests for him to explain linguistic details and obscure texts.

After Marcella's death Jerome wrote of her: "She never came without asking something about Scripture, nor did she immediately accept my explanation as satisfactory, but she proposed questions from the opposite viewpoint, not for the sake of being contentious but so that, by asking, she might learn solutions for points she perceived could be raised in objection. What virtue I found in her, what cleverness, what holiness, what purity.... after my departure, if an argument arose about some evidence from Scripture, the question was pursued with her as the judge." Jerome also explained how Marcella was able to teach and give spiritual counsel, even to male priests.

"And because she was so discreet and knew about what the philosophers call in Greek 'to prepon', that is how to behave appropriately, when she was thus questioned, she used to reply as if what she said was not her own, even if the views were her own, but came either from me or from another man, in order to confess that, about the matter she was teaching, she herself had been a pupil. For she knew the saying of the Apostle, "I do not, however, permit a woman to teach lest she seem to inflict an injury on the male sex and on those priests who were inquiring about obscure and doubtful points."

Jerome and his contemporaries were hypocritical in allowing a woman to teach and counsel men only if she passed her opinions off as from a man. But in a patriarchal society, where women were restricted within both secular and religious society, this loophole must have given women scholars freedom to communicate their spiritual wisdom and their hard won knowledge.

Marcella lived an ascetic life but unlike Paula was moderate in her practice. She fasted but not excessively. She was generous; Jerome wrote of her that she chose "to store her money in the stomachs of the poor rather than keep it at her own disposal". But, at the urging of her mother, she also gave much of her wealth to her brother's family.

Women as writers

The one thing these godly and studious women did not do was write books. In the fourth century Paul's refusal to allow women to teach was seen as referring especially to writing. Religious controversy was regarded as the province of men. The only books written by women that have been preserved were not theological, devotional or Biblical commentary. A poem on the creation and the incarnation using phrases from Virgil has survived. This poem, written around 351 shows its author, Proba, as intelligent and well educated in Roman literature and Christian thought. A travel book has also been preserved. Egeria was a pilgrim who gives an interesting insight into pilgrimages in the fourth century. The group would stop at each site for reading and for prayer and she found that, when asked where any incident from the Bible happened; local guides were always ready to identify a nearby location. It is clear that she was not the only lone woman traveller. She records her delight when reunited with a nun she had met earlier, who was also on a pilgrimage.

There is one woman whose teaching was written, although not by her. She is also the subject of the only ancient 'biography' of a woman.

Macrina (c330 – 379) was from a Christian family. She influenced her brothers, leading them into a stronger faith by precept and example, two of her brothers became influential Bishops. After she died one brother, Gregory, Bishop of Nyssa, wrote her life story. He starts by writing "If indeed she should be styled 'woman' for I do not know if it is fitting to designate her by her sex, who so surpassed her sex." Macrina dedicated herself to virginity after the man her father had betrothed her to died, living with her mother and raising her youngest brother. Gregory writes that she persuaded her mother "to share the life of the maids, treating all her slave girls and menials as if they were sisters". After her mother's death Macrina was the Abbess of a community of women. She lived a life of service to God and her fellow men. Her brothers admired her, seeing her as less contaminated by the world, and church politics, than they were. Her story tells of the work of women's communities at that time. She was involved in teaching and caring for the poor and sick and during a famine she rescued baby girls left to die by the roadside, and cared for them.

What sets Gregory's book apart from other biographical writing about fourth century women is the accounts of miracles arising from her prayers. He seems to feel embarrassed to write of miracles performed by a woman and refers only to one healing in detail, with brief references to other healings and a miraculous replenishment of her store of grain, which enabled her to give local people relief throughout a famine. He writes of Macrina's spiritual insight and understanding, and of a conversation they had when she was dying. "She discussed various subjects, enquiring into human affairs and revealing in her conversations the divine purpose concealed in disasters. Besides this she discussed the future life as if inspired by the Holy Spirit." Gregory wrote a treatise 'On the soul and the resurrection' based on this conversation. It was cast as a platonic dialogue with Macrina in the Socratic role of teacher. Some have doubted whether this dialogue records Macrina's words but it is difficult to explain why else Gregory would do such an unconventional thing as putting a woman in a platonic dialogue. His contemporaries would have regarded this portrayal of a woman in a teaching role as inappropriate.

Women as carers

Ascetic women did not only devote their lives to study and meditation and seeking personal holiness. They were also heavily involved in caring for the poor and needy. The wealthy were generous with their money towards everyone but themselves, and sometimes their families. Both well to do women and those with nothing to give but their time and skill, were prepared to spend time and energy nursing the sick and caring for those in poverty. Fabiola founded the first hospital for the sick poor. Marcella, Paula and Olympias all gave generously of their wealth. We know less of ordinary Christian women but the information we do have indicates that many were involved in hands on care of those in need. Not just as individuals, many women's monasteries provided food, shelter and nursing care. Monks and clerics seem to have been reluctant to touch people for fear of arousing sexual feelings in themselves or the other person. Christian women were less inhibited and were prepared to offer hands-on care. Julian the Apostate demanded that his pagan priests practice charity and pointed out "No Jew is ever seen begging and the impious Galileans support not only their own poor but ours as well."

This makes it clear that Christians continue to offer sympathy and care to those in need and were not discriminating against non-Christians in their giving. Christian writers of the time were preoccupied with abstruse theological points and the need for a chaste lifestyle. It is helpful to be reminded that ordinary Christians were continuing to love their neighbours as Christ had taught. It was Christian women, not men, who were most involved in both giving and physical caring.

Women and friendship

Ascetism for a woman was socially liberating. One thing that stands out about these women was the closeness of their friendships, not only with each other but also with men. Several of the Early Church Fathers accepted women as companions and fellow scholars. They would warn young men of the dangers of women's wiles but could sincerely admire these women whose ascetic lifestyle made them 'honorary men'. Jerome saw no reason why Origen's ideal of an unrelenting ascetic labour of the mind, should not be extended in its full rigors to mature educated women. He depended on these women for emotional support. His competitive nature soured his relationships with male colleagues but he was less threatened by a woman's ability, and so felt free to share his learning with them and appreciate their knowledge and wisdom.

Another close friendship was between Olympias (c361 - 408) and St John Chrysostom. Olympias lived in Constantinople under the eye of the Emperor and, as a great heiress, was married to a member of his family. Her husband died shortly after the marriage, leaving her a widow at twenty. She immediately expressed a wish to consecrate her life to God. In an effort to control Olympias and her inheritance she was put under control of a guardian until she was thirty. At times clergy were banned from visiting her. Despite opposition, she persisted in living an ascetic life and giving generously to the church and to charity. When Olympias became thirty the Emperor was out of town and the bishop ordained her as a deaconess, despite her young age (the age qualification for a deaconess was sixty.) This can be seen as a kindly act, freeing her from the constant pressure to remarry she had endured for ten years, but the move also secured her wealth for the church. Olympias lived in seclusion with a community of 250 consecrated women based in her house. She met her mentor and friend John Chrysostom, when he was appointed bishop of Constantinople. He described her as "Like a town, a haven, a wall of defence, speaking with the eloquence of example and through your suffering instructing both sexes". Under his influence she began to focus her giving on the poor and needy, rather than the support of clergy or church buildings. John Chrysostom's lack of interest in politics made him a poor choice for bishop in Constantinople, which was a hotbed of politics, religious and secular. After seven years he was exiled and was never allowed to return. Although he and Olympias did not meet again, they corresponded regularly until his early death. Olympias was not allowed to leave Constantinople; both secular and religious authorities were concerned to keep her wealth where it would benefit the City. However, within the City she was able to live the life she chose and exert a positive influence on her society. Her willingness to accept other women to live in her household must have provided many vulnerable women with a refuge. John Chrysostom's letters to Olympias have been preserved. He expressed his dissatisfaction with a long distance relationship.

"To those who love one another to be spiritually united is not enough, they also need one another's physical presence for otherwise a large part of their joy is removed.   Even St Paul felt anguish when separated from those he loved.   It is hard for a soul in solitude to have a conversation with another soul and so, for true consolation, a man needs the friend's presence so that he can speak and listen in turn."

This acceptance of women as intellectual companions was not, of course, universal.   St Augustine's writings make it clear that he did not see women as suited for intellectual companionship.   He suggested that if God had intended to give Adam a companion, instead of a mother for his children, he would have created not Eve but a second man.   Augustine sought to live a life of the mind and spirit and his closest relationships were with the men who shared his intellectual and spiritual life.

Women in public life

In the fifth century, when real power seems to have passed from the Emperors to ambitious nobles, court eunuchs and barbarian military leaders, several women in the imperial family took a role in politics. These women were exceptions but, as in most patriarchal societies, women had much more indirect power and influence in practice than in theory.

A woman who took a prominent role in public life was Pulcheria, the eldest sister of Theodosius II (408 – 450).   Theodosius became Emperor at the age of seven and when, six years later, his Regent died or retired Pulcheria was appointed in his place.   Records of the fifth century are scanty and they do not give information on how a teenage girl persuaded powerful men to appoint her as Augusta (Empress) and

Regent.   Pulcheria, declared herself dedicated to perpetual virginity and persuaded her sisters to do the same.   As Regent she supervised her brother's education and ruled the Empire in his name until he reached his majority.   Edward Gibbon, in his Decline and Fall of the Roman Empire, wrote of Pulcheria: "She alone among all the descendents of the great Theodosius appears to have inherited any share of his manly spirit and abilities." He gave her the credit for the relatively peaceful reign of Theodosius.   Pulcheria trusted the management of military and political affairs to officials, as her father had done, but she was more active and interested in the business of governing the Empire than her brother proved to be; she also took a close interest in church affairs.

When Theodosius died in 450; Pulcheria chose his successor.   She entered into a formal contract of marriage with her choice for Emperor; giving him a claim to the throne by making him a member of the imperial family.   She insisted on a marriage in name only and remained true to her vow of chastity.   She picked well; Marcianus managed to end the previous policy of appeasing Attila the Hun with increasingly large sums in gold, without starting a war.   He was extremely popular in Constantinople, as was Pulcheria.   Pulcheria died three years after his accession and was later declared a saint.

Christian women, especially ascetic women, had more freedom in the fourth and fifth centuries under Christianity.   Stories of individuals show the spiritual, intellectual, and even social, freedom that women who lived ascetic lives could enjoy and how they served both God and their fellow men.

10. THE FALL AND RISE OF ROME

The decline of centralised Imperial power in the Western Empire led to a period once called the Dark Ages. There are fewer records from this period; the tribes who now ruled Europe had an oral culture not one based on writing. However, the idea that the period between the Roman Empire and the Norman Conquest was a dark age was the idea of Victorian historians.

Collapse of the Western Empire

At the beginning of the fifth century the Western Empire began to break up, troops were withdrawn from distant provinces like Britain, and the Emperor's control and power in the West faltered. Rome was sacked by the Goths in 410. From then onwards, the authorities in Constantinople had no real jurisdiction in the West; although in theory Italy continued under Byzantine leadership for several hundred years. In the sixth century Justinian briefly re-conquered Italy but from the seventh century the Eastern Empire was too busy resisting militant Islam to contemplate further involvement in the west.

Earlier chapters looked at Rome and the Eastern Empire, since most information available on the early church is from that area but from now on the focus will be on women in the western church. Differences in practice between the churches in the east and those in the west began to emerge, including differences in the way they treated women. In the East they continued to ordain deaconesses long after Rome banned them in the sixth century. As a result it was only in monasteries that women could teach and give pastoral care. However, the Church in the west allowed women, usually midwives, to baptise infants in situations where there was a risk a baby might otherwise die unbaptised.

Growth in the power of the Papacy

One reason why the churches in the east and west began to diverge was the growing power of the papacy. As the emperor's secular power in Italy decreased the Roman clergy increased their insistence that their bishop was not just the 'first among equals' but had authority over all other bishops. As the Emperor's jurisdiction in the west weakened a power vacuum was created, which some Roman clergy were eager to fill. This drive towards centralising decision making in Rome was a unifying force for churches in western Europe but it caused disputes with North Africa and the East, whose bishops were not prepared to accept papal authority. Ultimately it led to the division of the Church into Catholicism in the West and Orthodoxy in the East. This division stemmed less from relatively minor differences in theology, liturgy and practice than from poor communication and struggles over authority.

Pope Gregory the Great (590 – 604) is credited with laying the foundations of a powerful Papacy and his successors built on those foundations. Supporters of the Papacy were prepared to distort history to serve their purposes. A history of the early bishops of Rome gave most early 'popes' the status of martyrs. This 'history' dates to the eighth or ninth century but purports to be much older. It was written for a purpose; as was the Donation of Constantine, which appeared in the same period. This was a letter, allegedly written by

Constantine in 312, in which he entrusted both secular and religious affairs in the west to the Bishop of Rome.   Both documents were intended to enhance the status of the papacy and show that papal authority stemmed from the Apostolic authority of Peter and the Imperial authority of Constantine.   They appeared at a time the Papacy was trying to extend its power over secular affairs.   R W Southern comments on the Church's attitude to, and use of, forgeries in medieval Europe.   "It is important to understand the importance of forgeries as vehicles of ideas in the early period.   They did not have the vulgar associations of modern forgeries.   The primitive age (700-1050) had few records, but it had clear ideas of the past.   These ideas were based on accumulated traditions, legends, pious fabrications, and above all on a reluctance to believe that the past is largely unknowable.   Hence even learned and critical men easily believed that the past was like the present, only better; in a word that it was an idealized present.   Documents were therefore drawn up in which the theories of the present were represented as the facts of the past."

Neither of these forgeries is connected with the position of women but they are an indication of the way clergy were prepared to manipulate history and alter or destroy evidence, in order to show that the past conformed to their own ideas.   Given this attitude it is unlikely that any documents that dealt with women making a positive contribution within the church would have survived.   Documents were preserved when monks were prepared to devote many hours to copying them and those they chose not to copy have not survived.   This is why negative evidence is all that is left to indicate what women were doing in ancient and early medieval times.   Evidence that is literally cast in stone, like the epitaphs, which have been found describing women as 'presbytera', may have survived only because stone is more lasting.

One striking indication that women were less circumscribed than official histories imply dates from the ninth century. In the church of St Praxedis in Rome there is a mosaic of four women, the Virgin Mary, Saints Prudentiana and Praxedis and a fourth woman whose square halo indicates that she was alive when the mosaic was created. The inscription says Theodora Episcopa (bishop). Traditionally Theodora is regarded as the mother of Pope Paschal I, (817 – 824), who rebuilt the Church in the eighth century; as his mother she was given an honorary title. However it has been suggested that she is pictured wearing a head covering which indicates she was unmarried, which casts doubt on this identification. This mosaic bears witness to later efforts at censorship. An attempt has been made to obliterate the R and A at the end of her name, although the feminine ending for Episcopa has been left, indicating that the person with the chisel was not literate in Greek.

Double Monasteries

It does seem unlikely that any woman would have had such a prominent role in the church in Rome itself as late as the eighth century. However, in more remote parts of Europe there were women whose role in the church was as important and powerful as the role of bishops. They were the independent, authoritative abbesses who ruled double monasteries in Gaul and Britain.

Monasteries continued to be a significant factor in religious life and expression and in northwest Europe religious houses were founded where both men and women lived, accommodated separately but under the same rule.   In these monasteries the abbesses were in overall charge of both men and women.   Double monasteries developed especially in rural areas in the less urbanised countries of Gaul and the British Isles.   It was not desirable for a community of women to live in isolation during a time of almost continual warfare and the presence of monks provided the women's community with protection and with priests to conduct their services.   The laws in Gaul and in Anglo-Saxon Britain allowed women to own and bestow property and this must have facilitated the establishment of double monasteries, which were usually founded by, or on behalf of, highborn women.

The Conversion of Britain

Christianity spread to England before the time of Constantine but little is known about the early English church; there are no well-known names associated with it, except St Alban the martyr.   Christianity must have come to Britain through ordinary people who crossed the channel and shared their faith with those they met.   After the withdrawal of the legions the Romano-British culture, which had grown up while Britain was a province of Rome, continued to flourish for a time.   During this period British Christians evangelised Scotland and Ireland.   The most famous of these missionaries was Patricius, now known as St Patrick (c 385 – 461), who was instrumental in the conversion of Ireland.   Later, when Roman Britain and Christianity were overwhelmed by an influx of Anglo-Saxons, it was the church in Ireland that kept alive the flame of Christianity and classical learning. The incursions of Anglo-Saxons seem to have overwhelmed the British church and initiatives to convert the Anglo-Saxons came from overseas.   Irish Monks, the descendents of Patrick's converts, travelled back to the mainland to evangelise the Angles in Northern England and the Picts in Scotland.   A couple of generations later St Augustine of Canterbury arrived in southern England, sent by Gregory the Great to evangelise the Angles there.   He and his successors worked in southern England to bring the Anglo-Saxon leaders from their pagan beliefs to faith in Christ. Recently historians have begun to doubt the story of the Anglo-Saxons conquering England in a bloody conflict and have surmised that there was a more peaceful infiltration.   Certainly they seem to have received missionaries civilly, even when they didn't accept their message, and there were no martyrs in Britain to match those among missionaries to the Germanic tribes on mainland Europe.

Women in the Celtic Church

The Celtic church which, although seen as part of the universal Church, had developed separately because of its remoteness, did not emphasise women's role in bringing sin into the world by tempting men, which was a feature of the teachings of Augustine and his contemporaries.   The church in the British Isles had been established long before this strand of theology developed. Among Celtic, Anglo-Saxon and Scandinavian peoples women had more freedom to act independently, they had more legal rights and more freedom to make decisions about their own lives.   Thus the Celtic church saw women more positively.   This is probably why double monasteries, ruled by an abbess, seem to have been more prevalent in the British Isles.

St Bridget

St Bridget (c451 – 525) was the daughter of a couple converted by Patrick. She founded an abbey in Kildare and became its Abbess. It is impossible to disentangle historical fact from legend in the life of St Bridget. It is clear however that she was a forceful woman who had a great deal of influence both among the poor and the rich and powerful. When she decided Kildare needed a bishop she chose and appointed one. Abbots were more important than bishops in the Irish church, the Irish sometimes referred to the pope as the 'Abbot of Rome', so it is quite possible an Abbess had the power to appoint a bishop. The story goes on to suggest Bridget and the bishop argued over who had greater authority. St Bridget founded a number of communities in Ireland, each of which she visited regularly.

Hilda of Whitby

Hilda (614 – 680), who was a member of the Northumbrian royal family she was baptised with the whole court when her uncle the King was converted to Christianity after marrying Ethelburgha, a Kentish Princess who was a Christian. Hilda, who was probably a widow, had intended to enter a French monastery but St Aiden persuaded her to return to the North instead. After a few years as abbess of an existing monastery Hilda founded the earliest double monastery in England in the area that is now called Whitby.

Hilda seems to have been a remarkable woman. According to Bede, the main authority on her life, her wisdom was famous and she counselled both ordinary people and powerful nobles. Under her charge Whitby became a place of learning and Bede reports that she trained five future bishops and a future archbishop. She also trained women including her successor as abbess who was, like Hilda, literate, influential and independent. St Hilda encouraged the arts. When a local herdsman, Caedmon, developed a poetic gift Hilda nurtured his talent and made him a monk so that he had time to write his songs about God's creation. She probably also arranged copying of the Scriptures and other books; beautiful illuminated manuscripts were a characteristic of the Celtic church; the Book of Kells and the Lindisfarne Gospels are the supreme examples. When Hilda became an Abbess there was no higher education in England; both clergy and sons of nobles were sent overseas to study in Ireland or mainland Europe. In less than a hundred years this situation was transformed and Northumbrian monasteries were centres of learning renowned throughout Europe. Hilda must have contributed to this change.

Under Hilda the Abbey at Whitby became the burial place for the Northumbrian royal family. It was also the site of a Synod, called in 663 by King Oswy. This King had married a Christian Princess from the South. After he too became a Christian he found it annoying that when he was celebrating Easter, according to the Celtic date, his wife was still fasting because she followed a Roman dating for Easter. He called the Synod of Whitby to decide whether Northumbria should follow the practices of the Celtic or Roman churches. The decision at the Synod was made not by learned clerics, who each argued the case for their own church, but by Oswy himself. Initially he inclined to the Celtic side. It is said he changed his mind when the advocate for Roman practices gave St Peter as the authority for their style of tonsure and explained that St Peter had been entrusted with the keys of heaven and hell.   Oswy felt he could not afford to offend the gatekeeper who could exclude him from heaven.   In this way the momentous decision was made that the English church would follow Rome, the Celtic Church elsewhere in the British Isles remained independent for longer.

In the century following the establishment of the Abbey at Whitby a number of other double monasteries were founded and run by women, many like Hilda of royal blood.   Eventually there were sixteen double monasteries in England.   They were important religious centres and the double monastery at Ripon became the burial place for the kings of Mercia. Barbara Mitchell writes:

> "While it lasted this unique system educated many women and enabled their abbesses to hold positions of responsibility and power unattained by women before this century."

The double monasteries that flourished in Britain and Gaul were a high point for women in the church.   Independent, intelligent and educated women were able to carve out a role for themselves in religious life.   They were highly respected by their contemporaries and had considerable influence.   They could worship God with little or no interference from male clerics.

11. THE CHURCH AND THE BARBARIANS

In the last centuries of the first millennium Christianity was moving forward but the significant developments were not centred in Rome but among the barbarians who had overrun Roman Europe. This chapter will focus on the part women played in bringing Germanic tribes to Christianity.

A growing church

Mission was always central to Christianity; Christ had commanded his disciples to "Go and make disciples of all nations" and they had obeyed. We do not know how many Christians there were by the time of Constantine but they were certainly a sizable minority within the Empire and had spread far beyond its boundaries. The Catacombs of Rome, with their miles of passages with niches for bodies stacked to the ceiling on each side, are evidence of just how many Christians there were in this one city during the two and a half centuries before persecution ended and Christians could safely bury their dead in the open. In the fourth century the newly recognised faith penetrated more deeply within the Empire itself and outside its boundaries. Christians quickly became the majority within the Empire especially in cities; rural areas were more conservative and slower to accept Christianity. In the fifth and sixth centuries a real effort was made by Christians to evangelise the world beyond the frontiers of the old Roman Empire. Missionaries penetrated inland into Africa; East Syrian Missionaries journeyed across Asia, preaching and starting

121

churches, venturing as far as China.   During these early centuries Christian communities were established across the known world: in China, India, Armenia, Southern Arabia, Iberia, Persia, Mesopotamia, Ethiopia and the British Isles.

From the seventh century Christians in the west tackled the daunting task of evangelising Europe's pagan tribes.   English Christians, whose church was the most learned and flourishing in northern Europe, had a vital role in the conversion of mainland Europe. Abbesses and nuns contributed to this but were not the only women involved.   Christian princesses were often married to pagan rulers for political reasons.   They were sent away to live among people they had been brought up to consider barbarians.   They practiced their faith in pagan courts and there are stories of the impression the goodness and kindness of these princesses made.   Their quiet witness was often influential in persuading their husbands to accept the missionary monks who converted them to Christianity.

Boniface and Leoba

The man who evangelised the area that is now Holland and Germany was St Boniface (c 675 - 754) who was born in Crediton in Devon but spent most of his life in mainland Europe.   He has been described as the greatest English Missionary.   Boniface is known from writings about him and from some of his own letters.   He corresponded with several Abbesses; asking them to pray for his work when he was facing difficulties and asking for copies of the Epistles of Peter to be made and sent to him.   Later he wrote asking for monks and nuns to come and help him in his work.   Initially a group of twelve, six men and six women, travelled across the channel to join him.   The most prominent of these recruits was Leoba, a kinswoman of Boniface, whose presence he had requested because of her reputation for learning, wisdom and goodness.

We know about Leoba (710 – c780) from her biography, written over fifty years later by Rudolf, a monk in the Monastery where she was buried. He never knew her but did speak to others who had spoken to nuns who had known her and had the notes of another monk who, before his death, had collected first hand information about her, intending to write her life. Leoba was in fact a nickname given to her by her mother, it means 'beloved', but it seems to have stuck and she was known by it all her life. She was born in Wessex the only child of elderly parents, who regarded her birth as a miracle and dedicated her to God in thanksgiving. She was placed in the double monastery at Wimborne as a child. A letter she wrote as a girl introducing herself to Boniface has been preserved, she asks him to pray for her parents but also includes some Latin verses of her own composition which she asked him to criticise. She was studious and devout but "Above all she was practising charity, without which, as she knew, all the virtues are void." The Abbess who educated Leoba was a forceful lady who did not allow any men, even bishops, into the women's side of her monastery. Leoba lived among women and Rudolf specifically says that she modelled her conduct on the other nuns; no masculine influence formed her character.

Boniface appointed Leoba as Abbess of the largest monastery for women in his care and she remained there for the rest of her life. She continued to study; Rudolf writes:

"So that through the combination of her reading and her quick intelligence, by natural gifts and hard work, she became extremely learned. She read with attention all the books of the Old and New Testaments and learned by heart all the commandments of God. To these she added by way of completion the writings of the church Fathers, the decrees of the councils and the whole ecclesiastical law."

She concerned herself with teaching women about God and educating the nuns in her charge; in time all the Abbesses in the area had been her pupils. Rudolf writes that she also had common sense "She always kept the practical end in view." She gave practical help both to local villagers and to strangers, her monastery kept 'open house' for passing travellers. Rudolf attributes several miracles to her in her lifetime and others after her death. The elderly Boniface sent for her just before he set out on his final evangelistic journey, during which he was martyred. He begged her to remain at her post after his death and extend the scope of her work. He asked his successor and other senior monks "to place her bones in his own tomb so that they who had served God during their lifetimes with equal sincerity and zeal should await together the day of resurrection."

Leoba's work did not end with Boniface's death. She seems to have taken his place as a wise and godly counsellor. Charlemagne frequently sent for her to come to his court and she was a friend and mentor of his Queen, Hiltigard. Rudolf writes:

"The Princes loved her, the Nobles received her and the Bishops welcomed her with joy. And because of her wide knowledge of scripture and her prudence in counsel they often discussed spiritual matters and ecclesiastical discipline with her."

When Leoba died she was buried in the monastery church with Boniface, although not, as he had requested, in the same tomb.

Christianity originally grew from the bottom up, attracting ordinary people and gradually penetrating the upper echelons of society. Missionaries in northern Europe worked from the top down. They approached tribal rulers to persuade them to be baptised as Christians; after their conversion the missionaries would evangelise their peoples. For Boniface founding monasteries, for men and women, was vital - they became centres for the practice of Christianity among ordinary people. After the first six nuns had been working with him for a time another party of forty more English nuns joined him. We know that one of these also became Abbess of a double monastery and set up a school to teach local children Latin, Greek, mathematics, botany, literature and music.

Boniface and his monks preached to princes and made missionary journeys to pagan tribes but it was the nuns who were responsible for establishing Christianity within communities. Rulers can decree a change of religion but changing hearts and minds is a longer and more complex task. The nuns taught the local women both directly and through example. Women were the key to the spread of Christianity, as they had always been, it was they who taught children and passed on their faith, pagan or Christian, to the next generation.

Changes in the Church

Charlemagne and his successors took considerable interest in church affairs and encouraged education for the clergy. This led to what is called the Carolingian Renaissance, which was both intellectual and artistic. They tried to revive classical Latin, rather than encouraging priests to use a language the people could understand; a decision which would have long term consequences. Services became

125

incomprehensible to lay people, and the mass became a mystical rite, which the congregation watched, rather than a service of worship in which they took part.

The influence of Christian missionaries on pagan tribes was not all one way. The church absorbed some of the underlying assumptions of the newly Christianised tribes. These overlaid other assumptions, based on Greek and Roman ways of thinking, which had dominated Christian thought and practice in the past. The tribes did not educate their children in logic and reason and the superstitious element in religious life became more prominent. Miracles, instances of supernatural intervention, had previously been healings or similar events. In the middle ages the supernatural entered daily life, not just in the 'miracle' of transubstantiation but also in mundane 'miracles' like crosses appearing on loaves of bread.

Suppressing double monasteries

Double monasteries were well run and valued by their communities but they were not popular with Rome. The clerical hierarchy was bound to disapprove of institutions that gave so much equality and power to women. In 787 the Council of Nice forbad the founding of further double monasteries; although allowing those already established to remain. Many double monasteries in England were destroyed during the Danish invasions. But it was the hostility of Rome that ensured they were not rebuilt, or were rebuilt only for monks. By the end of the ninth century Double Monasteries had almost disappeared. With their disappearance the Church lost one of its most effective tools for spreading the faith, and education, among ordinary folk.

12.   REFORMING MONKS AND POPES

By the tenth century Europe was largely Christian, at least nominally. The church ceased to expand and began to be more introspective and to notice the corruption that had infected it.   For the English the eleventh century was pivotal; during it invading Normans destroyed the Anglo-Saxon kingdom.   England had been suffering for many years from incursions by Viking raiders but it was still one of the most civilized societies in Europe.   When that society disappeared many of the rights of ordinary people were lost.   In the feudal society established by Norman conquerors women lost the freedom and status they had under Anglo-Saxon Law.   The society where double monasteries had flourished was destroyed.

Cleaning up the monasteries

By the tenth century many monasteries had become lax in their practices and sometimes in their morals.   A number of monks decided reform was necessary and started new foundations with far stricter rules.   Their ideas spread rapidly until there were reformed monasteries all across Europe.   Their regimes were more austere and as the Abbott of the original monastery had authority over all subsequent foundations, a new system of centralised authority arose. This was the heyday for establishing and building monasteries.   Most of the great medieval monasteries were established between the tenth and twelfth centuries.

The new monasteries were built for men and opportunities for women in religious life declined. The few that remained were generally restricted to the rich and the nobility, nuns were now expected to provide a dowry before admission. During this period pressure was put on nuns to live a completely enclosed life. Some communities of nuns had always led a contemplative life but others, like Leoba and her nuns, were involved in their communities. Cloistered nuns were confined to a life of prayer, contemplation and domestic labour; the only outreach they were allowed was to educate girls within the Convent. Nuns who could not work for their community had no forum for winning public respect, which in turn must have led to a decline in their own self-esteem. The restrictions on community, social and educational work must have been a real loss to communities and also to nuns, since not everyone is suited to the contemplative life. Confinement, living together with almost no input from the world outside, must have put psychological pressure on women's religious houses. The restrictions seem particularly cruel when you consider that many nuns were not there from their own choice. Noble families would make provision for unwanted sons and daughters by sending them to be monks or nuns. It is not surprising that some women's communities had problems with rebellious or immoral nuns.

One reason for the popularity of founding, or endowing, monasteries was the system of penance that had grown up in the early medieval age. Heavy penances were imposed for serious sins; up to three periods of forty days fasting in the course of a year, possibly for several years. The effects of this were ameliorated by a system of substitution. A person could pay a monk or nun, to undertake the penance on their behalf. This system supplied a strong motivation for people to endow a monastery where monks and nuns could undertake penances for them and pray for their souls. The doctrine of purgatory, which had been gaining ground since the sixth century, increased this motivation with the suggestion that a person should pay for their sins in this life lest they find themselves paying in the next.

Doctrinal Changes

During this period the role of the priest had been transformed. He was no longer a pastor working with, and for, his congregation but a man apart with an almost supernatural role. Eucharist had been transformed into a sacred rite. Increasingly the idea took hold that during the mass the bread and wine became literally, rather than symbolically, the body and blood of Christ. It is not clear quite when this idea emerged. Catholic historians trace it back to the second century while others believe it developed hundreds of years later. During this period it was formulated into the doctrine of transubstantiation. It was attractive to clergy and people in a time of growing superstition and by the twelfth century was generally accepted. The raising of the host by the priest was regarded as a supernatural event; the moment when it became God and this moment became the centre of worship. Stories were told crediting the host with miraculous powers. The Eucharistic wine was restricted to the clergy. It was felt that if it was shared with laity the risk of spilling consecrated wine was too great. From this time the Eucharist was a priestly rite; all women, and most men, were excluded from sharing fully in the sacrament, which Christ himself had ordained for all

Christians.   Transubstantiation eventually became official Church dogma in 1215.

Scandal and the Papacy

The last centuries of the first millennium were a low point for the Papacy.   The office had become a tool in the hands of powerful Roman families; who appointed their candidate with no thought for their suitability to carry out religious duties.   The story that one of these popes was a woman, Pope Joan, was widely accepted for several hundred years after the story's first appearance in 1250.   The story relates that Joan disguised herself as a man in order to study and later teach.   She was elected pope but her gender was revealed when she unexpectedly gave birth during a procession.   The story has some credibility; there were other women who had successfully lived as men.   A number of stories tell of female saints who passed as men in order to escape from abusive men or an immoral life and some at least seem to have been based on fact.   There really were women who lived as monks or hermits and whose gender was only discovered at their death; one had died only a few years before the story of Pope Joan appeared.   A more recent example is Dr James Barry, who attended medical school, passing as a boy, and practiced as a male doctor all her life, even serving in the Crimean War.   However it is likely that the story of Pope Joan is apocryphal as its earliest source is hundreds of years after the various dates suggested for her reign.   It probably owes its survival to protestant polemics against the papacy and, more recently, to feminist historians, who include Pope Joan among the women whose memory has been suppressed by a patriarchal church.

The story of Pope Joan may have been invented but there were popes during this period who were far less suited to religious office than a godly woman would have been. By the middle of the eleventh century there were three rival popes. The family who currently controlled the Papacy had appointed a boy of twelve as Pope Benedict IX. The teenage Pope set about a career of crime and depravity; he formed a gang, who roamed the city at night and was notorious for his involvement in theft and rape. Eventually there was a popular uprising; Benedict was banished and an alternative pope appointed. His powerful family got Benedict reinstated but he wanted to marry and decided to sell the papacy to a relative. The purchaser, who became the third Pope, was superficially more suitable. He was older, already ordained and famed for his 'virtue', which meant he was chaste. Unfortunately he was also famed for his avarice and greed. Encouraged by these events the second Pope returned to the City and captured the Vatican by force. Benedict, spurned by the family of the girl he hoped to marry, regretted his bargain and returned to Rome with a small army. Faced with three rival Popes, each occupying a different part of the city and who might at any time stop excommunicating each other and start actual fighting, the Romans sent a plea for help to the Holy Roman Emperor in Germany. The Emperor arrived in 1046 and deposed all three popes, appointing in their place a German Bishop. The time was ripe for reform to spread from the monasteries to Rome.

Papal reform and Papal power

The German Bishop the Emperor appointed was the first of a series of reforming Popes who transformed the papacy and the Church over the next seventy years.   The Gregorian reform is named after Pope Gregory VII, an Italian who was an influential advisor to several Popes, before being elected himself in 1073.   The new men, influenced by monastic reformers, were determined to end corruption and laxity in the church and decided this could be done by freeing the church from all lay influence, including the role secular rulers had had in appointing bishops.   They banned the buying and selling of church offices.   Gregory VII, who as an Italian was concerned to increase Roman power, took the assumption of papal power further.   He took advantage of the fact the current Emperor was a minor and issued decrees that were designed to free the Papacy from all secular constraints and give it power over secular affairs.   His 'Dictatus' gave the Pope authority to depose all other rulers, secular and religious, and to repeal any sentence they handed out.   The pope, he decreed, must not be judged by anyone, there was no appeal against his sentences and he could absolve subjects from oaths of fidelity made to unjust rulers.   Finally he ruled that 'the Roman Church has never erred and, according to the testimony of scripture, it never will err'.

Gregory VII's unilateral power grab was not unopposed.   Once the child Emperor grew up he and Gregory were locked in conflict, with many clergy, alienated by Gregory's reforms, siding with the Emperor.   A bitter war followed.   Eventually the Emperor, who had occupied Rome, was forced to retreat when an army of Normans from Scilly came to Gregory's support.   The Normans and their allies, who included many Saracens, burnt and sacked Rome.   Pope Gregory has the distinction of being the only Pope to have initiated the destruction of Rome by a partially Muslim army.   When the Normans left the devastated city Gregory had to go with them, fearing the vengeance of the people he had betrayed. He died in exile but with his unshakable self-righteousness still in place.

The realities of power do not rest on a papal edict. A decree is no protection against an army and the only real powers Popes had outside Italy were those of interdiction and excommunication; clumsy and often ineffective weapons.   However, the efforts of Gregory's successors to exert the power he had claimed over secular affairs put the papacy in the centre of medieval political machinations.   Like many later revolutionaries, the papacy found it easier to tear down existing structures than to build something that suited them better. For example, papal support helped William I to conquer England but the proud Norman kings proved even less amenable to papal demands than the Anglo-Saxon kings they had displaced.

The most powerful and destructive papal interventions in international affairs were the Crusades, the first started in 1095. Not only men but also women went on Crusades.   The chronicler in the Abbey of Disibodenburg in Germany, the monastery where Hildegard of Bingen grew up, recorded: "Not only men and boys but many women also took part in this journey. Indeed females went forth on this venture dressed as men and marched in armour".   The Chronicler expresses his disapproval of this.   "Since men were marching together with women as mentioned above, unclean deeds of fornication and abomination transpired among them.   For this reason they well deserved the wrath of God."   The crusades caused havoc in the Middle East but also brought change in Europe; Crusaders brought back new ideas and new, to Europe, diseases. By the eleventh and twelfth centuries a society that had been largely rural saw an influx of people into towns.   Many of the newcomers lived in poverty and without the social support they had enjoyed in their villages.

The decrees of Gregory had lasting and damaging consequences; later popes expanded on the idea that a pope can absolve people from any oath or undertaking and were prepared to justify any amount of bad faith.   During the Crusades Muslim rulers found they could not trust Christians to keep treaties; as the Pope would always absolve them for breaking oaths made to unbelievers.   Consequences also followed the assertion that the Church cannot err and that Scripture proves it. This, and other doctrines promulgated at the time, made it undesirable for laypersons to have access to the Bible.   The gap between its teachings and those of the Church was too great and Bible study by those outside the church might lead to unanswerable questions.   From this time on groups who provided translations of the Scriptures in the vernacular, for ordinary people to read, were generally treated as heretics.

Reform in monasteries and in the wider church had been overdue but the form it took disadvantaged women, excluding them from what was becoming an increasingly masculine church.   The next chapter will look at the reform that impacted most directly and painfully on women.

13. MISOGYNY TRIUMPHANT

This chapter will look at how compulsory clerical celibacy was introduced into the Church. It had been regarded as an ideal for centuries but the decision to impose it on all priests came at a cost. It was women who paid most of the price. The imposition of celibacy was not universal, Eastern Orthodox churches continued to allow clergy below the rank of bishop to marry.

Concerns about the priesthood

Clerical reformers were concerned about the low level of education and of spiritual understanding of ordinary parish priests. The minimum qualification for a priest was the ability to recite the creed and the Lord's Prayer. Many local priests had little or no understanding the Latin Mass, nor could they read the Scriptures or devotional books for themselves. Their grasp of the things they were supposed to teach their congregations was poor; ignorant themselves they could do little to enlighten their parishioners. Another concern was that many priests, and bishops, regarded their jobs as hereditary, it was normal at the time for sons to follow their father in his trade and this practice extended into the Church. This led to confusion over the distinction between a priest's own property and Church property and some priests left church goods to their children. In contrast monasteries were rapidly accruing land and wealth. The Reformers wanted to preserve church property in parishes and at the same time get rid of clergy wives, who were another source of lay influence over the Church.

Compulsory Celibacy

The reformers believed that the way to deal with this problem, while also increasing the spiritual authority of the priesthood, was to impose compulsory celibacy on all priests. While clerical celibacy had been regarded as the ideal since the fourth century only monks and a minority of clergy seem to have practiced it. The monks who now controlled the Papacy were determined to impose celibacy on all clergy. From 1039 a number of church councils forbade priests to marry and in 1059 it was suggested the laity should be encouraged to boycott all ministry by married priests. Many clerics, both married and celibate, objected to the imposition of compulsory celibacy citing both Scripture and tradition in support of their views. They pointed out that it was voluntary choice that gave celibacy its value and making it compulsory would destroy this value. Accusations of homosexuality were made against the reformers. It is certainly noticeable that only one of the churchmen, who were so outspoken against 'immorality' when it involved clerical wives, also spoke out against homosexual relationships. It was pointed out by contemporaries that making celibacy compulsory would result in priests committing much more serious sexual sins and would attract homosexuals into the clergy. This prophecy proved accurate, the Church has been wrestling with problems resulting from the sexual activities of priests ever since.

Expelling the wives

Medieval marriage was not a church sacrament and had few formalities. If two people consented to a permanent relationship and had intercourse they were regarded as married and concubinage was recognised as a secondary marriage. Now clergy wives were told they were whores and their children were declared illegitimate. Many priests chose to leave their churches rather than their wives and families. Those who could not face losing their vocation and livelihood saw their families cast out without any provision for their needs. Some wives were enslaved as church serfs, others were driven to suicide.

Ignoring all protests, Gregory VII suspended all married priests in 1074 and enforced the decrees of his predecessors with a heavy hand. In France alone four bishops were suspended for tolerating married clergy. So many bishops were suspended in Germany that all of them sided with the Emperor in his dispute with Pope Gregory. Gregory's high-handed actions, and especially the way he encouraged lay people to judge their priests, alienated many moderate clergy. Encouraging congregations to rebel against their priests led to riots and violence. By the end of his life Gregory was in exile and had lost the support of most of the church. But Gregory and his supporters had turned the tide of public opinion against married priests and this ensured that the advocates of compulsory celibacy won. In 1127 provision was made for disciplining and even enslaving clergy 'concubines' as wives were now called. Finally in 1139 the marriage of priests was made a legal impossibility.

Clergy wives were seen by some as a financial asset and some undoubtedly supported their husbands financially. One group of priests, objecting to compulsory celibacy, claimed that "Unless they were maintained by the hands of their women they would succumb to hunger and nakedness." Later a bishop trying to enforce celibacy found "The excuse of almost everyone was 'this can in no wise be because of our poverty'". In parts of Christendom that were distant from Rome eradicating clerical marriage probably took longer. It is possible that in England married priests were able to live out their lives with their wives in peace. This may have been due in part to a loss of moral authority by the papal legate sent to England in 1125. A contemporary, Henry of Huntingdon, wrote "For in the Council (the papal legate) dealt with wives of priests very severely, saying it was the greatest sin to rise from the side of a whore (i.e. wife) and go to create the body of Christ. Yet having created the body of Christ that same day he was caught after vespers with a whore." The next generation of priests in England were celibate and by the end of the twelfth century there were no legally married clergy, even in distant parts of Western Christendom.

Clerical wives are very much invisible women – until the last few years they have been written out of history. Some historians writing of the Gregorian reform hardly mention compulsory celibacy as an issue. Few include any references to the considerable opposition there was to enforcement, or refer to the way it devastated individual lives. Just as the medieval church ignored its pastoral responsibilities to these women so history has ignored their suffering.

Papal propaganda and Peter Damian

To counter the opposition to compulsory celibacy the Popes and their advisors travelled widely around Europe preaching against clerical marriage. If they could convince ordinary people then angry congregations would force priests to comply. The most prominent of these papal enforcers was a hermit monk, Peter Damian, who preached an uncompromising message; "For holiness to revive amongst the Western ministers marriage must be banned utterly, those with concubines must be hunted down. Such men should be deposed and their women, as an example to others, should be sold into slavery." Peter Damian was sent to Milan where the clergy and the people had resisted a call for celibacy. By a mixture of hell-fire preaching and forged 'ancient' documents he defeated the local Archbishop and changed public opinion; the Milanese clergy were force to renounce their wives for fear of the mob.

Peter Damian was a man with no mercy for anyone, even himself; as a penance he would recite the entire book of Psalms all the while flogging himself, it must have taken hours. He was moderate in some of his views but bigoted on all issues relating to sex. He had a gift for propaganda and is credited with originating two new words. The first was to call married or co-habiting clergy 'Nicolaitans'. This was a reference to a text in Revelation "Yet this is to your credit: you hate the works of the Nicolaitans, which I also hate." (Revelation 2: 6.) It is not known what the "works of the Nicolaitans" were but it was certainly not a reference to clerical marriage. The other word Peter Damian originated was 'sodomy', unlike his colleague he was outspoken in his hatred of homosexuality. The identification of the sin of Sodom with homosexuality has only a slight basis in the Old Testament story of the destruction of Sodom but as propaganda it was brilliant. It implied that God especially hated homosexuality; a view certainly not supported by the few references to it in the Bible. The propaganda value of Peter Damian's word was not lost on those who hated homosexuality and it is still used by them today.

To reconcile clergy to celibacy it was necessary to denigrate and even vilify women; a strain of real misogyny in the Church originated from this time. Although the clergy had been concerned to control women's involvement in the church, and several of the Church Fathers had produced theological reasons for setting limits on women, there had been few signs of a personal animus against womankind. Peter Damian is one example of a new attitude. One of the least pleasant aspects of human nature is the way that groups of people decide that another group, which they regard as inferior but also fear, is sub-human and so not entitled to be treated with humanity. It is difficult to read the words of some late medieval clergy without feeling that they saw 'woman' as a separate subhuman race, inferior to man but dangerous. The analogies they used to describe women are of animals and they express no concern or care for them as people or as individuals.

For Peter Damian the only good woman was the Virgin Mary; he venerated her and declared that her bodily assumption was even more glorious that that of her Son. But he seems to have preached with real hatred against ordinary women.

"I speak to you, O charmers of the clergy, appetising flesh of the devil, that castaway from paradise, poison of the minds, death of souls, companions of the very stuff of sin, the cause of your ruin. You, I say, I exhort you women of the ancient enemy, you bitches, sows, screech-owls, night-owls, blood suckers, she-wolves.... Come now, hear me, harlots prostitutes, with your lascivious kisses, you wallowing places for fat pigs, couches for unclean spirits."

Peter Damian must have had virtually no direct experience of women; he had been the last child in a very large and poor family and, orphaned at a young age, was brought up by an older brother and placed as a child in a monastery school. It is ironic that he is said to have owed his life to a priest's wife. When he was born his mother rejected the baby and did not want to feed him. He was dying of malnutrition when the wife of the local priest visited and persuaded his mother to change her mind. A priest's wife saved the newborn baby, who was to grow up to be the scourge of clergy wives.

Apart from the sufferings of the families of clergy, other women must have suffered from the separation of the clergy from ordinary people. A priest's wife had status in the community and could give pastoral care and guidance to women; the woman who saved Peter Damian's life as a baby is an example of this. The mistress/housekeepers, who took the place of wives in the lives of priests who preferred a stable sexual relationship to using prostitutes, could not fulfil that function. The clergy were protected from the influence of women and women were supposed to rely for spiritual guidance and pastoral care on men with no understanding of the pressures and pains of their lives.

Consequences of compulsory celibacy

The factor that reconciled most priests to celibacy was the power that it gave to them as part of a strong masculine elite. The papacy was a

141

major player in European politics and Churchmen held influential positions in national politics. From this time on high churchmen were always close to political power; often acting as right hand men to kings and emperors.

The imposition of compulsory celibacy had many consequences. One was an increase in immorality among the clergy. Not all priests were suited to a life of chastity and they had no alternative to sin. This must have eroded their moral standards. From this time the presence of prostitutes was a constant factor in church circles. When Church Councils were held priests, bishops and cardinals would flock into the town but so also would innumerable whores, who saw a large gathering of clergy as a profitable business opportunity. Compulsory celibacy set the clergy apart, putting a barrier between them and ordinary men and women. They no longer shared the pressures and preoccupations of everyday life, and they no longer had a wife to help them understand them. More was now expected of them; the clergy had set themselves above ordinary Christians, so when they failed to meet the expectations they had raised people were disillusioned. Anti-clerical feeling increasingly became a factor in medieval life. A proliferation of lay sects, orthodox and heretical, developed as lay people sought a more direct experience of God.

Medieval images of women

Compulsory celibacy increased the hold that two differing images of women had on the medieval imagination. One was the Virgin Mary, who was increasingly seen as having been sinless from birth. Although the idea of the immaculate conception of Mary did not become official church dogma until the nineteenth century it was widely held during the middle ages. Celibate clergy encouraged the veneration of Mary, the only woman a celibate could legitimately love. She increasingly became seen as the channel through whom God's mercy came down to men and women. A whole theology of Mary was developed, much of which survives to this day in some Roman Catholic Churches. Christ was seen as the dispenser of God's justice rather than as personifying his love and mercy; people were encouraged to seek those qualities in his Mother. The church had instituted a system of penances and indulgences, the latter were promises of forgiveness for past or future sins granted by the pope, usually in return for a service, such as fighting a crusade, or for money. Lay people were encouraged to see priests as the source of absolution, rather than seeing forgiveness as coming directly from God. The clergy had placed themselves between God and lay people.

The Virgin Mary had ceased to be a relevant role model for ordinary women; so another exemplar was needed. A legendary 'Mary Magdalene' became the most popular saint, after the Virgin. Traditionally Mary Magdalene has been identified as a loose woman; so much so that the name Magdalene was for centuries used to describe a prostitute. This came about after Pope Gregory the Great, over 500 years later, identified her as the woman who washed Jesus' feet with her tears and who was described as a sinner (Luke 7:37). Popular opinion identified the nature of her sin as sexual. There is nothing in any of the Gospels to support the idea that Mary was a repentant prostitute. It is true the Gospel says she had demons cast out of her but other people from whom Jesus cast out demons seem to have had symptoms we would now ascribe to psychosis or epilepsy. Mary was no longer seen as the biblical friend and disciple of Jesus but as a profligate woman who after meeting Jesus, lived a life of penitence for past sins of the flesh.

Life stories were invented for Mary Magdalene; one popular version included her becoming promiscuous after being jilted on her wedding day by the apostle John leaving her at the altar to follow Jesus. She was one of several saints who were 'discovered' to have European connections after the pilgrim's route to Palestine became too dangerous. French clergy claimed that after leaving Palestine she had lived in Provence, as an evangelist and later a hermit, and France became the centre of her cult (In a similar fashion St James became associated with Compostela, and Joseph of Arimathea with Glastonbury.) In an age that venerated relics, many relics of Mary Magdalene appeared. Churches which claimed to have individual body parts were upstaged by two French monasteries which both claimed to have her body buried in their precincts. Both claims received papal approval, though from different Popes. It is easy to suspect the motives of later churchmen who encouraged the tradition of her being a reformed prostitute. Maybe it was, consciously or unconsciously, a way of neutralising a woman whose position among the disciples they found embarrassing. In 1969, the Roman Catholic Church officially overruled Gregory's identification but it is still widely accepted – it makes a good story.

As a role model Mary Magdalene was a continual reminder of the sexual guilt that was projected on to women. All the teaching about the evils of clerical marriage had blurred the distinction between marriage and prostitution, so Mary Magdalene was seen as a role model for wives as well as other sexually active women. In most medieval eyes only a lifetime of virginity could rescue women from the contagion of sexual sin; married women could only aspire, at best, to a second rate spirituality. There was, however, one group of women for whom the story of Mary Magdalene was helpful. The image of the repentant prostitute was a powerful one in medieval minds and provided a pathway out of prostitution for women who needed it.

The papacy's "great reform" and the introduction of compulsory celibacy changed the Church, and the lives of women, forever. The Gregorian reformers created the Roman Catholic Church, as we know it. Many innovations in practice and doctrine, which were introduced in this period, have survived into the twenty-first century. It could be suggested that Gregorian reformers were also responsible for the creation of the Protestant church. All the issues that alienated people from the church at the time of the Reformation: selling indulgences, compulsory celibacy, transubstantiation, discouraging lay people from reading the Bible and the cult of Mary; originated or were further developed in this period. Without the legacy of Gregorian reform later reformers might not have felt compelled to leave the Catholic Church.

14. GIFTED NUNS AND NEW RELIGIOUS HOUSES

During the period when the Papacy was trying to make the Church a solely masculine preserve the Church was graced with a number of gifted and godly women who made a positive contribution to Church life.

Making the most of limited opportunities

The twelfth century was not a good time to be born a woman. Barstow writes: "That women's roles were curtailed in both secular rights and in monastic opportunities from around 1100 on has been well documented. To these handicaps may be added the degradation to which clerical wives were subject when their marriages were challenged by enforcement of celibacy. The combined force of these disadvantages ushered in the era that has generally been agreed upon as the low point in female status in the medieval west."

In the twelfth century scholarship moved out of monasteries into the new universities in Paris and Oxford.   These were hot houses of exciting intellectual endeavour but were only open to men. The great tradition of women scholars was cut short. Women no longer had opportunities for study, and exclusion from theological and classical studies changed the nature of the education provided by nuns. Hilda of Whitby had educated bishops, later nuns could only teach young girls. Unless her family paid for private tuition a medieval girl's only educational options were a convent, taught by nuns who had had no access to higher education, or learning domestic skills in an aristocratic household.

The elaboration of canon law preoccupied many of the clergy and a number of medieval popes were canon lawyers. As the Church built a system of law designed to regulate all aspects of life, disillusioned believers turned away from reason and legality, towards mysticism and a more emotional faith. Women were in the forefront of this movement and many noted medieval mystics were women. Their visions gave them an authoritive voice, often used to speak out against clerical corruption. Deprived of access to the reason and logic that characterised medieval male scholarship women received encouragement, insight and even, some claimed, knowledge through visions.

Nor was mysticism the only interest of medieval nuns. Deprived of the chance to use their talents in academic study, or charitable work, they turned to other outlets including the arts and natural philosophy (science). The first poet and playwright to write in German was a nun, Hroswitha. She disliked the Latin comedies of her era and wrote six new comedies in the vernacular. They were not only the first plays written in German but were also the first domestic plays written since classical times. She took Terence as her model but her favourite subject was holy virgins who preserved their chastity through trials and perils. In a historical play set in a time of persecution, three virgins are saved from the attentions of a lustful general. He had locked them in a kitchen but when he arrived to rape them he was blinded and started caressing the pots and pans instead; their virginity, although not their lives, was saved. In her last two plays she tried a different theme, the repentance and salvation of fallen women.

Herrad, a twelfth century abbess, compiled a book that covered history, religion, philosophy and science. It was intended to educate the nuns and novices and includes all that a well educated nun should know. In her introduction she describes its composition. "Like a bee inspired by God I collected from diverse flowers of sacred scripture and philosophic writings this book which is called the Garden of Delights.

Hildegard of Bingen

The most brilliant of these intelligent and gifted women was Hildegard of Bingen (1098 – 1179). She had mystical experiences from childhood but was not just a mystic. She was interested in music, medicine, herbal remedies, and what would now be called psychology. Hildegard was born in Germany and sent as a child to live with Jutta, a woman six years her senior who was probably a relative. They lived together in separate quarters attached to a male monastery. They came under the authority of the Abbott but when other women joined them Jutta became Abbess of the nuns. Hildegard took her vows at fourteen and lived a semi-enclosed life from that time. We know nothing of her life with Jutta except she had a woman's education; music and a little Latin learnt from reading the Psalms. Judging from her later works we can only assume she spent those years educating herself from the monks' library and helping Jutta manage the small group of women who had joined them. She also learnt about herbs and medicine. The monastery ran a dispensary for local people, including women in childbirth; Hildegard learnt about life, giving her a surprisingly wide knowledge for an enclosed nun.

Hildegard was thirty-eight when Jutta died and she was made Abbess; although remaining under the authority of the Abbot. One of the monks encouraged Hildegard to start writing down her visions, which she had previously tried to suppress. This seems to have transformed her life. She describes how when she was forty-two "The heavens opened and a fiery light of the greatest brilliancy coming from the opened heavens, poured into all my brain and kindled in my heart and my breast a flame." She also describes the process of her visions; they did not come in dreams, a trance or a delirium but were something she watched with an inner eye. Some modern writers have suggested that her visions were a form of migraine; this theory provides an explanation for Hildegard's poor health and frequent illnesses. The monk who advised her to write down her visions devoted the rest of his life to acting as her secretary. He transcribed her apocalyptic visions, probably tidying up her Latin grammar but not interfering with the content. Hildegard's three visionary works of theology were widely read and a number of copies have survived. The Abbot reported on her visions to his archbishop, who in turn sent her book to Pope Eugenius III, who gave her papal approval. She became a noted figure and women from good families joined her. Eventually she moved to a new monastery she had built in Bingen. The monks were reluctant to let her go; they were often annoyed by Hildegard's actions but appreciated the international reputation, and the donations, she attracted to their monastery. Disputes with the Abbot continued for years, until eventually Hildegard won independence for her nuns and herself; buying their freedom with a generous financial settlement on the monks. In later life Hildegard travelled quite widely in Germany. The monks who wrote her life shortly after her death have left a description; "Hildegard – not only inspired but actually driven by the Divine spirit – went to Cologne, Trier, Metz, Wurzburg and Bamberg and announced the will of God to the clergy and laity".   She did not allow disapproval of women preachers to stop her and her sermons, like parts of her theological books, were trenchant criticisms of corruption in the Church.   She gives a vivid picture of the church as a woman whose face, clothes and shoes have become dirty because those who should be beautifying her, the clergy, were instead soiling her.

Hildegard also produced books on medicine and herbal lore.   These books are catalogues of information from classical and local sources and also include descriptions of different personality types and of relationships between the sexes.   She did not live in a prudish age and, although Hildegard was undoubtedly a virgin all her life, she writes frankly about sexual relationships and procreation.   Her comments on herbs include information on those with anti-fertile properties.   Hildegard's books were illustrated, with vivid pictures of her visions, and her words were set to music.   She is now best known for these musical compositions, which were rediscovered in the 1980s.   We do not know if she herself composed the music to accompany her words or if one of her nuns set them to music; but this music was produced and sung by Hildegard and her nuns and it will be forever associated with her name.

Hildegard lived to a good old age.   She had a wide correspondence with emperors, kings, popes and abbots and also responded to requests for advice from many ordinary people.   She gave encouragement to at least one other female mystic.   In her letters to powerful men she expresses timidity and acknowledges her weakness as a woman but this was probably a convention, she is forthright in expressing her views even when they are critical of the recipient of the letter. A medieval woman had to emphasise her own inferiority, otherwise men would not be receptive to her words. At times Hildegard was outspokenly critical of her clerical correspondents, even Popes. She also rebuked the Emperor when he attempted to deal with his conflict with the Church by appointing an anti-pope.

Hildegard received support from male clerics, including her devoted secretaries and a number of bishops and popes. However she was also subject to mistreatment from German clerics who disapproved of her, or were jealous of her fame. The Abbot who had authority over her for most of her life was often unhelpful. Even after she had won her independence he made life difficult for her by refusing to replace her secretary, when he died. The spite of local clerics followed her until the end of her life. When Hildegard refused to let them disinter a body from the graveyard at Bingen these clerics responded by forbidding the nuns from singing and participating in the Mass. Hildegard protested strongly in letters to the Archbishop who eventually reversed the decision of his cathedral chapter. Six months later Hildegard was dead.

Women and the reformed monasteries

Monastic reform movement was a masculine affair. The reformers built monasteries for men but left women out of their plans. The first person to change this was the Abbot of Cluny, whose monastery was the centre of the earliest group of reformed houses. He started a monastery specifically for female relatives, including wives, of men joining his Abbey. This woman's community was situated two leagues (six to eight miles) from Cluny but was totally under the Abbot's control. The Cistercians, the other major group of reformed monasteries, were less worldly and lived in isolated frontier areas. They didn't make any provision for women; their whole way of life was masculine. Their most revered Abbot, St Bernard of Clairveax, pointed out the dangers of any easy association with women: "to be always with a woman and not to have intercourse with her is more difficult than to raise the dead. You cannot do the less difficult: do you think I will believe you can do what is most difficult?" However the monks were unable to exclude women, who wanted to be associated with this new puritan movement. The Cistercians did not actively reject the many women's communities who affiliated themselves with their Order; nor did they take authority over them. For a time the abbesses of these Cistercian monasteries seem to have had a lot of authority and independence; this was certainly so in Spain where some letters between the King and an Abbess have survived. This freedom ended in the thirteenth century when the Cistercians tried to exclude women from their Order and, when that failed, clamped down on them; subjecting them to firm controls and insisting on the nuns being enclosed, so they could no longer manage their own affairs.

Women and the new Orders

Many new religious orders were founded in the twelfth century. Initially many included women; even the military orders, the Templars and the Teutonic Knights, originally accepted women. Other, less militant, orders were more attractive to women. One popular itinerant preacher founded a double monastery at Fontevrault. It had separate accommodation for men and women but a shared chapel. As in some earlier double monasteries the Abbess ruled over both the men and women. This female rule was said to symbolise the authority Mary had over Jesus, her son, and later the Apostle John her 'adopted' son. Fontevrault started by receiving anyone who wished to devote themselves to the religious life and initially especially welcomed reformed prostitutes. However, within a generation its inhabitants were almost all from the nobility and included royalty. This is probably why it survived when the papacy again restricted double foundations. In 1141 it was decreed that a women's foundation must be at least two leagues from a men's monastery and the nuns must be under the authority of an Abbot. Patricia Ranft points out that there is a clear pattern in the early history of many of these new religious orders. Most foundations accepted women initially but later, sometimes immediately after the death of the Order's founder, the leaders who succeeded him restricted or excluded women.

The Premonstratensians

The Premonstratensian Order was immensely popular with women, possibly because it was one of the few orders that welcomed them. Sources tell us that ten thousand women joined in the Order in its early years. However, after the death of the Founder, the monks almost immediately started to try and separate themselves from the nuns. Since the nuns were confined to their cloisters, and had to be based two leagues from the men's house, providing services for them was a burden. The Pope supported the women, pointing out that many of the Order's assets came from donations by, or on behalf of,

153

women and if the monks expelled the women they would have a right to take with them much of the Order's wealth. Two subsequent Popes reiterated this judgement. Despite this the monks began suppressing double monasteries and before the end of the century the Order's leaders had decreed that no further women were to be admitted to the Order, "since the times are dangerous and the church is burdened beyond measure". The reasons behind the decision were expressed by one Abbot less diplomatically:

"We and our whole community of canons, recognising that the wickedness of women is greater than all the other wickedness of the world, and that there is no anger like that of women, and that the poison of asps and dragons is more curable and less dangerous to men than the familiarity of women, have unanimously decreed for the safety of our souls, no less than for that of our bodies and goods, that we will on no account receive any more sisters to the increase of our perdition, but will avoid them like poisonous animals."

The remark about women's anger implies that the women protested at the destruction of their way of life and appropriation of their assets. However, even with papal support the nuns could not stand against the determination of the monks. In 1198 a fourth pope issued a bull forbidding the acceptance of any more women in the Order; the reason he gave was concern for the women's welfare, a concern they probably didn't appreciate. Not everyone, male or female, accepted this Edict, Ranft points out that women's houses, and even some double monasteries, were founded after this date. In 1270 a stronger edict expelling women was issued, this may have succeeded, since by then there were alternatives for women seeking a religious life.

The Gilbertines

Another example is the only new Order founded in twelfth century England. Gilbert of Sempringham in Lincolnshire wanted to found a monastery but could not find male volunteers. So he approached several women who were living reclusive religious lives in the district and they agreed to join his foundation. They were established in a house next to his Church and served by women of the town. Gilbert agreed to these serving women joining as lay sisters, opening up the order to working class women. In time Gilbert made his house a double monastery, the job of the monks was to assist the nuns and he laid down that the monks controlled external, and the nuns internal, matters. Again, after Gilbert's death, his successor reduced the power of the nuns and ensured all future Gilbertine foundations were only for men. By the middle of the thirteenth century the monks care for the nuns, whose welfare had originally been their primary task, was so neglectful that some nuns lacked the basic necessities of life.

Heloise and The Order of the Parcelete

There was one new order that was founded by a woman. Heloise (c1098 – 1164) was an exceptional and gifted Abbess whose fame rests not on her many abilities but on her relationship with Peter Abelard, the most noted theology lecturer of his day. Heloise was a beautiful and intelligent girl and her uncle persuaded Peter Abelard to lodge with them in return for tutoring her. Peter Abelard seduced Heloise, who became pregnant. Abelard married her secretly, to pacify her uncle, but he was determined it should not become known. As he was only in minor orders he could legally marry but he feared it would ruin his career as the most celebrated theologian in Paris, if he was known to be married. Heloise was content to be regarded as his mistress but her uncle became increasingly disturbed and demanded Abelard acknowledge the marriage. Eventually he hired thugs to break into Peter Abelard's lodgings and castrate him. Abelard was devastated; he retreated into a monastery and asked Heloise to take vows as a nun. This has been seen as a great tragic romance but more recent authors have pointed out that in a modern context it could be seen as an abusive relationship. Abelard was a middle-aged man in a position of trust as Heloise's teacher, and she was in her teens.

Many years later Heloise wrote to Abelard "Thy passion drew thee to me rather than thy friendship, and the heat of desire rather than love." Whatever his feelings Heloise had loved him deeply, and still did. Her integrity shines out in her letters; she tells him she does not expect any reward from God for her service to him because she became a nun for love of Abelard not love of God. Heloise was an exemplary nun and in time was chosen as abbess. Then the local bishop decided that he wanted the nun's property and expelled them, leaving the nuns homeless. This is an indication of just how vulnerable nuns were at that time with no protection against clerical rapaciousness. Hearing of their plight Abelard offered them 'the Parcelete', an isolated group of buildings his students had built. Abelard had tried to live as a hermit but such was his popularity that his students had followed him, leaving Paris to study with him in rural seclusion. Abelard had since moved to a monastery so the abandoned buildings were available for Heloise and her nuns. At Heloise's request Abelard prepared a 'rule' to govern the life of her community. However, Heloise revised the rule herself before introducing it so, unlike most contemporary convents, her Order of the Parcelete was not governed by a rule devised entirely by men.

Our knowledge of religious women of this time is limited, their contemporaries only wrote about those who were celebrated or lived dramatic lives. In the twelfth century women were regarded as inferior, weak physically and morally, and many women seem to have accepted this evaluation. It was a time when the Church struggled to free itself from any 'taint' of feminine influence and in doing so exhibited a distressing level of misogyny. The large majority of women lived quiet, dependent lives. Even in the secular world of politics few women had any influence. An exception was Eleanor of Aquitaine, who went on a crusade, married two kings, raised two more, and ruled England for years on behalf of her favourite son Richard I. But most women were confined to home or cloister and had little opportunity to assert themselves. Only a few exceptional women made their mark on religious life.

15. POWERFUL CLERICS AND POWERLESS WOMEN

It might seem that by the twelfth century the clergy completely controlled and confined women's input into religious life. The power and control of the papacy was at its height in the first half of the century but women continued to seek ways of worshipping God more directly and of serving him and their fellow men.

A male elite

The ecclesiastical establishment was now a masculine hierarchy that excluded lay people. Nuns were cloistered and unable to take a public role and laywomen were intended to be passive under the authority of priests. However, the clergy was not always successful in controlling women's religious life; it is not easy to suppress the abilities and aspirations of more than fifty percent of the population. Not all nuns accepted enclosure and laywomen sought ways to serve God. Freeing the church from all feminine influence was an impossible task, although in the short run it was partially successful. Studying a list of the women who were prominent in medieval religious life it is very noticeable how few lived in the thirteenth century. In the twelfth century there were gifted nuns; in the fourteenth century there were exceptional women following a religious life outside the confines of religious houses. But of the generations in between only a few of the many women who lived under a misogynist clerical hierarchy at the height of its power, have been remembered.

In the thirteenth century European scholars rediscovered the works of Aristotle and he was accepted as the final authority on scientific and many other issues. St Thomas Aquinas, the greatest scholar of his age and a prolific author, devoted much of his life to reconciling the works of the pagan Aristotle with the Bible and traditions of the Church. When they clashed he accepted the Bible but on non-religious matters he followed Aristotle without hesitation. Aristotle's theory, that a female was the result of a sperm which had failed in its task of conceiving a male, was accepted as fact by medieval thinkers and appeared to justify the Churches attitude to women.

St Clare and poverty as a way of life

The two most important of the new orders were the Dominicans and the Franciscans. They were inspired by a wish to return to the *vita apostica* and were mendicant friars, itinerant teachers and preachers who their founders intended should live in poverty, begging for their sustenance. Clare joined the Franciscans in 1212 after being impressed by the preaching of St Francis. Like Francis she came from Assisi and like him she left a rich and noble family to take a vow of lifelong poverty. The Order known as the Poor Clares was founded, with Clare as its head, soon after and was the only women's order given papal protection. Jacques de Vitry, later a French bishop, gave a contemporary description of their life in 1216.

"By day they enter the cities and villages devoting their attention to activities that others profit from, and at night they return to their hermitages or to a solitary isolated place to contemplate. The women in fact, live together near the cities in various hospices. They accept no wages but live by the labour of their hands."

Clearly at this time the women were working among the people like the male friars.

It could not last. In 1218 the Pope appointed a Cardinal to oversee all Franciscans, including the Poor Clares. The Cardinal insisted the nuns must be enclosed and must follow a Benedictine rule rather than the one devised by Clare. He also condemned their commitment to poverty. Clare appealed to the Pope who supported her and issued a bull praising poverty. Unfortunately when the Pope died the same Cardinal succeeded him as Pope Gregory IX He reversed papal policy by reissuing the bull after changing all the parts he disagreed with, and forced Poor Clare Houses to accept possessions. Clare seems to have accepted being cloistered without much protest, she probably realised this was a battle she could not win, but she was an intelligent and determined woman who continued to fight against other restrictions. When the Pope ordered friars not to preach to the nuns without special permission she organised a hunger strike and the Pope gave in. To the end of her life Clare fought to retain the Poor Clares' commitment to poverty and to her own rule. She was eventually allowed to introduce her rule in her own monastery, but only for her lifetime and in the one establishment. The practice of real poverty was not something a property obsessed clerical hierarchy found acceptable. In theory no monk or nun owned possessions but their institutions were wealthy. The Cistercians avoided any display of riches in their churches and way of life but they still accumulated wealth. They used it to acquire land and property so the order became one of the greatest medieval landowners. Not all nuns were as willing as Clare to accept confinement in a cloister with resignation. A few convents disregarded the papal bull confining them. One group at least defied the church openly and literally threw the document back at the bishop who delivered it.

Confession

A new church sacrament had been introduced, one which provided priests with a method of observing and controlling lay people The practice of confession to a priest grew out of the penitential movement of the twelfth century and was formally adopted as a requirement for all Catholics in 1215. Up to the middle of the thirteenth century the emphasis was on the penitent's inward repentance but later there was an increasing insistence on a priest's role in giving absolution. Thomas Aquinas, a theologian who, like Augustine, was more influential after his death than in his lifetime, supported this change. He defended the practice of a priest saying "I absolve you" rather than "May Almighty God grant you absolution." Like many other changes in church dogma and practice in the later Middle Ages this practice emphasised the power of the Church not the power of God.

Every Catholic, man and woman, was required to confess to a priest at least once a year, many women confessed much more frequently. The confessional relationship became an important one and was a support to many women but it was open to abuse. Guidelines written for priests on the practice of confession suggested that an important aspect was surveillance and testing for heresy; it suggested the model for the confessor should be the inquisitor. Inquisitors were a new breed of priest whose purpose was to root out heresy, so in following this model confession would have a strong element of interrogation and an emphasis on ensuring orthodoxy. In some ways the practice of confession may have increased women's religious freedom. The

Church could allow them to develop their spiritual lives, confident that a close eye would be kept on their beliefs and actions.

Elizabeth of Hungary

Elizabeth of Hungary (1207 – 1231) provides a disturbing example of abuse by a confessor. As a baby she had been sent from her home and family to Bavaria to grow up with Ludwig, her future husband. It was a good marriage, they had three children and Ludwig loved his wife, indulged her piety and supported her generosity to the poor. She would dress simply and visit paupers, especially women in childbirth. Ludwig allowed Elizabeth to have Conrad of Marburg, a priest whose main task was to be the Pope's inquisitor in the area, as her spiritual advisor and confessor. Conrad developed a strong hold on her despite his unreasonable behaviour, which included whipping her for failing to attend a sermon he preached.

When Ludwig died, on his way to the Crusades, Elizabeth's life fell apart. Her brother in law made himself King in place of Ludwig's young son and banished her without possessions or an allowance. Elizabeth was forced to live in abject poverty with her children and a few loyal women. When her husband's companions returned with Ludwig's body, months later, they forced her brother in law to provide for her. Unfortunately she was given the town of Marburg as her residence, which put her back in Conrad's clutches. Like many battered wives she seems to have been complicit in her own abuse and made no effort to escape his domination. In time the Pope became her guardian and appointed Conrad to act for him, so she lost any opportunity of escape. Elizabeth lived not in Marberg castle but in a small house where she established a hospital and tried to continue her charitable work with the poor.   She was subject to continual emotional and physical abuse from the domineering Conrad.   He extracted a promise of total obedience from Elizabeth and then parted her from her children and her ladies, substituting harsh servants of his own choice.   A famous legend about Elizabeth relates how she disobeyed a tyrannical husband to give bread to the poor but this story twists the facts.   It was not her husband but her spiritual advisor who forbad her to give money to the poor; when she started giving bread instead Conrad stopped that too, even when she tried to share her own crusts with beggars he forbad it.   Conrad wanted total power over her. Elizabeth escaped her tormentor by dying at the age of twenty-four.

Conrad was as cruel and unjust as an inquisitor as he was as a spiritual advisor.   His persecution of nobles for suspected heresy roused opposition from the King, Barons and Bishops.   He was eventually murdered by some of his victims.   Pope Gregory IX, the Pope who had insisted the Poor Clares must give up their life of poverty, supported Conrad throughout these events.   When told of Conrad's behaviour he replied "the Germans have always been mad, so a mad judge is all they deserve".   He was furious at Conrad's murder; his successors thankfully ignored his suggestion that Conrad should be recognised as a saint.

The Beguines

With nuns confined to their cloisters women who wished to live an active, rather than a contemplative, religious life began to do this outside the monastic system.   The largest and most successful of these spiritual movements was the Beguines.   This was a genuinely innovative and wholly female initiative.   Beguines started quietly in

163

the late twelfth century near Liege and spread rapidly in Germany and elsewhere in the thirteenth century.   Matthew Paris, the English Chronicler, wrote in 1243 that there were reported to be two thousand Beguines in Cologne and neighbouring cities alone.   Research by Southern has confirmed that a large number of property transactions involving women who were described as Beguines took place in Cologne between 1250 and 1400.   The Beguines were not an organisation but a spontaneous movement whose practices were alien to a stratified medieval church.   Beguines were women who wished to live a life that combined spirituality and compassionate service to those in need.   They lived in their own homes or in small groups in ordinary houses.   They took vows to live a simple, chaste life dedicated to the service of God.   Unlike monks and nuns they took vows not for life but for as long as they chose to live in this manner. They earned their living by their own labour, observed daily times of worship and undertook care of the sick, the old and the poor. Beguines had no theological quirks and were totally orthodox in their views.   They had a strong element of mysticism and the Eucharist was of immense importance to them, they saw it as uniting them with Christ; this kept their lives centred on the Church.   Initially there was no official opposition; although some Beguine women appear to have got into trouble for resisting sexual advances from their priests.

Beguines saw serving their fellow men as an integral part of their service to God and knew they could not do this if they joined a religious order.   Some Beguines may have been women who couldn't find a place in a monastery because they had no dowry and they probably provided a refuge for many unmarried and widowed women, who would otherwise have been alone and vulnerable.   But most chose their way of life because they wished to live a life of service to God without taking lifetime vows and accepting enclosure. One of the earliest Beguines, Mary of Oignies, was married and, persuaded her husband to join her in living a chaste life devoted to serving God.

Beguine mysticism focussed on the love of God. They desired to become close to Christ and in doing so sought to live a life like his, showing God's love to others as he had done. Many lived ascetic lives, especially at the beginning of their spiritual journey, but this was not done as a penance, as was usual in the medieval Church, but out of a wish to share Christ's sufferings. Beguine mystics wrote books of spiritual guidance and Beguine women relied on the Holy Spirit and other Beguines for spiritual counsel. Malone comments on this:

"Hence many of the Beguine writings sketch out the stages of the spiritual and mystical journey and become the guides in the journey for hundreds of their followers. It is not difficult to imagine the consternation of the ecclesiastical establishment as these often unschooled women, who had neither received nor even sought a mandate to teach, were now, in effect, running schools of biblical and mystical learning in the vernacular languages. It may even have been this departure from the sacred and exclusive ecclesiastical Latin language that most brought the Beguines to clerical attention. Indeed the Beguine writings are among the earliest and most brilliant examples of vernacular literature in Flemish, German, French, Italian and Dutch".

Unlike contemplative nuns the mystical experiences of Beguines did not take them out of the world but into it. They earned their own

165

living and their wish to follow in the steps of Christ involved them in work in the community. They identified with their Lord's care for those in pain or need. The Beguines can be seen partly as a response to the needs of the poor in the fast growing towns and cities. The Clergy had been slow to adapt to an urban rather than a rural society. At one point the city of Antwerp had only one priest to meet the needs of its fast growing population. The care for the poor, old and sick provided by Beguines must have been invaluable in towns whose populations had mushroomed with incomers from rural areas, many unemployed and living in destitution.

Initially the Beguines had a low profile, they demanded little of the clergy and did not seek attention. A few clerics befriended them and acted as their advocates within the Church. The most prominent of these was Jacques de Vitry, the priest who also wrote about the Poor Clares. He was devoted to Mary of Oignies, he wrote her life and sought support for the Beguine way of life from the Pope, who gave it half-heartedly. In time the Church became increasingly suspicious, feeling that so much piety hinted at heresy. In 1274 the Council of Lyons prohibited all religious groups that had been founded since the Council in 1215. From that time increasing pressure was put on Beguines to marry, join an existing order or follow an accepted monastic rule. Convents they joined were enriched by the arrival of Beguines with their own brand of spirituality. Beguines who chose to continue their own way of life risked being accused of heresy and many were persecuted and even burned at the stake. The Beguines left their mark on the church as religious Orders adopted the idea of lay adherents. They also left their mark on the Church calendar. The celebration of Corpus Christi Day started in the Liege area, in response to the vision of Juliana of Cornillon, a Beguine working among lepers. The Pope made it official and it was adopted throughout Christendom

The twelfth and thirteenth centuries were not a good time to be a woman. The Church controlled people's daily lives in hundreds of ways, large and small. Many priests regarded women as inferior beings, whose very gender implied guilt. Nor did the Church provide opportunities for religious women as it had in the past. Despite these restrictions, many women managed to live holy lives outside the confines of the monastic system, at least for a time.

16. MYSTICS OUTSIDE THE CLOISTER

As nuns were so heavily controlled some women tried to serve God without the restrictions that being a cloistered nun imposed. In the fourteenth century a number of them succeeded in living godly lives in public, without finding themselves confined in a convent.

Decline in papal power

The first half of the thirteenth century is regarded as the zenith of papal power; in the second half of the century the popes were preoccupied with their conflict with Holy Roman Emperors. The Popes involved the French Kings in their dispute. This proved to be a mistake; in the fourteenth century France virtually controlled the papacy and the French popes chose to be based in France, at Avignon. The papacy did not return to Rome for over seventy years. Even after an Italian Pope settled back in Rome, the French Cardinals refused to accept him and appointed a series of rival popes, this schism lasted another forty years. This confusion, and a resulting decline in the reputation and power of the papacy, gave women the opportunity to satisfy their religious aspirations. Most of the roles they found were outside convents.

Marguerite de Porete

Marguerite de Porete (d. 1310) was almost certainly a Beguine, although we know almost nothing of her life. In 1296 she wrote a book on mysticism 'The Mirror of Simple Souls'; like other Beguine literature it focussed on divine love and was designed to guide others on their spiritual journey. But the Bishop of Cambrai chose to condemn the book as heretical and he publicly burned it. Despite the threat of excommunication Marguerite continued her itinerant teaching ministry and may have added to her book. She sent the book to three theologians who endorsed it, though they suggested it was not really suited to 'simple' souls. Their approval did not protect her; she was reported to the Chief Inquisitor and imprisoned in Paris. She refused to recant or even to recognise the authority of her inquisitors. Marguerite was condemned, on the grounds that certain phrases in her book, taken out of context, were heretical, and was burned at the stake. Like her Lord she went to death in silence impressing observers by her dignity.

There were probably political motivations behind the decision to put her to death. Earlier that year King Philip of France had annoyed the Pope by burning fifty-four Templars for alleged heresy; burning Marguerite was probably an attempt to appease him. It is worth considering what the Inquisitors found so dangerous in her teaching. This was an age of faith and reason. Theologians like Thomas Aquinas were not frightened by natural philosophy (science), they believed that everything they learnt about the world would tell them more about God. (Modern scientists who are Christians still find his words applicable.) Medieval scholars patterned their views on Aristotle and for them faith and reason went together. Marguerite de Porete on the other hand believed in Faith and Love; in her book she writes of the death of reason, overcome by the paradoxes of love. She writes of the greater Holy Church of Love and the lesser Holy

Church of Reason.   Inquisitors, who prided themselves on their reason and knew little, if anything, of love, found this unacceptable. Marguerite's death did not end her influence; her book continued to circulate and was eventually republished, accredited to an anonymous monk.   It was no longer regarded as heretical but was not identified as Marguerite's work until 1946.   Marguerite was alleged to have been strongly influenced by the teaching of Meister Eckhart, the German mystic; but the reverse appears to be true, Eckhart seems to have been influenced by Marguerite.   He spent time in Paris two years after her death and would have heard about her and seen her book.   His work was widely influential in Germany and, although he had problems with the ecclesiastical authorities, his teaching was never formally condemned.

Fourteenth century women prophets

Prophecy was an important role for men and women in the very early church.   Although prophesy as part of Sunday worship died out within a hundred years or so there have always been people, many of them women, who spoke out as 'prophets'.   In the Old Testament prophets are men and women who brought God's message; often this was a message warning the Jews of the consequences of ignoring their side of the covenant God had made with them at Sinai.   Mediaeval prophets denounced the corruption and vice they saw in the church and its disregard for the teachings of the New Testament.   Hildegard of Bingen seems to have been a prophet, among all her other roles, and in the fourteenth century other women also denounced corruption and vice in the church around them.   These women pronounced God's message to a Church hierarchy that had left him out of their calculations. Men must have been aware of the state of the church but it was so powerful that few spoke out against the behaviour of its leaders. It seems to have been women, whose gender prevented them having careers or power in the church, who were prepared to speak out against the abuses they saw around them.

The middle of the fourteenth century was a very difficult time for Europe. The Black Death, devastated the continent, plague killed at least a third of the population. With no theory on the causation of disease or understanding of how it spread, an atmosphere of fear prevailed. Many saw the plague as a judgement of God. Others blamed the Jews for poisoning wells and reacted with violence against them. During the same period France and England were locked in the hundred year's war and the moral authority of the Church was damaged by schism with two, or occasionally three, warring popes. It must have been a time of great uncertainty and dread. A few women intervened in Church affairs in this period; several women had a 'prophetic' ministry, denouncing clerical corruption and vice.

Birgitta of Sweden

Birgitta (or Brigitta) of Sweden (1303 – 1373) was a mystic and visionary. She was a daughter of a pious and wealthy family. She married at the age of thirteen and had eight children. Her husband supported her religious devotion but it was after his death that she was able to develop her religious aspirations. As a widow she started to live an austere life and encouraged others to do the same. She founded a double monastery; following a rule that she believed Christ himself had dictated to her in a vision. The monks and nuns did not mix but they shared a church, carefully arranged so they could

171

worship together but not see each other. She wrote down her visions in Swedish and two priests, who later wrote her life, translated them into Latin for her and her 'Book of Revelations' was well received. A few years later, now middle aged, she travelled to Rome to seek papal approval for her rule. She stayed in Rome for the rest of her life as it took twenty-four years to persuade a pope to agree to her request. Since Birgitta was wealthy and influential in Sweden, the Church hierarchy listened to her but it was many years before her rule was approved. Once it had papal approval her Order grew and it survives today.

Birgitta was extremely critical of the vice and corruption she observed in Rome and did not hesitate to denounce it. She sent letters to Avignon insisting that the Popes should return to Rome and end the corruption and vice she observed in the Roman church. Pope Urban V did return for a short time, and approved her rule during his visit, but he found the people of Rome rebellious and the palaces and churches neglected and returned to his magnificent palace in Avignon. Birgitta warned him that if he left Rome he would die and this prophecy came true when he had a stroke and died shortly after.

The Beguine idea of lay people living a dedicated religious life in the community was copied. A group called the Brothers and Sisters of the Common Life followed a similar model and flourished in the Low Countries; their most famous member was Thomas a Kempis, author of 'The Imitation of Christ'. Friars, both Dominicans and Franciscans, started what they called tertiary orders, which operated like Beguines. The name implied that monks were primary, nuns secondary and lay people tertiary. These orders of lay people, living in their own homes or communal houses, came to play an important role. Some tertiaries were married and others lived a celibate life. When pressure was put on Beguines to disband many of them became tertiaries.

St Catherine of Siena

The most famous tertiary was St Catherine of Siena (c1347 – 1380), her contemporaries greatly admired her and she became a cult figure in her own lifetime. She lived with her family in Siena and joined the Dominican Order as a tertiary not a nun; possibly due to a wish to retain control of her own life. Her ecstatic trances and visions started during childhood and Catherine vowed to serve God and never to marry. Her family reluctantly accepted this decision and for three years she lived as a recluse in her room, undergoing extreme fasts and depriving herself of sleep; permanently ruining her health. Catherine had a vision in which, watched by the Virgin Mary, she underwent a mystical marriage ceremony with Jesus. (Nuns were called the brides of Christ so when lay religious women had this type of vision it served as an acknowledgement of their consecrated status.) This vision changed Catherine's life; she left her room and went to Siena to visit hospitals, prisons and the very poor. There are stories of the selfless love she gave to those in need and she attracted other women to join her in this work.

After three years of caring for the poor and sick Catherine experienced another vision in which she underwent a mystical death. This time she felt called to go out from Siena to 'save souls'. For the last ten years of Catherine's short life she travelled in Italy and to Avignon. She wrote many letters and a book of revelations based on her visions; all by dictation as, like most women of her time, she had not been taught to write. Catherine was involved in mediation at every level in the Church. She loved the Church but she spoke out strongly against the corruption she saw within it. Catherine believed that the best remedy for the ills of the Church would be a strong papacy. She went to Avignon and eventually managed to see Pope Gregory XI. She hoped to persuade him to return to Rome and call for a new Crusade. He did return the papal seat to Rome and Catherine may have influenced that decision but neither he nor his successor called for the Crusade that Catherine hoped would unite Christendom. In her desire for peace in Christendom she seems to have been oblivious to the dubious morality of buying unity at the cost of starting a war elsewhere. Despite her efforts Catherine was powerless to avert the Schism that led to a separate line of popes based in Avignon. She died aged thirty-two, her body worn out by the abuse she had inflicted on it. She had become a medieval celebrity and her reputation has continued to grow. In 1970 she was made a Doctor of the Church.

It is interesting to compare Catherine's fate to that of Marguerite de Porete. They were both mystics and were both critical of corruption within the church. Maybe the difference was that Marguerite was wholly centred on God whereas Catherine loved both God and the Church. Her criticism was tolerated because of her support for the Papacy. Unfortunately her hopes that a strong pope would tackle clerical corruption and immorality were not realised. Reform within the Catholic Church did not come until the Reformation forced the papacy's hand.

Julian of Norwich

As well as nuns and laywomen there was another religious way of life open to women that was particularly popular in England. Anchorites were enclosed for life in small two or three roomed cells attached to a parish church. They had three windows to the world, one to the church so they could participate in services, one for their servant to bring them food and one for visitors seeking spiritual counsel. They were not part of a religious foundation and came under the direct authority of the local bishop. Women were especially drawn to this life; in twelfth and thirteenth century England there were 92 female and 20 male anchorites.

The most famous of these Anchorites was Julian of Norwich (c1342-1416). We do not know Julian's real name, she is known by the name of the saint to whom her church was dedicated. She was a religious woman who lived with her parents before her enclosure but we do not know where. She seems to have had a good education; although like other medieval women writers she plays this down. She lived in difficult times; war, plague and poor harvests led to famine and social unrest, culminating in the Peasant's revolt. In provincial England she was far away from the corruptions of the papacy but Henry Despenser, her local Bishop, was noted for his pride, extravagance and the cruelty with which he suppressed both rebellious peasants and Lollards; so she cannot have been ignorant of the lack of Christian love and Christian virtues shown by many clergy. However, Julian mentions none of these things in her writings and was uncritically loyal to the Church.

At the age of thirty Julian was taken seriously ill and was not expected to recover. After the crisis of her illness had passed she had a series of visions or 'showings', which took place over a period of twelve hours while she lay quietly on her sickbed. After her recovery she became an anchorite and spent her life meditating on these visions. She wrote an account of them soon after her illness and another longer version 'Revelation of Divine Love' some years later. Julian's spiritual thought was profound and original and her book is still read. Many of her showings deal with the passion of Christ; like Beguine mystics she focussed on the love of God. She was also concerned about the problem of sin and of evil and had a more sophisticated and spiritual definition of sin than many clerics, who were obsessed with sins of the flesh. The main subject of all her visions is God's love for fallen humanity. A striking element in Julian's writing is her emphasis on the motherhood of God and of Christ. This idea was not new, it appears in the Bible and in some other writers, but Julian was the first to make it central to her view of God. Julian did not accept the patriarchal view of God held by her contemporaries; she emphasised that God is both mother and father. Both Marguerite de Porete and Julian of Norwich reminded people of God's love and of the central importance of love in Christ's teaching. The books they wrote have helped many Christians over the centuries to grasp the centrality of love in the Christian faith.

Margery Kempe

The only reference to Julian outside legal documents and her own writings is by a contemporary who also lived in Norfolk. Margery Kempe (1373-?) was the subject of the first autobiography written in

English; a copy of her book survived in a family library and was re-discovered in 1934. It is an extraordinary story of a woman who was in many ways very ordinary. Margery was illiterate and dictated her story but her personality comes over clearly. She was the daughter of a successful merchant who was mayor of Bishop's Lynn (now Kings Lynn) five times. Her religious life started when she had postnatal depression after the birth of her first child; she recovered after receiving a vision of Christ. For a few years she carried on her normal life and started two unsuccessful business ventures. Reading her description of her actions it seems quite possible that she had bipolar disorder and started them during a manic phase. These failures led to much criticism from her family and neighbours and she turned to religion for solace. Margery began to have mystic experiences, at first in the form of hearing celestial music. In keeping with her nature her spiritual meditations were often practical; when she meditated on the life of the Virgin she saw herself serving her, providing for Mary's bodily needs, procuring lodgings for her on the way to Bethlehem and begging for white cloths to swaddle the baby Jesus. This down to earth element is typical of Margery. She uses the spiritual terms of other mystics and, like St Catherine, she had a vision of a 'mystic marriage' to Christ, but she anchors her mystical experiences in everyday life. Her book is a fascinating and vivid record of her life but it is difficult to imagine anyone using it as a spiritual aid.

As a mystic Margery had a major handicap in fourteenth century eyes, she was married and her husband was not prepared to accept a chaste relationship. Margery's life can be seen as an attempt to assert that her experience of sexual intercourse did not make her a spiritually second class Christian.   She was encouraged by stories of married saints like Birgitta of Sweden.   It was after many years, and the birth of another thirteen children, that she persuaded her husband to give up his marital rights.   She bribed him with a promise to pay his debts and he agreed.   From this time they mostly lived separate lives and Margery travelled widely.   She went on pilgrimages overseas, travelling as far as Jerusalem, Rome and Santiago de Compostela in Spain.   She also visited places of pilgrimage, and senior clerics and holy men in England.   She was hampered by opposition and accusations of heresy, since the piety of her life made people think she was a Lollard (a follower of John Wycliffe).   Eventually she was prompted to return home to nurse an ailing, and soon senile and incontinent, husband.

It is easy to have a negative view of fourteenth and fifteenth century clerics but many showed patience and kindness in their dealings with Margery; although her wealth may have had something to do with this.   In her early years, when she was in a state of high anxiety, her local priest seems to have heard her confession and given absolution up to three times in a single day.   Some clerics rejected her, but many of them were patient with a 'difficult' middle-aged woman. Archbishops and bishops received her, and monks and priests who she approached advised and encouraged her.   One form Margery's spirituality took was weeping noisily and uncontrollably over the sorrows of Christ, during the Mass and at other times.   This was disruptive to church services.   One friar did preach against her but surprisingly other clerics tolerated her presence.

"Another time Bishop Wakerying, Bishop of Norwich, preached at Lynn in the said church of St Margaret, and this creature (Margery) cried and wept most violently during his sermon, and he put up with it most meekly and patiently, and so did many a worthy clerk, both regular and secular, for there was never any clerk who preached openly against her crying except the Grey Friar".

One priest was encouraged to accept her by reading the life of Mary of Oignies, who had also wept abundantly when she thought of Christ's passion and death. This priest spent many hours writing down the ninety-nine chapters of Margery's book as a record of God's dealings with her.

During the thirteenth and fourteenth centuries many women sought to live a religious life outside a convent. These included a widespread movement, the Beguines, and individuals following their own inspirations. Birgitta and Catherine were prepared to take on the Church establishment in their desire for reform; there were others living quiet, holy lives far from the centres of power.

17. HERETICS AND OUTSIDERS

The late medieval church struggled with heresy, with both groups and individuals whose views were unorthodox. This chapter will look at how women fared in some of these groups.

There was no problem with heresies in the western church between 500 and 1000. This is often attributed to the fact that during these years life was a struggle to survive. It may also be due to the fact that by 500 AD Christian thinkers had established the New Testament canon and the basic doctrines of the church; reducing uncertainty about what Christians should believe. The papacy was a unifying force in this period and the Church was not yet a monolithic institution likely to provoke rebellion. The Gregorian reforms changed this. The Church became centralised and politically powerful; establishing its authority over almost all aspects of daily life. The corruption, avarice and vice of the clergy were proverbial. Unsurprisingly opposition to the Church increased and people sought alternative ways to relate to God. The later medieval Church was not tolerant of outsiders; Although there was limited official toleration of Jews; the killing of Jews in medieval times was generally a result of mob violence not direct action by Church or State. Christians who failed to conform to the beliefs of the Church were another matter. Heresy was regarded as the equivalent of high treason and therefore worthy of death.

Cathars

The first heretical group to be more than a local challenge to the new powerful papacy were the Cathars. This belief was brought back by returning crusaders, and was encouraged by disillusionment with the clergy. A major centre was Languedoc in Southern France, which was then an independent country. Anti-clerical feeling was strong in Languedoc, even among Catholics, and the secular authorities there were less than zealous in their support of the Church. It was therefore the Languedoc Cathars who most concerned the papal authorities.

Cathars were dualists who saw all matter as evil; they condemned all sexual relationships, even in animals. They had two classes, 'Perfects', who had made themselves pure by extreme fasting and abstention from sexual relationships even in marriage, and other believers whose duty was to support the Perfects. Only Perfects were saved and only Perfects could pray directly to God. Perfects would not eat meat, eggs, or dairy produce because of their associations with sex; they ate fish, because they believed fish did not mate. The austere life of a Perfect gained them great respect, especially when contrasted with the self-indulgence of many Catholic clergy. Women could become Perfects but could not progress any further; the Cathar hierarchy seems to have been male. One source includes a list of Perfects; forty-five percent were women, but the same source indicates that the percentage of women among ordinary believers was much lower. Most Cathar women seem to have followed their family into heresy; a reversal of the usual pattern of women bringing their families into Christian faith. The Cathar heresy did not provide women with a positive alternative to the Church.

The Church's initial response to the Cathars was to convert them. St Dominic went among the Cathars living in poverty as an itinerant preacher and founded the Dominican Friars so others would follow his example. The Friars had some success, but progress was slow and the Papal legate was impatient. Then he was assassinated. Pope Innocent III was infuriated and called for a crusade against Languedoc. The violence and horror that followed was directed against Catholics and Cathars alike. The Pope and Bishops remained unforgiving but they also had little control over the army they had conjured up. 'Crusaders' from Northern France were glad of an excuse to invade the prosperous South.

Catharism did not die out with the destruction of Languedoc. A fascinating study of the inquisitorial records for the mountain village of Montaillou, in the mountains between France and Spain, shows how it survived there, with the aid of a village priest who was a secret Cathar. The study shows how the asceticism, which had always characterised the movement, could be corrupted. The priest was a serial seducer and encouraged his lovers to think that, since all sex was sinful, adultery was no worse than marriage. He was eventually arrested and died in prison.

The Cathars would have been recognised as heretics in any period. Most other major heresies of the later middle ages were only heresies in the light of the newly defined dogmas of the Roman Catholic Church. The church in the first millennium would not have seen their beliefs as heretical and the churches that grew out of the Reformation came to see them as forerunners. These early reformers were concerned to spread the message of true Christianity and encourage reading the Bible. They spoke out against clerical abuses but they saw themselves as part of the church and worked for reform within it. Their followers remained within the church for as long as the Church would allow their practices and beliefs. When they left it was because their activities were no longer tolerated by Rome.

The Waldensians

Peter de Valdes (d. 1218) founder of one of these groups was a rich merchant in Lyons who had a conversion experience. Hearing of Christ's words "If you wish to be perfect, go, sell your possessions, and give the money to the poor, and you will have treasure in heaven; then come, follow me" he felt called to take them literally. He paid his debts and made restitution where it was due because of previous sharp business practices. He provided for his wife and daughters and paid some scholars to translate the Scriptures into French. Once he had done these things he gave away the rest of his money to the poor, literally giving it away in the street as coins or food. Peter became a wandering street preacher who told people of his experiences and read from the Bible in a language ordinary people could understand. Others joined him and they became known as the Poor of Lyons. The Church tried to forbid them to preach, unless specifically invited by a priest, but they refused to accept that the Church had authority to stop them telling out their message of salvation. Peter Valdes taught his followers that they all, women as well as men, had an obligation to evangelise and preach. According to inquisitor's reports there were illiterate women among them who had learned virtually all the New Testament by heart. Waldensians later went further and allowed laypersons, including women, to administer communion and baptism. The teachings of Peter de Valdes and his followers seem to have appealed to women and the sect attracted a much higher percentage of women believers than Catharism had done.

The Waldensians were condemned as heretics. In Strassburg in 1212 there was a crackdown on heretics, who were probably Waldensians, and eighty people, twenty-three of them women, were burned at the stake. Some Waldensians survived as secret believers passing on their faith in private, others by retreating to the mountains. In a remote Alpine retreat they were able to evict the inquisitors sent to persecute them and even to survive a Crusade called against them. After the Reformation most Waldensians joined Lutheran churches but some continued to worship separately.

Wycliffe and the Lollards

John Wycliffe (1320 – 1384) was an Oxford scholar and probably the foremost theologian of his day. His Bible studies made him increasingly uncomfortable with the dogmas and practices of the church. He was critical of papal indulgences, clergy taking money to pray for the dead, and compulsory celibacy. He stressed personal responsibility and the need for people to study Scripture for themselves. To facilitate this he and his friends translated the Bible into English. The Pope (Gregory XI) condemned his writings but Wycliffe had supporters at Court, including John of Gaunt, the powerful third son of the king. Wycliffe's anticlerical views were popular with nobles and other laity; but when he criticised the doctrine of transubstantiation this was a step too far for his aristocratic supporters. When they withdrew their support the English bishops condemned his opinions and exiled him to a remote country parish. While living there he encouraged the young men he had trained at

Oxford to travel the countryside with the English Bible, preaching to the common people.

Wycliffe had toyed briefly with the idea of woman priests, purely as an academic argument. One of his followers, Walter Brut, went much further and believed that women could preach publicly and could conduct the Eucharist. He based his argument partly on the Bible and partly on the fact that the Church did allow women to baptise – one of the chief sacraments. A number of papers written to refute Brut have survived, which is why his views are known.

Wycliffe was allowed to die in his bed but the Church hounded his followers, who were called Lollards. The English bishops persuaded King Henry IV to introduce the death penalty for heresy in 1399; although the English were not enthusiastic about burning heretics and numbers were quite small Lollards were driven underground. Among the common people Wycliffe's teachings survived and there were several later episodes of persecution, including one in the reign of Henry VIII over a century later. Although a few Lollard writings and sermons have survived, the main sources of information on individuals are the Church records of their interrogations and trials.

There is no evidence that Lollards had women 'priests' but their women did teach and give pastoral care to other women. A study of women among the Lollards has found evidence of only one woman, Alice Rowley of Coventry, who was involved in teaching both men and women. She was of higher social standing than most Lollards and this probably gave her the confidence to speak in mixed gatherings. This was probably also the reason she was not killed. She was broken by the inquisitor's interrogation and the last information available on her describes her being forced to walk to the scaffold, carrying wood for the fire and watch while another woman teacher, a close friend, was burnt at the stake.

In fifteenth century Europe laypeople who were seen to be earnest in their religious practice, and even people who showed integrity in their business and other dealings, were frequently suspected of heresy. Swearing became more common in parts of Europe as a way of demonstrating that the speaker was loyal to the Church. Ordinary church goers were not expected to be pious, or to allow their faith to affect their behaviour. In England Margery Kempe was several times accused of Lollardy because of her piety. She spent at least one night in prison before her innocence was established by the clerics who examined her to confirm her orthodoxy.

Ever since the Gregorian reform there had been people who had tried to 'reform the reform'. Some of these were excluded from the Church; others managed to stay within it. A few individuals, many of them women, were prepared to speak out against corruption and vice in the Church and again some were able to remain in the Church and others were accused of heresy. There was even a German Cardinal, Nicholas de Cusa, (1201 –1264) who introduced a few real reforms. He also exposed the Donation of Constantine as a forgery, undermining the Church's claim to secular power. The determining factor in deciding if an individual was tolerated or condemned for heresy seems to have been their attitude to the papacy. The Papacy was prepared to tolerate criticism from those who supported its authority, but any attack on papal privileges was unacceptable.

Anti-clerical feeling

By the end of the Fourteenth century anti-clerical feeling was rife across Europe. Chaucer's Canterbury Tales give us a picture of how the Church was viewed in England. In his group of cheerful pilgrims, or holiday-makers, the Church is well represented. The prioress was worldly in her attitudes and interests and ignored the rule that said she should be cloistered. The monk was obsessed with hunting. Three other clerics are portrayed as out to make as much money as they could. The Pardoner, who sold indulgences, is shown as the most corrupt of all. Only the parson, a local priest, is portrayed as a good man who practiced what he preached, "First following the word before he taught it." The folk tales and ballads of Robin Hood are even more revealing; in them men of the Church are portrayed as rich, worldly and cruel, the enemies of the poor and needy. Anti-clerical attitudes grew among both the intelligentsia and the general population. It is not surprising that people were receptive to critics of the Church. Disillusionment with the conduct of the clergy at all levels paved the way for the Reformation.

Witches

From the end of the fifteenth century the whole weight of the Church descended on another 'heretical' group; this time a group that did not actually exist. Medieval people were superstitious, remnants of half forgotten pagan beliefs survived in rural areas, practiced by local 'wise women'. But the 'cult' of witchcraft seems to have been almost entirely a figment of the imaginations of the inquisitors who investigated it.

187

Medieval theologians taught that spiritual forces could not be neutral, they were either of God or the devil. In 1484 Pope Innocent VIII issued a Bull calling for the destruction of all who used 'black arts' and he commissioned two Dominican Friars, to write handbook for inquisitors on the subject. Their book, Malleus Maleficarum (The Witches Hammer), was published a few years later. It was designed to help inquisitors identify witches and presented witchcraft as a serious challenge to the Church, which must be eradicated. The cult, they claimed, was almost entirely made up of women, a sex they considered to blame for almost all evil: "We find that nearly all the kingdoms of the world have been overthrown by women". (To prove this they cited Helen of Troy, Jezebel and Cleopatra, who, they suggested, had destroyed the Republic of Rome.) Witches, they said, entered into a sexual relationship with the devil, they believed that men could resist this temptation but not women, who were morally weak. "All witchcraft comes from carnal lust which is in women insatiable." Their book is a strong candidate for the most sexist and misogynist ever written; it remained in circulation for several hundred years, although banned by one Pope.

Malleus Maleficarum did emphasise the need to ensure witches had a fair trial; although their concept of a 'fair' trial included torture, which they saw as an acceptable method of extracting confessions. The book debates whether a plea bargain, a promise to save the life of a witch in return for a confession incriminating others, should be binding on the court or merely on the individual judge, who might hand over to someone else to pronounce the death sentence. The book also said witchcraft was a matter for the civil authorities, unless the witch was also guilty of heresy. However, this did not protect women as when the Church became distracted by the rise of 'heretical' Protestants, civil authorities continued to prosecute witches.

The idea of witchcraft took hold of the popular imagination and a belief that black magic was a serious threat was widespread. Seeking out witches became an obsession for some men in Catholic, and later in Protestant, churches. Persecution of witches reached its peak in the sixteenth and seventeenth centuries. So called witches, mainly middle aged and elderly women, were tortured until they confessed to entering into a pact with the devil and were then burned to death. Once accused there was often no way out. One method of investigation was the ordeal by fire or water; if the accused woman died it might indicate her innocence but too late to save her; if she survived the ordeal it was seen as evidence of how strong her magic was and therefore as proof of her guilt.

Even before the reformation there were a number of religious groups that were outside the church, though not always by their own choice. At the same time anti-clerical feeling was growing among the general population; not for religious reasons but because of a perception that many priests were greedy for worldly wealth rather than heavenly treasure. Disillusionment with the clergy paved the way for the Reformation.

18. WOMEN IN THE REFORMATION

The sixteenth century saw the most radical changes in the way Christianity was organised for over a thousand years.   Change was in the air and dissatisfaction with the Church and the clergy had reached a tipping point.   New ideas undermined the authority of the Church. The ideas of the Reformers had immediate appeal to those women who found the Church was not meeting their spiritual needs.

A time of accelerated change

In the sixteenth century cultural changes, which were later named the Renaissance, were changing the arts and encouraging new modes of philosophical thought.   New ideas were being put forward undermining the dependence on established authorities, which had characterised mediaeval Europe. This mindset made it more difficult to disregard the evidence of experience in favour of long accepted 'facts'; to ignore the lives of actual women in favour of the 'truth' that all women were sinful and inept.   Erasmus, the humanist scholar who laid much of the intellectual groundwork of the reformation, also rethought medieval attitudes towards women.   In a few of his 'Colloquies', Erasmus pictured intelligent, educated women debating with men.   His portraits were based on real women, like the daughters of his friend Thomas More.

The Church hierarchy ignored the warning implicit in the popularity of new humanist ideas, and the widespread negativity towards the clergy and continued to be deaf to pleas that it should tackle corruption; the Pope was preoccupied instead with building St Peters. The sale of indulgences continued; they were impossible to justify theologically but were the most effective way of raising money. Across Europe the uneducated and credulous were persuaded to part with their hard earned money to save themselves and their loved ones from purgatory. This distressed many less worldly priests, including a monk and university lecturer called Martin Luther. Luther had earlier been disillusioned by a visit to Rome, where he had observed the blatant laxity and vice of many Roman clergy. His subsequent studies had convinced him that salvation came only through personal faith in Christ. Incensed by the blatant money grubbing of a local campaign to sell indulgences he wrote Ninety-five Theses on the issue. These he nailed to the church door in Wittenberg with the idea of provoking local debate on the issue. He cannot have expected the consequences that followed.

Unfortunately for the ecclesiastical authorities the political climate in Northern Europe had changed since John Wycliffe's time. English Kings had suppressed the Lollards on behalf of the Church but the Elector of Saxony was prepared to protect Luther and his followers. The Church realised it had to deal with Luther directly. Luther was accused of denying papal authority; since papal authority was the only grounds on which indulgences could be defended. The situation could only end in Luther's submission or death, or in a breakdown of church unity in Western Europe. Luther was not prepared to back down. He had to go into hiding but was later able to live quietly in a region where a reformed faith was accepted. Others were not so fortunate; Luther's ideas precipitated religious, social and political upheaval across Germany and Northern Europe.

Katherine Von Bora

The new printing presses made the Reformers' writings widely available. Books were no longer handwritten and restricted to the privileged few. Luther's books soon reached educated laywomen and even enclosed nuns. Many German nuns became ardent adherents of the new ideas. The reformers were critical of clerical celibacy and monastic corruption and this encouraged many nuns to leave their convents. This was not easy in areas where the ruler was still Catholic. One group of a dozen nuns wrote to Luther who arranged for them to be smuggled out by a merchant delivering a supply of dried herrings to the convent. The story goes that the nuns escaped by hiding among the barrels that had transported fish. Those nuns who could not return to their families came to Wittenburg, where Luther settled them with families and sought husbands for them. Most of those of marriageable age were settled but arrangements for one, Katherine Von Bora (1499-1552), fell through. Luther tried to make another match for her but she sent him a message that there were only two men she would marry one of them being Luther himself. It is sometimes suggested that the least attractive nun was left on the shelf and Luther had to take pity on her; but the evidence indicates it was Catherine who chose him.

Luther had been encouraging friends to marry; now he felt he should set them an example. After the wedding the marriage was consummated in front of witnesses, as was the local practice at the time. (This practice is evidence that sixteenth century marriage was a social contract, which had to be 'ratified' physically, rather than a personal relationship.) Luther's marriage was not motivated by personal affection but once settled they got on very well. Katherine's presence improved Luther's physical comfort and his health. He once said, "Before I married the bed was not made for a whole year and became foul with sweat. But I worked all day and was so tired at night that I fell into the bed without knowing that anything was amiss." Not all Luther's friends were happy with his decision and in Catholic circles the marriage caused a scandal. Katherine was singled out for public criticism, and called an apostate for breaking her vows. Despite this the marriage was a success. Luther had suffered all his adult life from recurring depression and was constantly alert to the malevolent influence of the devil on his inner life. He told his friends that married life and love was far the most effective way of combating the devil.

Katherine was a competent, intelligent woman. She was also strong willed and independent; at times Luther called her "Lord Kathe". She ran Luther's home, and bore him six children, who she brought up along with four orphans She also contributed to their income by managing a farm some miles away. Luther called her his morning star because she would get up at 4am to fulfil her many responsibilities. Luther's house had a constant flow of guests, casual visitors, refugees fleeing persecution and resident students. As well as making them all welcome and providing for their physical needs Katherine seems to have been witty and wise, able to contribute to the discussions between Luther and their guests. The couple were always hospitable and charitable. In times of plague they took in the sick and their home became a hospital. Luther clearly loved and appreciated Katherine. He described her as "Preacher, brewer, gardener and all things else." Katherine can be seen as the prototype minister's wife, pioneering a new role.

The reformer's teaching on women

Luther firmly believed in "the priesthood of all believers" including women. But he did not translate this into practice and allow women to preach or take any office within the church. Luther wrote that women could baptise (as the Church had allowed for centuries) and could provide wise counsel and Bible teaching in private situations. He only allowed them to preach when no men were present, for example in convents. Luther had a traditional view of a woman's role "A woman is never truly her own master. God formed her body to belong to a man and to have his children". He put great emphasis on women as mothers and one surprising consequence of this was his suggestion that a woman whose husband was impotent, could either conceive children in an extra-marital relationship, with her husband's consent, or could leave him, go to another country and be morally free to enter into a new marriage. Luther saw motherhood not only a responsibility but also as a right.

Luther was not the only reformer to marry. Zwingli, Calvin and other former priests who led the new protestant churches also found wives. Marriage became the norm among protestant clergy; Catherine Von Bora was the forerunner in a long tradition of minister's wives who supported their husbands in their work. Many of the younger reformers who followed were more radical in their religious views but few questioned the accepted view of women. Protestants did not share the misogyny of many priests and did not demonise women or claim that Eve, and by extension all women, was responsible for evil.

But new churches were no more accepting of women as teachers, writers or leaders than the Roman Catholic Church.

Women's status in Protestant countries

Protestant ideas spread quickly through Europe and took root; especially in the north where the rulers were further from Rome and had less investment in the status quo. The religious status of a country depended on the views of its ruler and there was great turmoil as refugees fled from their homes to countries where they could worship as they saw fit. Historians argue as to whether women were better off in Catholic or Protestant churches. Writers usually suggest the situation within their own church was more positive. To some extent it depended on a woman's position. The reformers rediscovered the role of wife and mother and valued it highly, raising the status of married women. The role of minister's wife provided many women with an opportunity to be involved in meaningful work and to serve their community. It is easy for us to underestimate how important this was in a world where the idea of a 'career' for a middleclass woman was unthinkable. However, the Protestant churches did not offer so much to single women. Protestant women did not have the opportunity to live a dedicated life in a community of sisters. Single women, who might once have been 'holy virgins', were regarded as 'old maids'. Protestant widows who needed a refuge had no retreat of the kind offered to some of their Catholic sisters by convents. Protestant women also lacked religious role models; there was no protestant substitute for prayers to the Virgin and female saints. The status given to the Virgin Mary reminded Catholics of the heights to which a woman could rise, but protestant churches have reacted against what they see as an inappropriate veneration of Mary, and have played down the role of Jesus' Mother.

Women flocked to join the new churches and women spread the new ideas, often with little encouragement from their family and community. Women on both sides felt strongly and were prepared to take action for their faith. In Catholic areas nuns sought to escape the cloister but equally, in some protestant towns, other nuns fought to continue their consecrated way of life. In England after the dissolution of the monasteries they had no choice but to leave their convents. Only a few women were able to take a public role or exercise any power in church affairs and then usually only because they had high status in secular society. A few royal or aristocratic women, especially in France, took an active role in church politics but most women had no opportunity for action or influence outside their own small circle.

In England King Henry VIII had been encouraged towards reform by Queen Anne Boleyn and Thomas Cromwell, who were both convinced Protestants, but after his break with Rome he had turned against them for other reasons and executed them both. He remained a religious conservative despite his quarrel with the Pope; denial of transubstantiation remained a capital offence. Henry did allow publication of an English translation of the Bible but he and his advisors were wary of the social unrest, which had followed the spread of reformed ideas in Germany. A law was passed saying the English Bible could only be read by clerics, noblemen, merchants and gentry. Initially this law was intended to restrict readership to men but it was changed to allow upper class women to have access to a Bible. Many women took advantage of this opportunity, including

Henry's sixth and last Queen, Katherine Parr, who organised Bible studies for her ladies in waiting and other courtiers.

Another traditional attitude that reformers failed to challenge was the intolerance of diversity, which had bedevilled the church for centuries. Both Protestant and Roman Catholic minorities were persecuted for their faith.   During the political unrest which followed the reformation people were tortured and killed by both the Catholic Inquisition and by Protestant governments.   Women were included among the martyrs who suffered persecution and death rather than renounce their beliefs.

Anne Askew

One martyr whose story has come down to us in her own words, is Ann Askew (1521 - 1546), who was burned at the stake at the age of twenty five.   Ann was born to a family of Lincolnshire gentry with protestant views.   While she was still a teenager her father insisted on her marriage to a Catholic gentleman, they had two children but the marriage was unhappy.   Anne studied the Bible and was a gifted teacher but her husband was unsympathetic to her determination to share her faith.   Eventually he turned her out of the house and later seems to have been instrumental in arranging for her second arrest. Anne went to live with her brother in London and sought a divorce; citing in support of her plea St Paul's words that Christians should not be "unequally yoked" with unbelievers.   She continued counselling and teaching from the Bible.

Anne's request for a divorce was refused and the authorities arrested her.   They were unhappy with her views on transubstantiation; she was convinced that when Jesus said, "this is my body" he was talking symbolically but Henry's church still accepted the literal presence of Christ in the Host.   Influential friends at court were able to arrange for Ann's release on this occasion but two further arrests followed. The authorities did not want to put Anne to death but they were determined that she should renounce her views and cease to propagate reformed ideas.

It was Anne's misfortune that because she had friends in high places her interrogation became political.   Some members of the court were anxious to discredit Katherine Parr in order to replace her with a new queen from another powerful family.   Katherine was known to have protestant views and her enemies saw this as her weak point; since her behaviour did not give any scope for morals charges of the kind that had been used to discredit Henry's previous Queen.   Subjecting a gentlewoman to the rack was not only unusual, it was against the Law; but the Lord Chancellor himself supervised Anne's interrogation under torture; he was determined to make her betray the prominent men and women who shared her views.   Anne held firm, refusing to incriminate anyone, though tortured on the rack until she could no longer walk.   In her account of her 'examinations' it is clear the powerful men who confronted Anne did not intimidate her.   She refused to let her interrogators twist her words and whenever possible she used her extensive knowledge of the New Testament to justify her views.   She remained steadfast to the end and, when she was being carried to the stake, turned down the promise of a royal pardon if she would recant.   Her steadfast faith encouraged the three men who were executed at the same time.

Anne Askew's account of her examinations was published soon after her death, initially abroad.   The publisher expanded it considerably with his own comments but Anne's own words make up almost half the book. John Foxe in his book of Martyrs, published 13 years after her death, included her story without additional material. Both books were widely read and were an inspiration to English Protestants. The first book includes a ballad written by Anne Askew in Newgate prison. It is full of military images "Faith is the weapon strong / which will not fail at need / my foes therefore among / therewith will I proceed". The ballad also includes a prayer that God will forgive those persecuting her.   Foxe quotes another contemporary ballad about Anne Askew, which is very different; it begins "I am a woman poor and blind / and little knowledge remains in me". The aim of this ballad was to attack Stephen Gardiner, the man mainly responsible for the persecution under Mary, long after Anne's own ordeal.   As so often happens, once Anne Askew was dead her admirers were free to exploit her story for their own purposes.

Other female martyrs

Ann Askew was not the only English woman martyr.   In his 'Book of Martyrs' Foxe recounted the stories of a number of protestant women who died for their faith during the reign of Mary I, Henry VIII's fervently Roman Catholic daughter who reversed the English reformation during her short reign. Under Mary the Church burned a number of ordinary women at the stake because they would not abandon their beliefs.

Not all martyrs were Protestants.   Elizabeth I tried to make her Church of England as inclusive as possible.   But she was forced to regard Catholicism as treason, since the Pope had imposed a duty on all Catholics to depose or kill her.   It became a felony to receive or shelter a priest.   Margaret Clitherow (1556? – 1586), a York merchant's wife and a Roman Catholic convert, built a secret room to hide priests, several of whom were later martyred.   She prayed for the grace of martyrdom for herself.   Her prayer was answered when she was arrested and then executed for refusing to co-operate with the court; her refusal to make a plea was probably motivated by a wish not to involve her children and servants in giving evidence at her trial. In 1970 the Pope proclaimed Margaret a saint.

This chapter has looked at how the one Church of medieval 'Christendom', which had a virtual monopoly on all things religious, gave way to a number of different churches.   The reformation was the result of thousands of separate decisions made by individuals, who found study of the Bible and the ideas of the reformers met their spiritual needs better than their local priest and the rites of the Catholic Church.   A majority of the Reformers' followers were women.

19. THE COUNTER REFORMATION

For centuries ecclesiastical authorities had ignored calls for reform but the loss of most of Northern Europe forced the Papacy to start a process of reform within the Church. The Counter-Reformation was intended to be a masculine movement led by priests; but women were deeply involved in counter- Reformation spirituality and reform.   It was also women whose beliefs put them at the forefront of work to ameliorate the massive social problems of the sixteenth and seventeenth centuries.

The Council of Trent

The Papacy postponed calling a Council for several decades, despite the crisis, but in 1545 the Council of Trent started its deliberations. The Council made decisions that led, in time, to a system of education for priests and a reduction in the immorality and corruption that had alienated so many lay people. The resulting changes were slow but over the next centuries the Council's decisions led to real reforms. Conservatives dominated the Council and insisted that errors and mistranslations of the Bible should be accepted as providential, designed by God to glorify Mary and support other Catholic doctrines. With this attitude it is not surprising that the Council's reforms failed to move the Church towards reconciliation with their 'separated brethren'.   Like the Gregorian reform, the Counter-Reformation was masculine and centred on the clergy.   The Council did nothing to improve the situation for Catholic women and despite a strong groundswell of opinion in favour of clerical marriage the Papacy insisted that the Council must not weaken on compulsory celibacy. As one of the Council's final acts the Pope persuaded them to reinforce clerical control of religious women by ruling, yet again, that all nuns must be enclosed and live a contemplative life.

The Council was concerned with religious, and secular, politics, the spiritual impetus for Counter-Reformation came from elsewhere, especially from the work of two Spaniards. One was Ignatius Loyola, who founded the Jesuits and pioneered education for priests. The other person who inspired Catholic reform was a woman.

St Teresa of Avila

Teresa of Avila (1515 – 1582) was a noblewoman in Spain, a country where the reign of a woman monarch had given women confidence. Isabella of Castile was conservative in her religious views and a strong supporter of the Church. She and her husband established the Spanish Inquisition, which was controlled by the Crown not the Papacy and which became a byword for fanaticism. Jews, Muslims and later Protestants, all suffered under Isabelle's rule; but nuns flourished. Teresa entered a Carmelite convent at the age of 20, despite her Father's disapproval of her decision to become a nun. For ten years she wrestled with spiritual struggles and ill health. Then while reading 'The Confessions of St Augustine' she underwent a life transforming experience, in her autobiography she describes the change; "…another and a new life. Hitherto my life was my own; my life since... is the life which God lived in me." The following year Teresa began experiencing visions and ecstasies. She was a mystic in the Catholic tradition but, unlike earlier mystics such as

Hildegard of Bingen and Catherine of Sienna, she did not denounce the shortcomings of the Church. She loved it and felt unable to criticise it while it was under attack from protestant ideas. Teresa practiced, and encouraged others in, a life of prayer. Although liturgical prayer was part of religious life, mental prayer was not encouraged; it was seen as dangerous and as containing the seeds of Protestantism. An index of forbidden books produced in 1559 included many works on prayer. Despite this Teresa, encouraged by her Jesuit confessors, persisted in exploring methods of prayer.

Teresa always tried to be an obedient daughter of the church and relied on her confessors and other priests to affirm her actions; "I did nothing without asking the opinion of learned men". Teresa and her friends talked of founding a small convent where they could live according to the original, less lax, Carmelite rule but she did not consider it seriously until she had a vision. "So efficacious was the vision, and such was the nature of the words our Lord spoke to me, that I could not possibly doubt that they came from Him. I suffered most keenly, because I saw in part the great anxieties and troubles that the work would cost me." Her plans to found the convent of St Joseph were met with both encouragement and virulent opposition but eventually she was able to enter the new House and marked the occasion by changing her aristocratic name to the simple 'Teresa of Jesus'. St Joseph's was only the first of a number of small 'barefoot' Carmelite monasteries she founded. This involved leaving her contemplative life and travelling widely within Spain. Initially the Houses she founded were for women but later she also established reformed monasteries for Carmelite monks. Teresa faced a lot of opposition from those dubious about her mystical experiences. After the Council of Trent she also faced opposition because of her active life. Despite the fact she was a mystic, who advocated and practiced contemplation, she was also a competent administrator and her activities and travels were far from conforming to the ideal of the contemplative life. A Papal Nuncio described her as "A restless gadabout, disobedient, contumacious woman who promulgates pernicious doctrine under pretence of devotion." He also accused her of being ambitious and of teaching theology as if she was a doctor of the church. Teresa was confined to one convent and her friend and collaborator, St John of the Cross, was kidnapped and imprisoned. Eventually the Pope pronounced in Teresa's favour and she was able to continue her work.

Teresa was encouraged to write down her story by her confessors and wrote a number of books. The Inquisition confiscated the first version of her autobiography but she continued to write, rapidly in a discursive style and without any revision. Her books were intended to encourage her sisters in their spiritual development but they were also widely read by lay people. Most were submitted for censorship before being widely circulated, so some of her works exist in two versions. One passage that was removed by the censors was a defence of women. "Nor did you Lord when you walked in the world despise women; rather you always with great compassion helped them (And you found as much love and more faith in them that you did in men...is it not enough Lord that the world has intimidated us? ... so that we may not do anything worthwhile for you in public or dare speak some truths that we lament over in secret without you also failing to hear so just a petition? I do not believe, Lord that this could be true of your goodness and justice, for you are a just judge and not like those of the world, since the world's judges are sons of Adam and all of them men. There is no virtue in women that they do not hold suspect.... I see that these are times in which it would be wrong to undervalue virtuous and strong souls, even though they are women." (Way of Perfection Chapter 3: 7) The priests who censored her work felt this passage should not be included in the version circulated among lay people.

Teresa appreciated the need to look outward as well as looking inward; "Christ has no body now on earth but yours, no hands but yours, no feet but yours; yours are the eyes through which to look at Christ's compassion to the world, yours are the feet with which he is to go about doing good and yours are the hands with which he is to bless us now". Forty years after her death Teresa was declared a saint. Ironically, in view of the Papal Nuncio's accusation during her lifetime, in 1970 the Pope recognised her as a Doctor of the Church.

The Ursulines

In the sixteenth century social and political changes led to enormous social needs, which demanded a response from the church. It was women who first recognised this and responded. One example of this response was the Order of St Ursula, which was founded before the Council of Trent. They were active in providing hospitals and schools for the poor. The order was founded by a tertiary Franciscan Sister and continued to include women who lived in their own homes. Ursulines emphasised that all service was voluntary so nuns were not bound for life and could decide to leave, and ask for the return of their dowry, at any time. Ursulines provided a vital service, which the Church needed, so they managed to hold on to their freedom of action for a number of years. In France the order spread widely and had a reputation for providing excellent education. They opened their chapels during services so the public could hear them preach and teach. Ursuline nuns also travelled the roads of France teaching the common people, many of who had no other opportunity to learn since many parochial clergy were absentees. The Council of Trent had ruled that the catechism must be taught word for word without explanation. Ursulines disregarded this and adapted the catechism, when necessary, and gave explanations so that ordinary people could understand.

The control the Ursulines had over their own lives did not please the Church hierarchy, although they appreciated, and needed, their work. Gradually more and more restrictions were imposed on them. By the middle of the seventeenth century the French Ursulines were enclosed; undeterred some nuns continued teaching from behind their convent grille. A Sister in Paris taught a group of girls their catechism in front of an audience - teaching the public in reality if not in name. At times this audience included a future King, Louis XIII, and a future Pope, Urban VIII.

The English Ladies

Another group had more serious difficulties with the authorities. Mary Ward (1585- 1645) was a Roman Catholic from Yorkshire, who had a vision to educate women. She started an institute in the Spanish Netherlands to work with English immigrants and their children. The institute was successful and many English Catholics sent their children abroad to be educated there. But Mary and her co-workers were criticised by the local clergy because they did not follow a rule, or wear a uniform, and were not cloistered. Mary believed that God had called her to do the same educational work among women as the Jesuits were doing among men and thought that, like them, she would be able to get papal approval for her 'English Ladies'. She planned that they would not only teach but also care for prisoners and the sick and dying. She founded a number of houses in Germany and, after travelling to Rome to ask for Papal approval for their work, she started a work in Italy.

Mary Ward was vulnerable. As she was English she had no national church to support her, she was not rich and she had no powerful clerical sponsor although she had the support of some priests. She lived in Rome in real poverty for years while the Vatican considered her case; her ill health was probably due to lack of food and some residents in her Roman house died from malnutrition. The Roman authorities turned against the 'Jesuitess' despite the good work done by the 'English ladies'. A Bull was published suppressing her order and the Inquisition ordered her arrest and imprisonment on a charge of heresy. She was released after two months and the charge of heresy was dropped, without any evidence against her being offered. But the Bull was enforced and the English Ladies had to disband. Mary was allowed to continue to live with a few of her followers in Rome but, after becoming seriously ill, she left and returned to England. This indomitable lady started a school for girls in London, which was not easy at a time when anti-Catholic feeling was strong. When the political situation for Catholics deteriorated, and the strain of continual police searches was too disruptive, Mary moved back to Yorkshire, where she continued her work until her death. Women continued to follow Mary Ward's vision over the following centuries, often subject to clerical disapproval and persecution and only occasionally with short-lived papal approval. It was not until the twentieth century that the English Ladies, who are called Loreto sisters in America, were allowed to officially recognise Mary Ward as their founder.

Mary Ward was a loyal and dedicated Catholic, who only wanted to serve the Church and bring up girls to be good Catholic mothers. Despite this she was subjected to persecution, hardship and humiliation because of her gender; some of her enemies in Rome had even wanted her executed. Her crime was that, to quote the Papal Bull suppressing their work, she and her sisters had "carried out works by no means suiting the weakness of their sex". Their work was suppressed not because they had provided poor or unsound education, but because they had had the temerity to teach at all.

St Vincent de Paul and Louise de Marillac

Another group of women, who were involved in charitable work but did not wear a habit or live to a rule, avoided provoking opposition from the clerical hierarchy. This may have been because the innovator who inspired their work was a man and a priest.

In the seventeenth century France had multitudes of poor, driven from the countryside to the cities by poor harvests, plague and war. The Government, intent on making France the dominant power in Europe, didn't deal with the sources of the problem but reacted by suppressing and criminalizing the poor in an effort to make them invisible. Vincent de Paul (1581? – 1660) was a priest from a peasant background, who was determined to change attitudes to poverty. He preached to the poor but also set up charities to help them. He became involved with orphans, the physically and mentally sick and prisoners; he arranged training for servants and teachers and the distribution of food and goods to the poor. He sought help with these tasks from both fellow priests and lay volunteers. Vincent de Paul observed that the majority of his volunteers were women and that it was the women who were most efficient in getting the work done. "Men and women do not get along at all in matters of administration; the former want to take it over entirely, and the latter won't allow it...We had to get rid of the men. And I can bear this witness in favour of the women, that there is no fault to find in their administration, so careful and accurate are they". When he started a work in Paris he realised the aristocratic ladies there would not do menial tasks. A young peasant woman offered to organise a group of women to help. Vincent de Paul asked a wealthy widow of good family, Louise de Marillac (1591 –1660), to train them. In time Louise de Marillac became his full time lieutenant, organising what became the Congregation of the Daughters of Charity. There were only two hundred Daughters of Charity during Louise de Marillac's lifetime and the amount they achieved is astounding. They visited hospitals and were asked to take responsibility for all the nursing care. They started a work with foundlings, there had been a foundling hospital in Paris for many years but the care offered was so poor that not a single child had ever survived. Louise de Marillac changed this and organised care homes, foster care and trade schools for children. The Daughters visited prisons and gave practical help with cleaning, as well as instructing the prisoners. They provided care for the elderly, which included teaching them crafts so they could earn money and be independent. They also started the first elementary schools in Paris.

Vincent de Paul was trained in canon law and helped them avoid trouble with the Church authorities. They wore no habit and took private vows without witnesses. They had none of the trappings of a convent and the sisters were told that service to the poor must always take precedence over religious practices. But they studied the life of Christ and their work was underpinned with a deep spirituality. All over the world there are still people working to serve the poor, inspired by the vision of Vincent de Paul and Louise de Marillac.

The movement for reform in the Catholic Church was intended to be masculine and controlled by priests. But, despite discouragement, women were deeply involved in Counter-Reformation spirituality and reform. It was women whose response to their faith often put them at the forefront of working to ameliorate the massive social problems of the sixteenth and seventeenth centuries.

20 WOMEN IN PROTESTANT SECTS

Religious controversies continued in Britain in the seventeenth century. Those who were not satisfied with the Elizabethan religious settlement and wanted further reforms came to be known as Puritans. Not all puritans were content to stay within the established church; some joined new sects, which grew up during the reigns of the Stuart Kings, others emigrated to America in search of freedom to worship as they felt right. This chapter will look at the roles women took in these dissenting sects.

King James - Bibles and Witches

King James I, who succeeded Elizabeth as monarch and head of the English Church, resisted calls for further reform but did authorise the best loved English translation of the Bible. As head of the Church he encouraged the Anglican clergy to revisit the misogyny that had been so prominent in the Catholic Church. James came from Scotland, where the leading reformer had been John Knox, the author of "The First Blast Against the Monstrous Regiment of Women"; a book written to denounce two Catholic monarchs, Mary, Queen of Scots and Mary Tudor, Queen of England. James, whose intimate adult relationships were with men, encouraged his bishops to be firm with women and to preach against women's fashions. This may explain why unusually during the Stuart period Englishmen, other than puritans, were more extravagant and showy in their dress than their wives. The Anglican Church offered no role outside the family to women, although the Presbyterian Church, which was the official church in Scotland, did consider reviving the minor office of 'widow'.

James I fancied himself as a writer and one of his books had a baleful influence on the lives of many ordinary women. The King was fascinated by witchcraft; persecution of witches had been especially prevalent in Scotland. In his book on the subject he repeated the contention that women were twenty times more likely to be witches than men. Royal approval encouraged an interest in witch hunting. Even the Puritans, who rejected James' church, accepted the idea that witchcraft was a real problem. When Puritans went to found a colony in America they took these ideas with them; the most notorious witchcraft trial was at Salem in Massachusetts in 1692.

Puritans and Dissenters

Some European Protestants were forced into exile; German theologians and Dutch Anabaptists sought refuge in England and discussed their ideas with those they met, influencing the Puritans with their more radical religious ideas. The Dutch were able to return home when their country gained its freedom from Spain. But some of those whom they had influenced felt unable to continue to accept the English Church, and in their turn fled persecution. It was under Dutch protection that many separatists developed their ideas. They were able to return to England during the Civil War and the Interregnum; initially Oliver Cromwell, who was a Puritan himself, was more tolerant than the Stuart Kings had been, although it was to be another generation before dissenters had freedom of worship in Britain.

A number of puritans chose to emigrate; the Pilgrim Fathers who travelled on the Mayflower were the first of many who left Europe to seek freedom to worship in the way they believed was right. Unfortunately the new State of Massachusetts, founded by puritans, chose to perpetuate the intolerance they had suffered from in England. Like the British Government their leaders saw religious dissent as an attack on the State. Their perception of the community they were building as a 'city of God' made them intolerant of those who were not prepared to conform. Dissidents risked fines, banishment and even death. Women in the Colonies were a minority and so were valued and they had more rights than back in Britain; wife battering was punished severely and women no longer had to wear a veil in church. But the American puritans also saw women negatively; original sin was one of their central doctrines and their sermons often emphasised the fact that women were morally weak and easily deceived.

Anne Hutchinson

Anne Hutchinson (1591 – 1643) was born in England, the daughter of a puritan minister who was critical of many clerics in the established church. Her own faith was strong and she took advantage of every opportunity to study scripture in depth. At 21 she married William Hutchinson, a merchant. She was a wife and mother, eventually she had 15 children, she also served her community as a midwife. Her other interests were less conventional. She was not a passive Christian. She listened critically to sermons and was prepared to defend her own views if she didn't agree with the preacher. She and her husband were followers of John Cotton, a noted puritan minister, and when he emigrated to Boston they decided to follow him.

On Anne Hutchinson's arrival in Boston she was regarded with suspicion and was only allowed to join the Church after she had been examined by the Governor and other prominent men. She was known to have claimed to have had personal revelations from God and to have taken a critical view of some sermons and preachers. In Boston she started meeting with other women in her home on Sunday afternoons to discuss the sermon. In time more and more women wanted to attend and she had to hold several meetings. Then men also started to come; these included prominent men, even one who was for a short time Governor of the Colony.

Anne Hutchinson believed that local preachers were emphasising a 'Covenant of Works' rather than one of grace. She was not alone in her views; her Brother-in-Law was banished from the Colony for expressing similar opinions. The local clerical and civic establishment saw her as a threat to the authoritarian form of Government they had established in Massachusetts. Her neighbour John Winthrop, who was now Governor, felt particularly strongly. She was charged with 'traducing the Ministers' and hauled up before a civil tribunal. John Winthrop seems to have acted as both prosecutor and judge. Although she was pregnant for the sixteenth time she was force to stand in front of her judges all day for several days. Winthrop accused her of breaking the fifth commandment (to Honour her Father and Mother) by criticising her church 'Fathers'. She had no defence lawyer but defended herself strongly using her knowledge of the Bible. When she realised her judges were determined to find her guilty she told them "You have no power over my body neither can you do me any harm for I am in the hands of the eternal Jehovah my Saviour.   I am at his appointment....therefore take heed how you proceed against me; for I know that for this you go about to do for me God will ruin you and your posterity and this whole State."   She was found guilty and, after a further church trial, was banished from Boston.   During her trial her husband and some of her supporters had left Boston to found a new Colony in Rhode Island which was established with separation of Church and State, the model later adopted by the United States, and she joined them there.   After her husband's death she left Rhode Island for the Dutch Colony of New Amsterdam (New York).   While there Anne Hutchinson, her servants and most of her children were killed in an uprising by Native Americans, angry at their treatment by the Dutch.

Anne Hutchinson preached the equality of women and also spoke out on the rights of Native Americans but it was not these view but her religious opinions which led to her trial.   However, her Judges' anger was stronger because it was a woman who was defying them and setting up her beliefs against theirs.   Winthrop said her meetings were "A thing not tolerable nor comely in the sight of God, nor fitting for your sex."   The men who condemned her were totally unforgiving; when she lost the child she had been carrying during her trial they felt no guilt but instead claimed it had been a monster and its death was a punishment.   When she and her family were killed they rejoiced at what they saw as God's judgement on the woman they called 'the American Jezebel'.

Non-conforming Dissenters

Many Puritans, both those who remained in England and those who went to America, remained in the Anglican (Episcopalian) Church but others felt they had to be free to worship and structure their churches as they felt was right. Some dissenting sects believed in the spiritual equality of women and many of them were prepared to follow through on this and allow women lay preachers. They believed the call to preach came direct from God, through his Holy Spirit, and acknowledged that he might call women to this ministry. Women were attracted to these sects, which were so much more accepting of them than the established Church, and the majority of sects had a preponderance of women. Women preachers were subject to a lot of criticism and sometimes prosecution, leading in a few cases to their death. In some cases their families, or the authorities, regarded the 'enthusiasm' of dissenting women as evidence of mental illness and used it to justify confining them. The early Baptists allowed a number of women lay preachers and so did some other groups; but the sect who gave the most freedom to women was the Quakers, a group that developed in England during the Civil War.

The Friends or Quakers

The Society of Friends, or Quakers, founded by George Fox, allowed women to preach and teach. George Fox, the founder, encouraged, or allowed, Quaker women in London to set up separate women's meetings and which ran without masculine oversight or interference. One monthly meeting was to distribute money collected for charitable purposes and the other was to plan pastoral work. Women's meetings were responsible for planning and carrying out any actions needed to meet the needs of the poor, the sick and orphans. George Fox made the same discovery as St Vincent de Paul, women were best at organising charitable work. Women did not have any real equality even among the Friends but they did have scope to organise, preach and teach.

Mary Dyer

It was Quaker women who felt the call to spread their message and it was women who first spread Quaker ideas in many places; including London, Dublin and America, where they were persecuted by the Boston Puritans. Mary Dyer, who had been a follower of Anne Hutchinson, became a Quaker on a visit to London. She returned to find punitive laws in place to suppress Quakers, including the death penalty for those who refused to accept exile. Mary Dyer was immediately banished from Boston but returned again and again, in defiance of the authorities, in order challenge this draconian law. Eventually, after her third trial, she was hanged; a martyr for the cause of religious freedom. The death of a respectable woman, and one whose husband had a prominent role in another colony, was embarrassing. It was one of the factors that led to the law being repealed and eventually encouraged Massachusetts to relax its determination to maintain religious conformity.

Margaret Fell

The most prominent Quaker woman was Margaret Fell (1614 – 1702), who lived in Lancashire. Most Quakers were working class but Margaret was from the gentry. Margaret was convinced by George Fox and soon organised a Quaker meeting in her home. Until his early death her husband tolerated, but did not share, her enthusiasm.

Margaret became a Quaker leader and an apologist for their views, as a speaker and as a writer. She started the first women's meeting outside London and despite opposition she and Fox pushed for all Quaker Meetings to adopt the practice of women meeting separately to organise charity and pastoral care. Margaret was never afraid to stand up for her beliefs; she sought an audience with King Charles II himself to try and secure Fox's release during one of his imprisonments. She herself was imprisoned for several years and during this time she wrote "Women's Speaking Justified, Proved and Allowed of by the Scriptures". Margaret was also the first Quaker writer to advocate pacifism, a belief that was to characterise Friends in the future. George Fox's paper on this issue is the one that is remembered but hers preceded it by some months.

After many years of widowhood Margaret married George Fox, taking an unusual step in marrying outside her own class; he was the son of a weaver and her own family were landowners. Fox allowed her to continue to hold her own property, contrary to normal practice at the time, and with the help of her daughters she continued to run the family farm and several businesses. She made regular visits to the south to spend time with her new husband, who felt unable to leave his work. After his death she continued writing and leadership in the local Meeting but with age her influence waned. One of her last papers was an unsuccessful attempt to dissuade Quaker women from their new practice of dressing only in grey.

George Fox's enthusiasm for women using their gifts was not shared by his successors. Ten years after his death a meeting of male leaders forbad female leaders from meeting together and tried to limit women's contributions to mixed meetings. "Women Friends should be tenderly cautioned against taking up too much time in our mixed public meetings." However, compared to most denominations the Friends continued to provide an environment that encouraged women and allowed them to take an active role.

Toleration for non-conformists

The sixteenth and seventeenth centuries were a turbulent time in Britain and it was during this period that many of the religious denominations that make up the English speaking Protestant churches were formed. Women were fully involved in these dissenting churches; it was a time of comparative freedom for them during which many women were able to actively serve God and the church. The Toleration Act, passed in 1689, during the reign of William and Mary, gave non-conformists, as they had became known, freedom to worship in their own way, although it did not apply to Catholics. However, as the dissenting sects became accepted they also became less willing to ignore the views of their society and allow women to preach or take on leadership roles.

21 THE FIRES OF REVIVAL

This chapter looks at women's involvement in the religious revivals that swept through Britain and America in the eighteenth century. They came in the period known as the Enlightenment, a time of intellectual excitement, as old ideas were thrown out and a new viewpoint put man, rather than God, at the centre. The foundations of modern science had been laid in the seventeenth century but now philosophers and thinkers studied social science. They questioned past certainties and put forward new theories; but one certainty few questioned was the inferiority and subordination of women. Enlightenment authors suggested women should have their own separate sphere; following classical tradition.

The Eighteenth century English Church

The Enlightenment was secular and did not extend to the religious sphere; Spiritual and intellectual torpor characterised the Anglican Church. Voltaire observed that there was only enough religion in England "To distinguish Tories, who have little, from Whigs, who have none". The Government, which was usually Whig, appointed bishops and archbishops, so it is not surprising that few were chosen for their spiritual qualities. The Anglican Church was ripe for revival. When revival came it changed the lives of innumerable individuals and English society itself. It was a movement of the people, and initially had most effect among the working and lower middle classes. A French historian, studying British history considered that it was this revival that enabled Britain to avoid violent revolution, of the kind which was to engulf France.

Susanna Wesley

The revival in England originated with a small group of Anglican clergymen who, when they were at Oxford, were called 'Methodists' because of their determination to live according to 'the method laid down in the New Testament'. This group included, John Wesley (1703 – 1791) his brother Charles (1707 – 1788) and George Whitefield (1714 – 1770) who was a college servant not a student. George Whitefield was the more charismatic preacher and through his preaching he had a great influence in both England and America; but it was John Wesley whose dedication and gift for organisation changed English society.

One of the strongest influences on the Wesleys was their mother, Susanna Wesley (1670 – 1742). She was the daughter of a non-conformist minister and, as a minister's daughter, she had educational opportunities denied to most women. She was intelligent, strong in her faith and had a mind of her own. At the age of 13 she decided to join the Anglican Church; it says a lot for her and her family that she remained on good terms with her father despite this. She married Samuel Wesley, an Anglican clergyman, and for most of their married life they lived in a country rectory in the village of Epworth in Lincolnshire. There she brought up and educated her twelve surviving children. Life was not easy, money was short and her husband had a habit of alienating people. A parishioner once put him in prison for debt and a serious fire at the Rectory, which nearly killed the six-year-old John Wesley, was started deliberately.

Throughout her life Susanna refused to accept the religious or political views of her father and husband if they conflicted with her own sense of what was right; this sometimes led to conflict within her marriage. When Samuel went to London for a Church Convocation, leaving a locum in charge of his parish, Susanna was determined her children's religious education should not suffer. She started to hold evening prayers for them on Sundays. Their friends started to come too and then adults asked to join; eventually Susanna had a congregation of about two hundred in her home each Sunday. The curate was annoyed, since his services met with much less enthusiasm, and wrote to Samuel asking him to rebuke Susanna. Her letters to her husband have survived; she emphasises the responsibility she felt for those whose spiritual education had been entrusted to her. Samuel did not insist on her stopping; knowing the strength of her conscience he may have been reluctant to give an order she would not feel able to obey. The meetings came to a natural end on his return but her children had seen a woman's teaching having a real impact on people's lives. Susanna encouraged her sons to enter the church and she continued to give her children practical advice and spiritual encouragement, by letter and in person, until her death.

John Wesley and women

When he was 35 and already a clergyman John Wesley underwent a conversion experience that changed his life. From that time he devoted his life to spreading the message of salvation as an itinerant preacher. He remained an Anglican all his life, and encouraged his followers to do the same, but his enthusiasm did not endear him to his fellows and many vicars refused him permission to preach in their churches. For Wesley the important question was always whether the Holy Spirit blessed an action, as indicated by spiritual results. This way of looking at things made him willing to challenge accepted ideas: it led him from the security of a pulpit to a lifetime of travel and preaching to large crowds in the open air; it led him to follow his Mother's advice and approve lay preachers; and in time it led him to accept women in leadership. Early Methodism appealed to the disenfranchised and marginalized; it predominantly attracted women and working class men. It was organised in bands, small groups linked by gender and way of life, and larger classes, of mixed gender and age. As women outnumbered men in the Methodist movement they not only led female bands but also were approved to lead mixed classes of up to two hundred men and women.

As John Wesley's attitude to women evolved so did the roles he allowed them to take in public. First he approved of women 'testifying', telling of their own experiences; then 'exhorting', encouraging others to spiritual growth; finally he accepted them 'preaching', which involved teaching from a biblical text. At the heart of Wesley's decision to approve both lay preachers and women preachers was his acceptance that some individuals had 'an extraordinary call'. At each step he was convinced by the spiritual results from speakers who would not previously have been encouraged, to speak in public. The Methodists never formally appointed 'itinerant' women preachers in the same way as they appointed male itinerant lay preachers but John Wesley encouraged a number of women to get involved in itinerant preaching. Some worked with their husbands but single women were also involved. During just one year Sarah Crosby, one of these women preachers, travelled 960 miles, led 120 public services, addressed 600 classes and spoke at a number of evangelical meetings in private homes.

The Countess of Huntingdon

A few aristocratic women were also involved in the revival; as patrons they funded preachers and Methodist schools, many run by women. The most prominent patron, both socially and in the extent of her involvement with the Methodist cause, was Serena, Dowager Countess of Huntingdon (1707-1791). She worked closely with both Wesley and George Whitefield. She did not preach in public herself but arranged drawing room meetings, where a reluctant Wesley preached to her aristocratic peers; in later life she also funded evangelistic campaigns, travelling herself with the preachers. She built chapels and founded a college to train young men with evangelical beliefs, who were rarely accepted as students by the Universities. Her school prepared them to work in both the established and dissenting churches. The Countess later broke with Wesley when she adopted George Whitefield's more Calvinist theology. The idea of the elect, those who were predestined to be saved, may have been more comfortable for an aristocrat than John Wesley's belief that everyone, however degraded, had freewill and could be saved if they chose to repent and trust in Christ. The Countess continued to fund the school but sacked the staff and replaced them with Calvinists. Many of her students became ministers in the chapels she built. She appointed them and gave them counsel and advice, acting in the role of de facto bishop. The chapels became known as The Countess of Huntingdon Connection and still operate under her name.

In England the freedom of women to be active in Methodism barely outlasted John Wesley. After his death the movement was institutionalised and separated from the Anglican Church. In the conservative climate that followed the French Revolution the new denomination found women preachers unacceptable. Women were forbidden to preach in Ireland in 1803 and their activities were limited in England; although they were only formally banned thirty years later. Many prominent women were not given obituaries in the Methodist magazines because their preaching was by then considered embarrassing. But women preachers continued to be accepted in some breakaway Methodist organisations.

The Wesleyan revival touched the lives of ordinary people and changed the face of British towns and villages; even today most villages have a chapel as well as a church. One important contribution John Wesley made to British life was the way he gave the disenfranchised, working men and women of all classes, the opportunity to develop ministry and leadership skills. Even after women were silenced, lay preaching continued to be important in Methodism and allowed working men to develop skills in leadership and public speaking. This was one factor in making Methodists so central in the early socialist movement in Britain. The Tolpuddle martyrs, six agricultural workers who were sentenced to be transported for forming a Society, and who are seen as forerunners of the Trade Union movement, were led by a Methodist lay preacher.

Sarah Edwards

In America at the same time there was a revival, known as the Great Awakening. This movement also gave a new value to women, in contrast to the misogyny of some puritans. But its leaders did not give the same freedom of action to women that Wesley had done. In America a patriarchal mindset was not challenged by the new religious enthusiasm. The leading figure in the Great Awakening was Jonathan Edwards, a Congregational Minister in New England. He was a man of many gifts but unlike Wesley he did not give women opportunities to take on new roles, nor did he approve of laymen preaching. However, the person who influenced and helped him most was a woman, his wife Sarah Pierpont Edwards (1710- 1758). Sarah Edwards was a mystic, she had much in common spiritually with some of the mystics of earlier centuries. However, her setting was very different; she lived her life not in a convent but as a devoted wife and mother to their eleven children.

Sarah was born into a noted Puritan family, the daughter of a Minister who died when she was young. Even as a child her devotion to God was seen as exceptional and attracted the young Jonathan Edwards; he described her in a letter when she was only 13; "They say there is a young lady in New Haven who is beloved of that almighty being who made and rules the world, and that there are certain seasons in which this great being, in some way or other invisible, comes to her and fills her mind with extraordinary sweet delight and that she care for nothing but to meditate on him....She has a strange sweetness in her mind and a singular purity in her affections; is most just and conscientious in all her actions; and you could not persuade her to do anything wrong or sinful, if you would give her the world, lest she offend this great being." Four years later they were married and remained devoted to each other for the rest of their lives. Allen in his biography of her husband describes her: "There was nothing morbid or sad about her religion; she had no depressing experiences; her piety like her character was a joyous one, bringing with it light and gladness. She made the home at Northampton a centre of genial and attractive hospitality until it became almost like a sanctuary to which multitudes resorted as, in the course of years Edwards came to be looked on as a spiritual teacher and guide." The same author also wrote: "We cannot be wrong in assigning to Mrs Edwards a place in the great awakening hardly inferior to that occupied by her husband."

Sarah Edwards' greatest influence on her husband was not through her support and help in his work, important though that was, but through her deep devotion to God and her mystical experiences. In January 1742 she had a series of mystical experiences which Jonathan Edwards encouraged her to write down. It started when "I felt very uneasy and unhappy at my being so low in grace. I thought I very much needed help from God and found a spirit of earnestness to seek help of him, that I might have more holiness." The following day "The presence of God was so near and so real that I seemed scarcely conscious of anything else. God the Father, and the Lord Jesus Christ, seemed as distinct persons, both manifesting the inconceivable loveliness, and mildness and gentleness, and their great and immutable love to me." Her experiences continued through the week "To my own imagination, my soul seemed to be gone out of me to God and Christ in heaven, and to have very little relation to my body. God and Christ were so present to me, and so near me, that I seemed removed from myself." Some of her experiences were shared with others at the church and Jonathan Edwards, who had been away that week, returned home to find his wife overflowing with love of God and the beginnings of a revival starting in his church. The results of this experience remained with Sarah Edwards for the rest of her life. It gave her confidence; she was no longer anxious about what people, even her family, thought of her, only God's opinion mattered. Jonathan Edwards was an intelligent, contained and scholarly man; he had a deep understanding of theology, his books are still read.   But his understanding of the heart of religious faith owed much to Sarah's experiences.   He accepted that what she felt was of God and went on to describe her experience, without identifying her or mentioning her gender, in one of his books.   Jonathan Edwards died in his fifties and his wife followed him a few weeks later.   The results of their work and the revival they had fostered continued long after their deaths.

This chapter has looked at the involvement of women in the revivals which swept England and America in the second half of the eighteenth century.   Jonathan Edwards valued the spiritual contribution women made to the Great Awakening but never considered any change their roles.   In contrast John Wesley gave women freedom to use their leadership gifts.   But Protestant denomination and sects followed the same pattern shown in Catholic religious orders.   Charismatic founders might encourage women, but their followers reverted to a patriarchal model and excluded women from leadership.

22. FEMINISTS AND ABOLITIONISTS

The revivals of the eighteenth century had an influence that spread further than their immediate followers. One effect they had was to inspire men and women to tackle the social ills of their society. This chapter will look at one of the English women who were inspired to live out their Christian faith by seeking to help the poor and oppressed and at American women whose faith also inspired them to action. All these women had in common an interest in feminism, a hatred of the slave trade and a passionate interest in its abolition.

Hannah More and her sisters

Hannah More (1745 – 1833) was one of five daughters of an impoverished schoolmaster in Bristol As a child she was eager to learn, but although her father educated all his daughters so they could earn their living as teachers, he was ambivalent about female education and refused to teach Hannah Latin and mathematics, 'unsuitable' subjects which she longed to learn. Hannah's older sisters went into the only profession open to middle class women and started a school. The sisters had a gift for making friends and despite the fact that initially the headmistress was only twenty, and the sisters who assisted her were younger, the school prospered. In time Hannah and her younger sister joined the staff and the school provided a base and a living for all the More sisters for many years. Hannah was a gifted girl whose wit and knack for writing verse made her popular. At twenty she achieved the ambition of most eighteenth century girls when she made a 'good match'; she became engaged to a pleasant and wealthy man twenty years her senior. However, her betrothed's indecisiveness led him to cancel their wedding at the last moment and he subsequently postponed it several more times. After six years Hannah broke the engagement and refused his offer of monetary compensation for wasting her youth; she was now beyond what was considered marriageable age. However, a friend intervened and arranged an annuity of £200 pounds on her behalf and persuaded her to accept it. In her twenties she found herself a spinster with an independent income, able to follow a literary career.

Hannah became well known for her verses and wrote several plays. She was introduced to David Garrick, the foremost actor manager of his time, he helped Hannah by revising one of her plays and producing it, to considerable acclaim. Her career as a playwright came to an end when Garrick died and another play, written without his editing hand, was less successful. Hannah gave up plays although she continued with her writing. She spent a lot of time with Garrick's widow Eva, and became one of the 'blue stockings', a circle of wits and intellectuals, male and female. Her friends were intelligent and educated women and she got to know Doctor Johnson, Horace Walpole and Madame De Stael. Hannah herself became famous in her own right; in a print of the 'nine muses' Hannah was included with eight other noted English women.

In her middle years Hannah's religious beliefs became central to her life, religious revival was now entering the mainstream church. She maintained her old friendships but other more earnest friends and activities became increasingly important to her. One new friend was William Wilberforce, a young MP whose strong convictions led him to devote his life to the abolition of the slave trade. The Abolitionists succeeded in changing the law by first changing public opinion. Hannah worked with them on this; through her writing and her efforts to mobilise women she helped create one of the first pressure groups in British politics. One of her most famous poems was eloquent on the evils of slavery and racial prejudice:

"Fired by no single wrongs the countless host
I mourn, by rapine dragg'd from Afric's coast.
Perish the illiberal thought which would debase
The native genius of the sable race!
Perish the proud philosophy, which sought
To rob them of the powers of equal thought!
What does the immortal principle within
Change with the casual colour of a skin?"

For the rest of her life this issue was close to Hannah's heart, even after the abolition of the slave trade she continued to campaign against the existence of slavery overseas.

It was Wilberforce who encouraged Hannah More, and her sister Martha, to start a Sunday school in the village of Cheddar. When this was established they started a dozen more schools in other Mendip villages and towns. Sunday schools were a new idea and provided the only education available to the rural poor. Children from poor families had to work during the week to supplement the family income; so Sunday was the only day they were free to learn. Sunday schools taught not only religion but also reading, though not writing. Hannah persuaded the local farmers and clergy to support the idea and appointed teachers, working people who had, by their own efforts, achieved more education than their fellows. Initially most of these teachers were Methodists, who at the time were still part of the established church.   Hannah also believed in adult education and classrooms were used in the evenings to teach reading and practical skills to adolescents and women.   In time a few of the schools also offered full time education for those whose parents could afford to forgo their children's earnings.   Hannah and Martha also started women's clubs in the villages.   These were benefit clubs; in return for a weekly pittance women received sick pay, money for a new baby and death benefits.

Some historians have criticised the Sunday Schools movement, claiming it was designed to educate people to become industrious workers; in evidence they can quote from letters Hannah wrote to raise funds from conservative friends, in which she stressed the utilitarian advantages of educating the poor.   But these letters did not reflect her own motivation; her concern for the poor and desire to improve their lot was real and stemmed from her faith.   The education she offered was entirely voluntary, no one was compelled or pressured to attend.   Hannah tried to make lessons interesting, used rewards to motivate children and she banned corporal punishment in her schools.   She was also influenced by the concerns of recipients of her charities.   When she started benefit clubs it was local women who insisted that death benefits must be provided.   For many women saving for a decent funeral was more important than childbirth benefits and Hannah adapted her plans to their priorities.   The More sisters gave all girls on their marriage a pair of wool stockings, knitted by them personally, five shillings and a Bible.   This was popular and so were the special events they arranged.   They organised and funded yearly picnics for the children and their families and annual 'feasts' for the women's clubs.   It was Hannah who raised the necessary funds, from her many friends, but it was Martha who undertook much of the actual organisation.   It was also usually Martha who preached at these events, even on occasions when clergymen were present.   For the rest of her life Hannah worked for and supported these schools and clubs despite opposition and attacks on her reputation. In time Sunday schools were generally accepted; even by those who had initially opposed them on the grounds that they would make working people rebellious

Hannah continued to write: political and religious tracts for ordinary people and books, including a best-selling novel, her books were designed to encourage evangelical faith and moral behaviour among the upper classes.   She even wrote a book suggesting a system of education for Princess Charlotte, the heir to the throne.   Only the Princess's guardians appreciated it, the Princess found it boring. Hannah More also visited and corresponded with her many friends. Her friendships stretched from ordinary working people to minor members of the Royal family, taking in intellectuals, politicians and churchmen on the way.   She never neglected a chance to encourage the faith of those she knew, both in person and by letters.

Hannah More was an early proponent of the evangelical wing of the Anglican Church, which was to flourish in the nineteenth century. She had a strong connection to the 'Clapham Sect'; a group of Anglicans who were instrumental in initiating several major social reforms. Towards the end of her life Hannah was visited regularly not just by friends but also by numerous people who wished to meet the famous philanthropist and writer.

A contemporary of Hannah More was Mary Wollstonecraft (1759 – 1797) who in 1792 published 'A Vindication of the Rights of Women'. It called for better educational opportunities for women but its impact at the time was muted by Mary's self identification with the French revolution, whose excesses provoked a conservative backlash in Europe that lasted for decades, and by her atheism and irregular personal life. Mary Wollstonecraft's atheism put Hannah More off reading her book and she did not see herself as a feminist. If she had read it she might have realised how alike were their views on female education. In old age Hannah became increasingly conservative in her politics but more liberal in her views on gender. She admired Elizabeth Fry, who was working in prisons and for prison reform. She realised how acceptance of women's activities among the Quakers had given Elizabeth Fry her confidence in tackling difficult issues.

Hannah More died at the age of 88. Her writings have been largely forgotten but she is remembered not only for her part in the fight to abolish slavery but also by the physical legacies her practical philanthropy left behind. Several of the Schools she started continue to flourish, having been taken over by local authorities when education became compulsory. Her women's benefit clubs were only dissolved in 1951, when the welfare state was established to provide a safety net for the poor.

Hannah More came from an impoverished background and yet made herself part of the intellectual and social elite of her time. She pioneered women's involvement in social action in England and was active in the evangelical movement, which would be so influential in the Victorian age. Although she died before Victoria came to the throne her biographer has described her as 'the first Victorian'. She and her friends introduced two preoccupations that were to become an essential part of Victorian life. One was the importance of moral conduct and faith in the upper and middle classes and the other was the importance of social action as an outworking of religious belief.

Sarah and Angelina Grimke

In the year Hannah More died across the Atlantic two other women were starting their own political involvement. Sarah Grimke (1792 – 1873) and her sister Angelina (1805 – 1879) were born to a slave owning family in the South. Yet, far from taking slavery for granted, from early childhood they both hated it and were deeply upset by the cruel treatment they saw meted out to slaves. Sarah was bright but, like all girls in her society, was not allowed secondary education. She used to secretly teach herself at night from her brother's schoolbooks but when he went away to school her educational opportunities were over; her life shrunk to home and church. The young Sarah taught bible classes for black children and she longed to teach them to read, but this was against the law. At thirteen she got into serious trouble with her father when he caught her secretly teaching her personal slave to read. She later described this "The light was put out, the keyhole screened, and flat on our stomachs, before the fire, with the spelling book under our eyes, we defied the laws of South Carolina." Later that year Angelina was born and Sarah, frustrated in her attempt to widen her interests, took much of the responsibility for her sister's upbringing.

Some years later Sarah accompanied her Father north, seeking a cure for his mortal illness. She met a group of Quakers in Philadelphia and, after his death, moved north to join them, hoping for opportunities to fight for the emancipation of slaves. Anglelina followed her into the Quakers and subsequently joined her. But they were frustrated by the circumscribed role allowed to women by society and by the Quaker Meeting. A few years later they gained more freedom of action. Sarah broke her engagement, believing her Quaker fiancé would treat her as a vassal not a partner, Angelina's fiancé died and so did their brother. They were left without male relatives to control them.

The sisters embarked on an active career in the abolition movement almost by accident. Angelina wrote a moving private letter to a reforming newspaper supporting its work against slavery. The editor published her letter without permission saying he "could not, dared not suppress it". Other papers reprinted it and it was made into a pamphlet. The Grimke sisters found themselves famous. The Quaker elders were furious with them for failing to consult them before sending the letter. They moved to a more liberal Quaker group in Rhode Island and started working publicly for abolition.

Like Hannah More they both wrote books and pamphlets against slavery. Because they were Southerners of good family their work was read in the Southern States; unlike most abolition writers. They went a step further than Hannah More when they agreed to speak publicly. In 1837 they embarked on a twenty-three week lecture tour for the abolition movement. This tour ended with Angelina addressing the Massachusetts state legislature, the first woman ever to speak to a US legislative body.

The Grimke sister's faith was important to them and fuelled their work; their writings are religious in character; although they also deal with political issues.   Many fellow Christians were unhappy with their actions.   During their tour a group of Congregational ministers castigated them in the press for their 'unnatural behaviour' in speaking in public and especially for the way Angelina mentioned the unmentionable – the sexual abuse of slave women.   The Philadelphia Quakers finally expelled them altogether when Angelina married a fellow abolitionist who was not a Quaker.   After her marriage she ceased lecturing.   It is not clear why but it is possible that Angelina's husband's theoretical belief in an equal marriage was at war with his actual feelings and that he discouraged her from continuing in public life.   The Sisters continued writing and also ran their home and brought up Angelina's three children and two nephews, sons of their brother and a black slave.

Their experiences made the Grimke sisters very aware of the role of women in a male dominated society.   Angelina's writing continued to focus on abolition but Sarah also wrote increasingly on the issue of women's rights.   She believed "God created us equal;- he created us free agents;- he is our Law giver, our King and our Judge, and to him alone is woman bound to be in subjection and to him alone is she accountable for the use of those talents which her Heavenly Father has entrusted her."   In one book she wrote about the creation story in Genesis, pointing out errors of interpretation that were used to justify the subservience of women.   On the passage where God told Eve she would be subservient to her husband she wrote "the curse is a simple prophecy".   She believed God was telling Eve not what should happen but what would happen; once sin entered their relationship the physically stronger partner would inevitably dominate.   It may have been Sarah's work that later inspired an acquaintance, Elizabeth Cady Stanton, to write the Women's Bible.

Angelina shared Sarah's views; she once wrote:

"Whatever is morally right for a man to do, it is morally right for a woman to do.   I recognise no rights but human rights – I know nothing of men's rights and women's rights; for in Christ Jesus, there is neither male or female."

Angelina's work focussed on slavery; she appealed to southern women to oppose slavery because of the threat it posed to their marriages.   With unusual frankness she pointed out the evidence for this – the mixed race children fathered by white men on black slave women, who had no way to resist their owner's lust.

The Grimkes, like Hannah More, believed that women had a responsibility to speak out on issues of social justice; they were prepared to go further by speaking publicly as well as writing and as a result they met more criticism.   They did not share the width of her interests, probably because slavery was so central to the American experience.   For Hannah More slavery was something she heard about but not experienced; the Grimkes had personally lived with its cruelty and injustice.

Sojourner Truth

Not all abolitionists were white; a number of ex-slaves were involved in the movement.   Sojourner Truth (1790s – 1883) was born in captivity on a farm in New York and named Isabelle.   She was bought and sold several times and separated from her husband and children as slaves often were.   She was strong minded, even as a slave, and deeply religious.   In 1827 she was finally freed under a

State emancipation Law. She chose her new name because, she said, the Lord told her she was to "Travel up an' down the land, showin' people their sins and being a sign to them". From on then she was involved in singing and speaking at Camp meetings and speaking at secular meetings of both abolitionists and feminists. She did not have the security of being employed by any anti-slavery society, unlike most male ex-slaves who spoke out in favour of abolition, but she felt it was her duty to be an itinerate speaker. Her confidence in God's ultimate judgement was such that she felt able to put aside bitterness and pity slave owners. She remained uneducated and illiterate all her life but had great intelligence and common sense. She studied the Bible, getting others, generally children, to read it to her. With the help of a white friend she wrote her autobiography.

Sojourner Truth was a tall, gaunt woman whose bearing and eloquence made a powerful impression on audiences. One of her speeches is still remembered. In response to a clergyman, who had cited women's physical and intellectual weakness as an argument against the feminist cause, she recounted sufferings she had endured with the refrain "Ain't I a woman?" She met Abraham Lincoln and lived to see slavery abolished in the South, after the Civil War. She continued to speak both about her faith and her desire that all women, black and white, should be able to vote.

The history of the abolition of slavery, like most history, dwells on the actions of male abolitionists but women, both black and white, were deeply involved in the fight to free slaves and end a towering injustice which had led to so much cruelty and death.

23 EVANGELICAL FAITH AND SOCIAL ACTION

This chapter looks at the involvement of women in the evangelical movement which changed nineteenth century society, ushering in massive social reform and changing attitudes.

Victorian ideas on woman

In the Victorian era a new stereotype of woman emerged. A Victorian woman was expected to be gentle and self-sacrificing; she was a lady and so should set an example of high moral standards to her men folk and the 'lower orders'. In contrast to the medieval stereotype she was not seen as a sexual aggressor, but as virtuous and submissive to her husband. (It is this stereotype that makes Dickens heroines dull.) A Victorian lady was not expected to work but to stay at home and care for her family; if poverty forced her to work almost her only option was being a governess or school teacher.

This Victorian ideal woman was middle or upper class. Lower class women had to work; in industrial areas they worked very long hours in factories and mines, usually starting as children. Elsewhere domestic service was the only alternative to working in the home or on the land. In the cities some women, living in poverty, found prostitution or starvation were their only choices. There were over half a million 'surplus' women in Britain by the middle of the century so many women were unable to fit into the accepted pattern of marriage and children. Outside the cities women were involved in back breaking work in homes without modern conveniences and often also in managing small holdings; in America, as pioneers moved west, many woman had to undertake similar tasks in isolated settlements.

Evangelical Christianity became predominant in most denominations and a high moral standard was set; especially for women - double standards flourished in the nineteenth century. Women were expected to be religious, especially in America where religion was regarded as predominantly for women. Despite this most churches did not welcome women in any roles other than passive listeners, donors, or behind the scenes workers. Women were expected to keep silent except in women only meetings. In the early part of the nineteenth century it was more possible for women to take an active part in religious life in the United States than in Europe. As in England there were woman religious writers, of both devotional books and hymns. But Charles Finney, the leading evangelist in the second Great Awakening, encouraged women to get involved in supporting evangelistic work. In America there were even a few women preachers. They were mainly evangelists, fitting into the American pattern of revival meetings. These women testified to the call they felt from God to preach. They told of their own reluctance in putting themselves forward and the discouragement they had received from religious leaders. Despite opposition a number of women, both white and black, persevered with a preaching ministry.

Phoebe Palmer

The best known of these women was Phoebe Palmer (1807 –1874) a Methodist from New York. Many earlier women preachers had been single women, who, like the Grimke sisters, gave up speaking in public after marriage, but Mrs Palmer was married throughout her ministry. She started by arranging a weeknight meeting for the Promotion of Holiness. This she ran for twenty years; it was enormously influential and attended by many ministers and church leaders. A contemporary described her as "the Priscilla who had taught many an Apollos the way of God more perfectly". She was also involved in pioneering social work among the poor in New York. Mrs Palmer went on to edit a magazine, the 'Guide to Holiness' and to conduct evangelistic meetings with her husband. Mrs Palmer did not 'preach' but would give lengthy exhortations, not from the pulpit but from the communion rail, after a sermon given by her husband or a local minister; but she was the attraction and the effective evangelist. Mrs Palmer was reported to have been responsible for the conversion of 25,000 people as well as inspiring many thousands of Christians by her teaching on holiness and sanctification. The Palmers spent four years preaching in England and her example inspired a number of English women. These included Catherine Booth, who with her husband founded the Salvation Army, and who would develop women's ministry even further.

Women social reformers

In England women were more circumscribed and rarely had any public involvement within the churches. But one form of activity outside the home was regarded as acceptable for Victorian women - charity. Salvation came through faith but was demonstrated by works. For many women this was routine – they gave to the 'deserving' poor and made items for 'sales of work' to raise money for worthy causes. More active women taught in Sunday Schools; since the days of pioneers like Hannah More the Sunday school movement had become strong in England, America and several European countries. But the paradox of the nineteenth century Evangelical movement was that charitable causes allowed women, who were normally expected to lead quiet, moral and passive lives, to involve themselves in work which required them to be active, even forceful, and to be informed about evils which they would normally be expected to be ignorant about. In America women were involved in campaigning for the abolition of slavery, as British women had been earlier, and later in both America and Britain women were heavily involved in temperance movements.

There were women who were not prepared to accept the limits imposed on them. Their concern was not limited to the 'deserving poor' and they felt called to serve in ways that challenged their society. A few women, whose faith led them to devote their life to a cause, managed to make radical changes in that society. Elizabeth Fry (1780 - 1845), a Quaker of good family, went into women's prisons and changed them; both by her work with individuals and by persuading the authorities to reform institutions. Elizabeth Fry also encouraged respectable women to become nurses, predating Florence Nightingale's later and better known efforts.

Josephine Butler

One of the most interesting examples of a women social reformer who was inspired by her faith was Josephine Butler (1828 - 1906). She was born to a large and happy family with strong religious faith and good connections. A cousin was Lord Grey, who as Prime Minister presided over the passing of the Reform Bill and the abolition of slavery (1833). Josephine was intelligent and beautiful. Her faith was strong and she believed in prayer. She made a happy marriage to a man who accepted her as an equal partner in their life together. When they were first married he worked at Oxford University. She found the misogyny and prejudice of Oxford dons difficult; they refused to accept that a woman could contribute to any intelligent discussion. The family moved to Cheltenham and then Liverpool, which she found more congenial. The Butler's were evangelical Anglicans but they were not interested in the usual church centred concerns or in theological controversy. They were more interested in the teachings of Christ than the teachings of the Church. Nor were they into aggressive evangelism; Josephine Butler once wrote:

"The abrupt enquiry 'is such a one converted or saved' has seemed to me under some circumstances, as indelicate as the question would be, put to an expectant mother, 'is the embryo which you bear within you quickened?'" .

Josephine Butler might have continued a solely domestic life but she was shattered when she witnessed the accidental death of her only daughter. Grief drove her out of her safe environment; she said she "had an irresistible desire to go forth and find some pain keener than my own.....The only solace possible would seem to be to find other hurts which ached night and day; and with more reason than mine". Mrs Butler sought out outcasts and derelicts; she began to visit the Liverpool workhouse and sat and worked with the women who had been set to pick oakum, talking to them and later encouraging them to learn Bible texts. She befriended these women and even took a sick prostitute into her home. In time she persuaded the workhouse to arrange less unpleasant alternative work. She became aware of just how difficult it was for women who lived in a society that lauded the value of work and self-improvement but did not allow respectable women access to jobs. This led her to become involved in the fight for higher education for women and the founding of the first college for women at Cambridge University. Through these activities she became a practiced public speaker and developed skills in persuading reluctant authorities to act.

Mrs Butler's life took another abrupt turn when she was asked to lead the fight to repeal the Contagious Diseases Act. This Act allowed women in garrison towns to be stopped in the street if they were suspected of prostitution. Magistrates would accept a policeman's word and order an intrusive physical examination, which the Act's opponents compared to instrumental rape. If a woman was found to have a venereal disease she was confined to a hospital for three months. This Act was widely supported, as an effective measure against the spread of disease among the armed forces, but it treated women as less than human and some Christians opposed it from the start. Mrs Butler knew many prostitutes from her charitable work but it was not easy for her to agree to undertake this task – or for her husband to let her do it. It involved subjects that a well brought up Victorian lady was not supposed to know about let alone discuss. She described it as a call from God that, like Jonah, she initially tried to ignore. She eventually agreed to undertake the task and her intelligence and commitment made her formidable opponent to the Act's adherents. She mobilised Christian opinion in all denominations to oppose the Act. When the abolitionists were beginning to win the argument and the fight had moved into a political arena, a man took over leadership of the movement but the work of changing public opinion had been done. On the night Parliament made the decision to repeal the Act Christians all over England held prayer meetings. Later Mrs Butler turned her attention to people trafficking, then known as the white slave trade. She was concerned about the export of English girls, many only children, to work as prostitutes overseas. She was involved with WT Stead, a journalist, and the Salvation Army in the case that led to the raising of the age of consent in Britain.

The repeal of the Contagious Diseases Act was a resounding victory for the church at a time when its moral influence was waning. Persuading the medical, military and legislative authorities to change their minds about the Act was a Herculean task. Josephine Butler and her colleagues created an ecumenical movement at a time when denominational barriers were rigid. They harnessed the power of Christian opinion to protect vulnerable women. However, those interested have to read about it in social history books: led by a woman, and with such a shocking subject, the campaign doesn't fit into conventional church histories.

Octavia Hill

Octavia Hill (1838 – 1912) was another woman who was inspired by her faith to change society. She was from a middle class family who moved to London when her father's mental illness caused financial difficulties. Their mother educated Octavia and her sisters to earn their own living. Mrs Hill worked for the Christian Socialists and Octavia worked with her and was inspired by their vision of working individually to change the plight of the poor. At the age of fourteen Octavia was appointed to manage a toy factory where girls from a ragged school were taught to make toys. This work and her next job as secretary to the women's classes at a workingmen's club, made her very aware of the difficulties faced by the urban poor. Seeing the iniquities of poor housing, and the difficulties caused by landlords who were only concerned with their own profit, she longed to bring change. John Ruskin, who is better known as a writer and art critic, enabled her to bring her vision into reality by buying several houses for her to manage. Her method was to visit the tenants not only to get the rent but also to offer them help with any difficulties. It was also Ruskin who advised her to run the houses as a business, making a small return for investors. This advice paid off and as well as philanthropists buying property for her to manage other landlords asked her to manage their property, including the Anglican Church Commissioners. Her sisters and a growing number of women volunteers worked with her. Her methods were later copied outside London, not only in Britain but also in Europe and America. In time the Government consulted her when they considered social and housing policies.

Another of her concerns was that ordinary people should be given access to the countryside. She was a founder of the National Trust, whose aim was to protect endangered coast, countryside and buildings so they would be a heritage for ordinary people. She was also involved in the Charity Organisation Society, the precursor of social work in Britain. Octavia Hill was the founding inspiration for two modern professions, social housing management and social work.

Catherine Booth

A woman who combined a practical concern for the poor with direct involvement in church leadership was Catherine Booth (1829 – 1890).

She was born to a family very different from those of Josephine Butler and Octavia Hill. She only had a few years schooling due to ill health and because, far from valuing education, her very pious mother's main concern was to protect her daughter from contamination by the world. However, Catherine was intelligent and studied intensively the one book her mother found acceptable – the Bible. She is said to have read it through eight times by the time she was twelve. Catherine grew up to be a strong woman with strong religious convictions based on her own reading of the Bible. These included her belief that God approved the ministry of women. Catherine met William Booth, a pawnbroker's clerk turned preacher, and they fell in love and became engaged. They married when she was twenty-six and for thirty-five years she was his partner and his support, intellectually, physically and at times financially. William Booth had no formal training in theology and was strongly influenced by Catherine in both his religious views and in his concern for the poor.

Catherine was excited by the Phoebe Palmer's visit to the North East of England but was prevented from hearing her preach by illness and family responsibilities. However, when a minister wrote a pamphlet attacking Mrs Palmer, Catherine sat down and wrote a reply with cogent, biblically based arguments. She went further than Mrs Palmer in asserting that women should be free to preach from the pulpit. This caused considerable controversy when, with William's support, her work was published. Catherine had taught women and children for some time but, at a time when she was recovering from the birth of her fourth child in four years, she felt that God was calling her to full time ministry. Several months later she got up and spoke during a time of testimony in her husband's church. Her husband was as surprised as the congregation but immediately announced that she would preach at the evening service. Her career as a preacher had begun. Shortly after this William's health broke down and he went away leaving Catherine as acting minister for over two months. She soon became well known, and notorious, in the area as a female preacher.

Neither William Booth's emotional revivalism nor Catherine's preaching suited the increasingly staid Methodists; the resulting difficulties led them to decide to work independently. He resigned from his church and they worked together as revival preachers. They moved to London where William started working in a mission in the East End slums while Catherine spoke to more affluent groups in the West End. For a time she was the main breadwinner for the family. However, when a group of wealthy Methodists offered to build her a church bigger than that of Charles Spurgeon (a noted Baptist minister and preacher) she refused. When William inaugurated his 'Christian Mission', which eventually developed into the Salvation Army, its constitution reflected the views on gender he shared with his wife. Men and women were recognised as equal under God and women could undertake any role, including being in charge of a mission.

Catherine's pamphlet on women preaching, written years earlier, was revised and republished. It is a closely reasoned paper. She deals with all the texts used to restrict women, referring at times the work of biblical scholars and to the original Greek words. She gives many examples of women used by God both from the Bible and from among her own contemporaries. She also points out the difficulties caused by taking texts out of context. "In short there is no end to the errors in faith and practice that have resulted from taking isolated passages, wrested from their proper connections, or the light thrown on them by other scriptures, and applying them to sustain a favourite theory." Judging from the blessed results which have almost invariably followed the ministrations of women in the cause of Christ, we fear it will be found, at the great day of account, that a mistaken and unjustifiable application of the passage "Let your women keep silent in the churches" has resulted in more loss to the church than any of the errors we have already referred to."

Catherine had no formal role in the Salvation Army but was totally involved in it from its inception; she was called the 'Mother of the Army'. She supported William in his role as 'General' and encouraged his concern for the urban poor. She was particularly concerned with helping young prostitutes, who she saw as victims of poverty and male brutality. The opposition their work met, from both secular and religious authorities, did not discourage the Booths, who saw it as evidence that they were doing the Lord's work. The book on urban poverty, which was the inspiration for much of the Army's later work, was published just after Catherine's death from cancer and William testified that even while she was dying in great pain she had been involved in its production.

When Catherine died her funeral reflected her importance to her contemporaries. It took place at Olympia Exhibition Hall in London and there was a congregation of 36,000. The only reason the crowd was not larger was that the turnstiles were locked for safety reasons two hours before the start and 'late' comers were unable to get in. The Manchester Guardian said at the time that Catherine had "probably done more in her own person to establish the right of women to preach the gospel than anyone who has ever lived."

Catherine stands out; not only for what she achieved but also for her confidence in the rightness of women's ministry, which she communicated to her daughters and generations of woman officers in the Salvation Army. Her views would have been unexceptional a hundred years later but in Victorian times were unusual and it took bravery to advocate them publicly. Even after William's death the Salvation Army was more accepting of women in leadership than other organisations; although the most prominent women seemed to be members of the Booth family. These included Catherine's daughter Eva who ran the Army in the United States for many years and returned to England as General, the head of the Salvation Army.

Venerating Saints and visions of Mary

While protestant women were moving towards increasing involvement in a changing society Roman Catholic's were being encouraged to turn their backs on the modern world. In 1854 Pope Pius IX ended centuries of controversy by formally accepting as dogma the immaculate conception of Mary, suggesting that she, like Christ, was sinless. The veneration of Mary and other Saints, which had been growing since the Counter-Reformation, became more central to the faith of many Catholics. Pilgrimages to shrines and devotion to holy objects were popular. In this atmosphere a few, generally young and uneducated, women saw apparitions of Mary. The most famous of these was Bernadette Soubirous, who in 1858 reported that she had seen and spoken to the Blessed Virgin. As a result her home, Lourdes, became a place of pilgrimage, especially for those ill or in pain.

In 1864 Pope Pius IX published the 'Syllabus of Errors' a denunciation of all aspects of progress, liberalism and contemporary life. Among other things he condemned socialism, democracy and science. While Catholic intellectuals were horrified, most Catholics accepted his views as definitive. At the end of the decade he called a Council who defined the doctrine of papal infallibility. As Protestant women began to see new opportunities opening up for them, Catholic women were encouraged to concentrate on domesticity or life as a cloistered nun.

Therese of Lisieux

One woman who suffered under but also embraced these restrictions was St Therese of Lisieux (1873 –1897). She was born into a devout family and as a child was determined to follow her sisters into the local Carmelite convent, she entreated the Bishop and then the Pope himself and got her way when, at the age of fifteen, she was admitted as a novice. Therese had great aspirations, "To be Your Spouse, my Jesus; to be a Carmelite; to be, through my union with you, a mother of souls, surely this should be enough? Yet I feel the call of more vocations still; I want to be a warrior, a priest, an apostle, a doctor of the church, a martyr." There was no room in nineteenth century Catholicism for these aspirations so instead Therese embraced the restrictions of life in an enclosed convent. "Love, proves itself by deeds so how am I to show my love? Great deeds are forbidden me. The only way I can prove my love is by scattering flowers and these flowers are every little sacrifice, every glance and word, and the doing of the least actions of love". Therese subdued her desire to serve the Lord on a larger stage and concentrated on loving him and her fellow nuns. She died at the age of twenty-four, having never left her small convent community, but the writings she left behind had a powerful influence on a far wider world. The Church held up her goodness and piety as an example for Catholic women everywhere. Within thirty years the Pope had declared her a saint and, in 1997, Pope John Paul II proclaimed her a Doctor of the Church.

Nursing and teaching Nuns

Not all nuns accepted enclosure. During the nineteenth and early twentieth centuries many new religious Orders were started and many of these were Orders of nursing or teaching nuns. Communities across the world would have been poorer without these dedicated women; their willingness to serve the community was crucial in meeting the needs of the poor and downtrodden as well as the better off. The hospitals and schools which played such an important part in Catholic life depended on the sacrificial lives of thousands of nuns. Evangelical Christian women changed their society because of their belief that their Christian faith should not be confined to their personal lives but should also inspire them to work for a more just and compassionate society. Despite the restrictions imposed on them Roman Catholic nuns were also helping create such a society by providing nursing, social care and education for Catholic girls.

24. TO THE ENDS OF THE EARTH

A passion to spread the Gospel characterised the early church but over the centuries the task had lost its urgency. This chapter will look at how, after almost a thousand years, Christian men and women again felt called to evangelise the world.

Reading the history of missions is like reading church history; it can appear that women played no part - the actors are all masculine. Male missionaries, even those whose work produced little fruit, get more attention in histories than the most effective women missionaries.   Professor Stephen Neill's 'History of Christian Missions', first published in 1964, mentions only a few women peripherally and rarely attributes any value to their work.   "By the end of our period (1798 –1914) women in the missions greatly outnumbered men. This is explicable, in the light of the much slower development of education for women and girls in the younger Churches, and in many countries by the prejudice against any other career for girls than that of marriage, but the disproportion in the ranks of the foreigners has not been altogether to the benefit of the work." Thus he brushes off the work of the majority of missionaries. His views were not unique, even in the twentieth century many Christians denigrated the work of women missionaries.

Anne-Marie Javouhey

The first new missionaries were inspired by the counter-reformation not the reformation.   While most Christians were content to stay at home the Jesuits had carried Christianity as far as China and Japan. A number of Catholic women, mostly from France, felt called to go to Canada and started religious orders there, working in pioneering situations often with little support from their Church. The first person to send women as missionaries beyond the Western world was Anne-Marie Javouhey (1779-1851), a Frenchwoman who became a nun in 1800 and received a vision in which she was called to work overseas. She founded an Order of Sisters to do missionary work in 1805. In 1817 she sent a group of missionary nuns to Reunion and two years later another group to Senegal. In 1822 she followed them and worked in Africa for the rest of her life. Her work was hampered by years of battling with a power hungry French Bishop but by her death there were 900 Nuns in her order, serving across the world. Even Stephen Neill gives her a brief, if second hand, tribute in his reference to her. "Roman Catholic historians attribute the first renewal of African missions in the nineteenth century to the faith and enterprise of a woman, Anne-Marie Javouhey." Javouhey's nuns were only the first of thousands of Catholic nuns who were to leave their home countries and travel across the world to face hardship, illness and even war in their desire to serve God by caring for others.

Protestant missionaries

It was not until the nineteenth century that the Protestant churches became conscious of a responsibility to obey Christ's last command to his disciples, "Go and make disciples of all nations". The trickle of Protestants going overseas, which started when William Carey went to India in 1793, became a flood by middle of the nineteenth century and large numbers of missionaries continued to go overseas from Western countries in the first half of the twentieth century. From the beginning women were involved in this enterprise.

Missionary wives

Most of the early pioneering protestant missionaries were married and took their wives with them. Some wives did not share their husband's call and went overseas from duty, to accompany their husband not to share his work. Dorothy Carey, William's wife, opposed his desire to go to India and went with him reluctantly. She was an ordinary woman, barely literate, and felt overwhelmed by the strange environment. Her fears were realised when her son died in India and, overpowered by grief and fear of the unfamiliar, she became mentally ill and was confined, remaining in India until her early death.

A missionary wife who shared her husband's desire to serve was Mary Moffat. When she was twenty she fell in love with Robert Moffat who was working as a gardener in her father's nursery before going overseas. Two years later, in 1819, her parents allowed her to sail to Africa to marry him. The Moffats lived in the South African interior far from other Europeans, among an initially unreceptive tribal group. She coped uncomplainingly with life in the bush and with her domestic chores, learning to clean her floor with cow dung, like the locals, finding it the best way to discourage insects. The Moffats served together for 53 years. Robert was an evangelist, agricultural advisor and Bible translator but Mary saw her job as providing him with support and domestic comfort and bringing up their ten children. When they retired to England they left behind not only a flourishing church and a more prosperous agricultural base but also several children who were themselves working as missionaries.

Other wives shared their husband's call to the mission field and hoped to work in partnership with their husbands, evangelising the local women. Their lot was not easy; while their husbands could concentrate on mission work wives had other demands on their time. They had to fit evangelism around care for their children and household, had to cope with the stress of frequent childbirth and often with emotional trauma from the death of their children. The death rate of male missionaries was high, but that of their wives and children, was much higher.

Single Women Missionaries

From 1820 a trickle of intrepid single women went overseas as missionaries. A number were from the evangelical Anglican 'Clapham Sect', which had been so active against slavery and child labour. Mission societies were forced to recognise that male evangelists could not evangelise women, since in most countries women of good character were not allowed to associate with foreign men and were kept secluded from any man outside their family. Christianity, as always, needed women to evangelise and educate women. A Society for promoting female education was started, with links to the Church Missionary Society, and it sent out its first single woman teacher in 1834.

The first mission to actively encourage single women missionaries was the China Inland Mission. Hudson and Maria Taylor started the CIM to change the way westerners were trying to evangelise China. They wanted missionaries to leave the safe European enclaves on the coast and go into the vast interior, dressed in Chinese clothes and living as the Chinese did, so that they would not stand out as foreigners. For this great task Hudson Taylor was willing to recruit those not normally accepted by mission societies, artisans and single women rather than the usual middle class graduates. When he and Maria returned to China they took fifteen recruits, including eight women, six of them unattached. In time hundreds of single women went out under the CIM, many of them lived and travelled accompanied only by a Chinese Christian couple. Hudson Taylor realised that these single women were invaluable in training national Christians in leadership. As both Chinese and Europeans saw leadership as masculine, male missionaries overshadowed national Christians, who inevitably took a dependent position in relation to them. Female missionaries, on the other hand, were able to mentor national Christians quietly, leaving Chinese Christians to take a more public role in preaching and teaching. The growth of an indigenous church leadership owed more to the work of women missionaries than their male counterparts.

In the first half of the nineteenth century American women did not have the opportunities of their European sisters. In the United States it was regarded as totally unacceptable for a single woman to go overseas. A number of couples married on very short acquaintance because they both wished to serve abroad. Male missionaries were encouraged to marry, so as to reduce the risk of them starting a relationship with a local woman, and women who felt the call to go overseas were only allowed to go with a husband. Some of these marriages worked well but other couples, living in social isolation with a near stranger, ended up desperately unhappy. The woman sometimes found herself not only married to someone who was temperamentally incompatible but also contending with domestic chores, pregnancy and childcare, unable to do the work to which she had felt called.

Women's missionary groups existed in the United States but only for the purpose of raising financial and prayer support. Eventually American women took things into their own hands. They started societies specifically to send single women overseas to work with women and children. These societies were supported and run by women. The first was started in 1861 and others followed soon covering a range of purposes and denominations. These societies flourished until the second decade of the twentieth century, when mainstream missionary societies pressured the women's societies to merge with their denominational equivalents. As so often in the history of the church, once the value of work done by women was appreciated, men took it over. The women who had competently run the women's societies were not offered similar management opportunities in the denominational societies which absorbed them; so women overseas found themselves controlled by masculine Mission Boards with patriarchal attitudes.

Domestic restrictions or overseas challenges

By the last quarter of the nineteenth century large numbers of women were going overseas, to China, India and Africa. There were reasons for this; life at home was restricted, families were close and often introverted and churches expected women to occupy themselves with sewing circles, sales of work and church teas. Only a few exceptional women had any opportunity for public service. The women's missionary movement was not driven by feminism; but it was driven by a desire to be actively involved in the ministry of the church. The number of 'surplus' women, who never had, or had turned down, an opportunity to marry, were later augmented by the death toll of young men in World War I. Single women had few options; most were expected to live with their families and many had no opportunity to follow careers. A woman anxious to serve the church was encouraged to arrange flowers, organise the catering or raise money for charity; she had few opportunities and fewer challenges. Overseas the same woman might find herself coping with discomfort, ill health and danger but she would also have unlimited challenges and possibilities for service. It is no wonder that for a century many of the more intelligent and active single women with a strong Christian faith chose to go overseas as missionaries. Ex-patriate women were involved in all kinds of mission work, even pioneering in remote areas unexplored by Europeans. Single women went out as nurses, doctors and as teachers. The first female missionary doctor, Clara Swain, started work in India in 1870; she was an American, since this was before the English medical establishment allowed women into medical schools.

Women missionaries were heavily involved in education in the wider sense, not only mission schools. Isabel Kuhn (1901 – 1957) who worked with OMF (previously the CIM) in Thailand, pioneered the idea of short term Bible schools for women; planned for the wet season, when women could not work in the fields. Isabel Kuhn, and other women missionaries who copied her idea, trained many enthusiastic female evangelists who worked among village women in their own locality.

Many single missionaries adopted native children – usually unwanted baby girls. Most cared for a family of six to ten while continuing their other work but some made caring for children their life work. Amy Carmichael (1867 – 1951), whose work became well known through her many devotional books, organised care for over a thousand children.

Pioneer missionaries

Women were involved in work even in remote areas unexplored by Europeans. Mary Slessor (1848 – 1915) was a Scot and, like many successful missionaries, she was working class; her formal schooling had stopped at eleven when she started work in a mill (factory) to help support her mother and siblings. While working a ten hours day she also pursued her own studies and taught young men and girls the Bible in her spare time. When her wages were no longer essential to support her family she went out to West Africa. She felt called to Calabar (now part of Nigeria), an area known as the 'white man's grave'. Few Europeans had penetrated inland from the coast and the few that did soon died of the tropical diseases endemic in the area. It was a difficult area, damaged by the effects of the slave trade and, although the involvement of Europeans in the slave trade had ended, slavery itself was still practiced among local people.

Initially Mary worked, like other Europeans, on the coast. She found the lifestyle of middle class missionaries alien to her experiences but she remained there for over ten years. It was shortly after she received news of the deaths of her mother and sister in Scotland that the Mission agreed to her request to move inland to live among

Africans. From then she lived in an African house and ate African food. She abandoned the complications of Victorian women's dress, corsets, wide skirts, hats and even shoes. It is said she lived not just as an African but as a poor African, in an area where no other missionary had survived. Mary served the Africans around her as a preacher, teacher, nurse and foster mother to unwanted babies. Twins were regarded as evil in this part of Africa and were killed, so missionaries cared for many twins in order to save their lives. Mary coped with illness, opposition, spiritual warfare against witchcraft and loneliness. She fell in love and became engaged to another missionary but the marriage was postponed when the Mission Board refused permission for him to join her work, insisting he remain on the coast until a substitute could be found for his own work. Mary was not prepared to leave her work to join him and when he subsequently returned to Britain, on health grounds, the engagement ended. Her attempts to work with other women missionaries were not successful, but as she got older she had companionship and help from her adopted daughters. After more than twenty years she had established a work and a church, in the interior. She felt called to move on, leaving the work she had established to other missionaries while she started again even further inland. She worked there to the end and eleven years later she died peacefully, surrounded by her daughters and mourned by Africans and Europeans alike.

Three women who also chose to work in a remote area were Mildred Cable (1878 – 1951) and Francesca and Evangeline French. They were long-term CIM missionary teachers when they felt God was calling them to the remote and unevangelised North West. They moved to the border regions of China beyond the Great Wall. They did not settle in one town but had an itinerant ministry among the trading cities. Although no longer young these ladies faced hardships and difficulties without flinching. They crossed the Gobi Desert, one of the remotest regions in the world, five times. Eventually they were forced to leave when the Chinese government decreed that all foreigners must leave the area. Miss Cable subsequently wrote a number of books, which brought them fame as travellers as well as missionaries.

Women missionaries never allowed themselves to be restricted to 'safe' areas and many showed great courage under pressure. During World War II three lone women continued their mission's work in Morocco. The last missionary to leave communist China was a woman.

Charlotte Moon

Women missionaries provided a template for Christian women; an example of what could be achieved by women who were not hampered by the restrictions that bound women in their home churches. Some have assumed that these women must have been feminists but in fact very few were. They were focussed on their task not on themselves, on the needs of others not their own rights. One example of a woman who sometimes fought the restrictions imposed on her but who never challenged patriarchal attitudes was Charlotte Moon (1840 – 1912). Lottie Moon was a member of well to do Southern family and received a good education; she was one of the first group of women in the South to receive an MA. During the Civil War she had to stay and help her mother run the family plantation but during this time she also educated her younger sister and learnt four languages.   In 1871 she was one of the first single women to go to China with the Southern Baptist Missionary Society. Some years later she became engaged to a friend back in the States and contemplated leaving China.   However she found it difficult to think of leaving her work in China and was concerned that his theological ideas were becoming too liberal, so she broke off the relationship. She said to her niece "God had first claim on my life and since the two conflicted there could be no question about the result".

Once in China, like so many other women, Lottie Moon was expected to teach in a school for Chinese girls. She found this increasingly frustrating and, when she had mastered the language, she felt a call to evangelise more directly.   She also found it difficult working under the senior male missionary; whose desire to control every detail irked her.   Lottie Moon sent home regular letters and articles for a Missionary magazine, which helped those back in the States to understand more about mission work.   In 1883 an article of hers, "The Women's Question Again" was published, in it she expressed her feelings clearly.   "Can we wonder at the mortal weariness and disgust, the wasted powers and the conviction that her life is a failure, that comes over a woman when instead of the ever broadening activities that she had planned she finds herself tied down to the petty work of teaching a few girls." Two years later Lottie Moon left her teaching post and went to live alone in the interior, where she was involved in evangelism and teaching new Christians. Apart from two visits home she remained in China for 39 years, until her death at the age of 71.

Possibly Lottie Moon's most influential contribution was made not in China but the USA where her published letters, and her advice to the

Foreign Mission Board, had considerable influence. She promoted the idea that missionaries should not go overseas for life but should, for their health's sake, return home every ten years for a furlough. She was concerned about the poor financial support given to Southern Baptist Missionaries and wrote a letter suggesting that the women of the churches should address this, as women had done among the Methodists. In doing this she made it clear she was not challenging the male establishment: "In seeking organisation we do not need to adopt plans or methods unsuitable to the views or repugnant to the tastes of our brethren. What we want is not power but simply combination to order and elicit the largest possible giving" In this she was successful; the Lottie Moon Collection is still made every December among Southern Baptists and has raised over 1.5 billion dollars since it was set up in 1888.

Missionaries and social policy

Christianity usually arrived at the same time as colonisers and so was often identified with Imperialism. But the missionaries had little help from secular authorities, both the British government and the merchant traders generally opposed and tried to hinder missionaries; who would often interfere with their exploitation of native peoples.

Missionaries were instrumental in providing information that led to legislation against traditional religious or social practices, in the same way as years before they had energised the campaign for abolition by providing factual information on the mistreatment of slaves. This work was a benefit mainly to women, not only to converts but also more generally. African feminists have pointed out that traditional practices which caused pain or damage generally involved women and children, while those imposed on men were more benign. Practices that the missionaries opposed included: foot binding, which crippled Chinese women; genital mutilation (female circumcision); infanticide; suttee (burning a wife alive on her husband's funeral pyre) and other customs that made being widowed a nightmare in many Asian and Africa countries; and polygamy. It has been suggested that Christianity's role in this has been overstated, and change would have come without the missionaries' intervention. This may be true but longstanding cultural practices are resistant to change. Female circumcision is still widespread among African Muslims, even those living in the West, and is practiced in a few Christian tribes, although the church strongly condemns it. It is certainly true that the missionaries' efforts were less effective than those of the national Christian women who followed them in challenging cultural practices that harmed their fellow women.

Missionaries could be misled by their own cultural assumptions into opposing practices that, however undesirable, were not unbiblical. In Africa the church's opposition to polygamy led to mainly female congregations, since a woman in a plural marriage was accepted by most denominations but a man was expected to dismiss all but one of his wives before being baptised. This ruling led to great hardship when secondary wives were turned out of their homes with little or no support, a tragedy that echoed the plight of priest's wives when celibacy was made compulsory 800 years earlier. Missionaries were aware of the harm the church's ruling was causing but felt the principle of not accepting polygamy was important. They allowed their own cultural conditioning to lead them into taking an unnecessarily strong line – after all polygamy was practiced by Jewish

Patriarchs and must have been an issue in New Testament churches; since Paul instructed Timothy that an Elder must be husband of only one wife. No doubt missionaries were partly motivated by awareness of the scandal condoning plural marriage would cause among their supporters back home. In the South Pacific similar motives probably drove a desire to change patterns of dress to conform to Western ideas of modesty.

Reaching remote peoples

Encouraging indigenous church leaders was not the only advantage women had on the mission field. Women, as the 'weaker sex', are less of a threat to fearful and aggressive men. Women were able to go into situations where men could not. When Wycliffe Bible translators wanted to reach the remote Auca tribe in South America the five young men who made initial contact were killed. Instead it was Elizabeth Elliott and Rachel Saint, the widow of one of the young men and the sister of another, who reached the Aucas. They lived among the Aucas, with Elizabeth's small daughter, for several years.

One woman missionary who pioneered a new way to evangelise was Joy Ridderhof (1903 – 1984). Forced by ill health to leave her work in Honduras and return home to California after only one term; she longed to do something for the people she had left behind. She recorded a message and sent it to them. Soon missionaries working with Spanish speakers were asking her for records. She had spoken on the original recordings but realised that a foreign accent was off-putting and established a rule that all recordings must be made by native speakers. Missionaries working in other languages heard of her work and asked her to make records for use in their work. From this small beginning the work of Gospel Recordings (later Global Recordings Network) was born. She did not start out to found a mission but as it grew she established the principles she wanted. It was to be a 'faith' mission; she never asked for money and she also decided to give away the records free, believing she shouldn't charge for the Gospel. Despite this funds were provided and the work grew. She started travelling with a friend to make recordings, initially in Mexico but later further afield. She spent five years, travelling with two companions to remote places in Africa and Asia, recording minority languages, many spoken only by small tribes. Many other field recordists followed in her steps.

Joy Ridderhof was one of those people, like George Muller and Hudson Taylor, who did not discover new spiritual principles but who lived their lives in a way that illuminated Bible teachings that most Christians fail to take seriously. She lived by faith; she and her staff took no salaries. She believed in the power of praise and rejoiced in all that happened; praising God for setbacks as well as advances, believing that all was in God's control. She was an enthusiastic person with an infectious faith that touched many lives. She was also ahead of her time in recognising that oral learners need to learn by oral methods, especially storytelling, and that people groups, however small, are more responsive if they are told about Jesus in their heart language. The work she started continued for sixty years before a group of mission societies recognised this and started the International Orality Network to develop methods to communicate with the three quarters of the world's population who are oral learners.

There are GRN centres across the world and also bases, all staffed not by expatriates but by nationals. About six thousand languages have been recorded and many thousands have responded to hearing the Gospel in their own language. GRN has been far the most effective tool to reach small language groups and many churches have been planted as a result. Gospel Recordings was started by a woman and initially was mainly staffed by women; but now in only two of the twenty plus GRN centres does a woman lead the work; reflecting a lack of acceptance of women in a leadership role in many countries.

Patriarchal Mission Boards

Generally male mission boards and field directors have directed the work of women missionaries. Over the years many women have been deeply hurt by conscious or unconscious patriarchal attitudes. Women who had built up a work from nothing saw it handed over to someone with less experience whose gender made him more 'suitable' to lead it. One woman who has written with honesty about her experiences is Helen Roseveare (b. 1925). She was sent, against her wishes, to work in a rundown leprosy camp. She raised the money to build a hospital and worked with Africans on clearing the ground and building it. Then a young male doctor was appointed medical director of the hospital she had built. Helen Roseveare suffered much during her time in the Congo but she used her sufferings, which later included rape at the hands of rebel soldiers, to help other brutalised women. These included some of the Catholic Missionary Nuns who, like her, had suffered great trauma because of their call to serve God in Congo. She has written and spoken with unusual frankness of the difficulties and failures she met as a missionary and the difficulty of not being involved in decisions about her own work. Her honesty made her a valued missionary author and speaker, one who dealt with the realities of life and faith.

Many books have been written by and about women missionaries. Most are autobiographical, biographical or devotional. Books on Missiology and mission strategy and scholarly biographies of missionaries tend to be by, and about, men. Biographies and autobiographies of women missionaries are generally published as paperbacks. Women who had something to say about mission strategy usually said it indirectly, in biographies or autobiographies, not challenging masculine assumptions by openly 'teaching'.

The present and future

Western missionaries still work in some countries but they see their work as serving, not leading, the local church. Medical and social services are provided in some place but most see their main task as providing training and Bible teaching to the leaders and future leaders, including women, of national churches. In countries where a church has been established for many years this task also has been taken over by nationals. Although far fewer Western Christians are now prepared to leave home to work at a demanding and poorly paid task, the missionary movement has not died; it has merely changed its base. The majority of missionaries now come from the countries that were once on the receiving end. They are working in their own countries and, increasingly, overseas. South Korea probably now has the largest contingent of missionaries, certainly far more than from any western country. A few are coming back to Europe to share with post-Christian societies the faith that was once shared with them.

25 WOMEN IN NON WESTERN CHURCHES

This book has largely focussed on the Western church and the English speaking world. In the twenty first century the western church is only a fraction of the worldwide church.   In this chapter we will take a brief glimpse at in the role Christian women have played elsewhere.

Christianity is now the world's largest religious group and, despite the challenge from militant Islam, the church is vital and growing almost everywhere, except in post-Christian Europe.   It is not western missionaries who have driven the staggering growth of evangelical Christianity in China, Korea, Latin America and other places during the last fifty years.   Missionaries played their part in sowing seeds, but the most effective evangelism has always been by people from within a culture.   Women have had a vital role in this; one of the most effective means of spreading Christianity has always been ordinary women 'gossiping the Gospel' and sharing their faith with their families and friends.

Schools and Bible Women

Missionaries sowed the seeds of this growth, and an important aspect of this was the changes that Christianity brought for women. In many countries it was missionaries who introduced education for girls. For example we are so used to meeting highly educated Indian women that it is difficult to realise that in 1897 only six out of every thousand women in India were literate and only ten in a thousand had received any education. Almost all of these literate women had been educated

271

in mission schools. Many went on to educate another generation of girls in Christian schools and in the Government schools that followed. Female education was one Christian innovation which Indian Hindus adopted.

Missionaries, especially women missionaries, employed national women to help them with the task of evangelism. Many were widows, like the widows who had worked for Christianity in the early centuries. Most of these 'Bible Women' worked closely with missionaries as assistants; although some were employed to work independently. A few became noted evangelists and Bible teachers. Most of their work was with women but a few were so effective in their evangelism, and authoritative in their Bible teaching, that men also listened. Many of these women, working for low wages and often suffering persecution for their faith, were outstanding individuals. The system proved effective in training indigenous teachers and leaders for a growing national church.

China

Hundreds of missionaries lived, and many died, to spread the Gospel in China between 1807, when the first Missionary arrived, and 1951, when the last missionaries were turned out. Missionaries had been educating Chinese girls and modelling for them living independent and fulfilled working lives. Their example had also encouraged women to seek change. Christian converts in China painfully unbound their own, and their daughters, feet and Chinese Christian women started anti-foot binding societies, which in time led to the abolition of a practice which had crippled generations of Chinese women.

When the Communists forced all missionaries to leave in 1950-1 there were estimated to be 700,000 Christians. The Communists forbade all religious worship except in 'Patriotic' churches which had no overseas links and were controlled by the authorities. Even today the Chinese Government insists that they, not the Pope, appoint Catholic Bishops. Rather than accept the restriction on their religious freedom many Christians, Protestant and Roman Catholic alike, formed underground churches; willing to risk persecution by meeting in secret. Yet half a century after all missionaries were forced out there are millions, possibly a billion, Christians in China. Christianity spread in Communist China even during the Cultural Revolution. Communists imprisoned theologians and church leaders; sparing only those leaders who were prepared to work with them, but Christianity spread through personal evangelism, mainly by women. After a hundred years many educated Chinese women were established in independent careers. Bible Women, who had worked with women missionaries, had seen that women could have their own ministry. These women had a good knowledge of the Bible and were trained in evangelism. When church leaders were arrested they were able to take over as pastors in those churches that went underground to escape persecution. Some Christian women were imprisoned; Dr Su was imprisoned for six years as a spy because of her association with the American missionary who inspired her conversion to Christianity. After her release she joined the Three Self Patriotic Church but, like many others, she was disillusioned by the way it was controlled by the State. She left and started a house church; in time she was pastor for several house churches that had grown from the original one. She was not alone; after visiting China in 1981 Arthur Glasser reported that eighty five per cent of house churches' leaders were women.

There is no barrier to women's ordination in China but male leadership is more usual. As the numbers of Christians increased dramatically, and the political situation changed, male leaders returned, many released from prison after years of suffering. When David Aikman was doing research for his book 'Jesus in Beijing' only one of the Christian leaders he met was a woman. However, he found that eighty per cent of church members were women, an exceptionally high proportion. Cultural reasons may partly account for this; in the traditional Chinese religion of ancestor worship women tended the family shrine, so the idea that women represent the family in religious matters has deep roots. There may also be political reasons; under the Communist Party attending church is not a good career move. Men may feel it is unwise to embrace Christianity until after they retire. But one reason must be personal evangelism by women, who could most easily share their faith with fellow women. In the first decade of a new century the Chinese church may have a billion believers. While still a small minority in a vast country, Christianity is expanding fast; not only in rural areas among the peasants but also in cities among university students and educated professionals.

India

In India events have been less dramatic but Indian Christian women played a vital part in the growth of Christianity in their country. They taught in schools, worked in mission hospitals as doctors and nurses and worked with the poor and needy; after 1967 when the Indian Government started refusing visas to missionaries they took responsibility for Christian work with women in their country. There are thousands of Indian Catholic nuns mainly from Kerala, involved in education and nursing. Many became nuns because the exorbitant sums demanded for dowries meant their families could not afford for them to marry. Some are living in foundations started by Europeans and have had to adapt to a western lifestyle but other Orders are Indian. The best known of these Indian religious orders is the Missionaries of Charity. Its founder, Mother Teresa, was Albanian but this should not obscure the fact that those who joined her in her work were Indian and that they followed a lifestyle that fitted in with that of the people among whom they worked. The Order now has Houses all over the world, most of them started by small teams of Indian nuns.

Some Indian women tried to help ex-patriate Christians to understand and work more effectively within their culture. Pandita Ramabai (1858-1922) was a Hindu who had spent her childhood and youth as a pilgrim, travelling with her family to Hindu shrines and holy places seeking the truth. Her father had taught her to read Hindu Scriptures, suffering persecution as a result since this was regarded as the preserve of Hindu priests like himself. Sometime after his death she was asked to lecture Hindu women on their religious duties. She was dismayed to realise that the Hindu scriptures had a totally negative view of women, suggesting they were totally unworthy and their only hope was to worship their husbands. She became a reformer, working to raise the status of women, especially widows. On a visit to England she stayed with a friend who was an Anglican nun and became a Christian. Her independence of mind survived her conversion and she was not willing to fit into a denominational straightjacket.   She continued to lecture and also to preach, even speaking about her Christian faith in Hindu temples when given this unique opportunity.   She was critical of missionaries who were not prepared to work with the caste system and believed Christianity needed to be presented in a way that fitted in with Indian culture.   Her faith was a personal one, she followed Christ, not an institutional church, but she was a woman of prayer who saw her prayers for revival answered.   The large orphanage she founded to give girls a Christian education is still flourishing.

Many Indian women now work as evangelists and Bible teachers. Indian Christians have also been, and are still, working against the dowry system, which has had such a baleful influence on the lives of many Indian women.   They are also taking up the issue of female feticide, which has become a serious problem in India since modern technology enabled couples to find out the gender of an unborn child.

Africa

In Asia, as in the Roman and post Roman world, Christianity brought with it a respect for women, which attracted people who had been devalued and restricted all their lives.   This was not true in all parts of Africa, where a few tribes were matrilineal; in them women traditionally had more status.   African traditional religions allowed women priests.   The denominational churches, which were planted by missionaries, were led by men and some African feminists feel they reinforced restrictions on women.   Certainly African Bishops are emerging as a strong conservative force in the world wide Anglican church; for their views on women priests as well as on the contentious issue of homosexual priests.

As well as the denominations founded by missionaries there are more than 7,000 new African religious movements and churches. Most are Pentecostal and emphasise a ministry of healing. These sects have offered women more opportunities; they have women prophetesses, healers and pastors, mostly working subordinate to male leaders and mainly working with other women. A few new churches were founded by women, most of these were small but they included at least two wider movements, Mai Chaza and Alice Lenshina both had thousands of followers in Southern Africa; however, after their deaths their leadership passed to men. In several countries African Christian women, initially with some support from missionaries, developed women's clubs run by, and for, women. The attraction of these groups was partly social but their main purposes were Bible study, evangelism and pastoral work. They attracted thousands of women, gave women in the denominational churches opportunities for ministry and encouraged unity by crossing denominational barriers.

Christians living among Muslims

One area where Christians are struggling is the Middle East. Indigenous Christian Churches, many of which date back to the first and second centuries, are now threatened with exile or extinction. For centuries Christians lived among Muslims in what was the Ottoman Empire; they were often at a disadvantage, in employment and socially, but Governments tolerated their existence. This changed when an influential minority started to advocate an intolerance which was alien to most Islamic tradition. Now many Christians have been forced to emigrate; they no longer feel safe in their own homes and their own countries. Nor is this danger from

Muslim fundamentalism confined to the Middle East.   Many Christians in mainly Islamic countries, like Pakistan and Indonesia, live with the threat of persecution, either from the Authorities or from crowds, or individuals, whipped up in to a frenzy of hatred by Islamists.   Churches have been destroyed and church leaders arrested, leaving their families without support.   Ordinary Christians, sometimes even children, have been murdered by those who believe their faith justifies killing those who do not follow Islam.   It is usually, though not always, Christian men who are imprisoned, or die in police custody, but women and girls are as much at risk from random sectarian violence.   In some areas Christian women risk violent attack in the streets if they do not adopt Islamic dress and the rules on public behaviour imposed on Muslim women.

A new age of growth and martyrdom

During the twentieth century the Christian Church has grown faster than at any time since the first centuries after its founding.   The shrinking church in Europe has been more than compensated for by growth elsewhere in the world.   Another similarity to the early centuries is that in many countries the right of Christians to worship their God in their way is not recognised and in some the church has been declared illegal.   There were more Christian martyrs during the twentieth century than during the previous two thousand years.

Over the past fifty years the non-western church has grown in size and maturity.   National leaders have taken over responsibility for their churches and are beginning to take a lead internationally as well. Some countries see rights for women and gender equality as western ideas, not relevant to their situation, and try to restrict Christian women in the roles they can take. But women have played a vital part in the growth of Christianity in all the countries where there is now an active Christian minority or majority.

26. WOMAN'S PLACE OR WOMAN'S LIBERATION?

The Roots of feminism lie at the end of the eighteenth century and its first flowering was in the decades following 1870. This chapter will be looking at the effect on Christians of its second flowering a hundred years later. Relatively few Christian women were active in the women's liberation movement but its influence, if often indirect, was considerable.

Christian Feminism

Feminism was not a single movement but many: there was traditional liberal feminism, which thought in terms of women's access to politics and work; Marxist feminism, which concentrated on the economic disadvantages imposed on women; and radical feminists of various persuasions. These included a few who wished to create women only communities, rejecting what they saw as a irretrievably paternalistic society and excluding all men, even feminists and sympathizers. One thing almost all feminists had in common was an underlying anger about the way women had been, and were being, treated; this anger gave them an aggressiveness not everyone found attractive. It is important not to see feminism as just a female movement. Male sympathisers have always supported the struggle for women's rights, and only a minority of radical feminist groups excluded men. There have also always been women who identified with the status quo and opposed feminism and its aims; Women's groups were formed to oppose women's suffrage and later the ordination of women.

Among feminists who were interested in religion some came to regard the Bible and the teachings of the church as completely distorted by patriarchal attitudes. They blamed the patriarchal system not on the secular world, which had created it, but on the Church, which had supported it through the centuries, giving it moral authority. For a number of feminists their anger extended from a patriarchal church to what they saw as a male God and this led to a number losing their faith. Keeping their faith was especially difficult for Roman Catholic feminists; they did not have the Reformation to insulate them from the worst examples of misogyny in Church history. They also had to cope with a Church that still has a totally masculine hierarchy and officially still regards traditional teachings on women as infallible.

Reassessing Scripture

Since the 1960s there has been a flood of articles and books published that reassess the traditional interpretations of key texts about women. This was not new; Margaret Fell, Catherine Booth and Sarah Grimke had all written on the need to look at these passages in their context and to be aware of mistranslations and misinterpretations that had crept in. Elizabeth Cady Stanton (1815 - 1902) had produced 'The Women's Bible', two volumes of Biblical criticism, not that different from earlier work in content but different in motivation. She condemned much of Scripture as patriarchal and hoped to free women from institutional religion through her work. She did not find a receptive audience at the time, even among her fellow workers for women's rights. They feared associating the suffrage movement with a book that took such a negative view of religion. What was new was that the reassessment of Scripture was being done not by under-educated women but by biblical scholars, male and female, backed up by a wealth of recent historical and biblical scholarship. Many scholars demonstrated alternative ways of reading the key Pauline texts. These new interpretations took into account the context in which the texts were written and resolved the contradictions that had always existed between traditional interpretations and other Pauline texts which showed that Paul allowed and allowed women to take an active role in the early church. This re-assessment of Scripture freed Christians to challenge traditional patriarchal attitudes without rejecting the authority of the Bible. It is difficult to overestimate how important this was in encouraging an acceptance of women in leadership within many Protestant churches. These new insights were less helpful to Roman Catholic feminists who had to deal not only with how the Bible had been interpreted but also the unambiguous teaching of the Church on women.

Anti-feminist backlash

Many Christians were critical of the more militant twentieth century feminism and some were aggressively opposed to it. They accepted the results of the first wave of feminism; never suggesting that women should forego the political and educational opportunities early feminists had achieved; although many religious leaders had opposed them at the time. These opponents of the new feminism had a stereotyped view of feminists, which appeared to be based mainly on press reports. This stereotype was often based on more extreme radical feminists; especially the minority who rejected male society wholesale and regarded lesbianism as a positive political life choice. This minority provided better copy for reporters than those with more moderate views and fitted in better with conservative prejudices. Anti-feminist Christians see feminism as atheistic and destructive to family life and 'family values'. A few American fundamentalist writers have even suggested that 'women's lib' is responsible for all the symptoms of moral decline they identify and despise in modern society: rising divorce rates, abortion, venereal disease, and teenage suicide.

These religiously conservative writers recommended a pattern of family life which put the husband firmly in charge, with his wife and children living under his authority. They justify this model of marriage by a traditional interpretation of Paul's teaching on 'headship', which they present as the only 'biblical' one. They seem unaware that any first century Christian would find the modern nuclear family, which they idealise, completely alien to their own understanding of what a family should be. A more hard-line version of this teaching considers that even single women should live under male authority and those that have no husband should allow their Minister or Elders to direct their actions. Not all those advocating a hierarchical family and submissive 'feminine' behaviour have been men. Several books on these lines have been written by women; often they are wives of conservative church leaders, who must have encouraged their wives to write since, according to their views, a wife should only write with her husband's approval. Some anti-feminists eagerly seized on evidence of neurological gender differences, believing their existence supported their argument that women should be subordinate. This is based on a misunderstanding; few would dispute that there are neurological differences between the genders which give men and women different strengths. Feminists do not want to be like men but only to be treated with equal respect, and given similar opportunities.

Christian and post-Christian Feminist Theology

Theology is study of the nature of God and until recently it was exclusively the province of men. People tend to see things in their own image and until recently theology was written by men who saw God in the light of their own masculinity. Since the late 1960s women have been writing feminist theology in an attempt to reconcile women's experiences with Christian beliefs about the nature of God. This can be a difficult task, balancing the insights of feminism with the traditional beliefs of Christians, and not everyone has kept their balance. Rosemary Radford Ruether wrote that "Feminist theology draws on women's experience as a basic source of content and Truth" and it is this emphasis on women's experience, rather than on God, that characterises much feminist theology. Feminist theologians do not find fault with Jesus, the Jewish Rabbi who challenged religious and secular stereotypes and treated women as valued individuals; but some do have difficulty in accepting a redeeming Christ who was incarnate as a man.

Mary Daly (1928-) was brought up and educated as a Roman Catholic. In 1968 she wrote a book about feminism, which she hoped would be a factor in making the Church more accepting of women. The Jesuit College where she taught found the book unacceptable and dismissed her; but later, as a result of student protests, had to reinstate her and give her tenure. Seven years later, when the book was republished, she wrote a post-Christian introduction to her own book, which stated that she had changed her views and abandoned all hope of the Church. "A woman's asking for equality in the Church would be comparable to a black person demanding equality in the Klu Klux Klan." She continued to teach theology in a Catholic College, until 'forcibly retired' at the age of 71, but she no longer worships either God or Christ, believing instead in the creative energy of women communing with 'be-ing'.

There are other Catholic theologians who, unlike Mary Daly, still consider themselves Christians but who have widened their views to include non-Christian traditions. They have substituted 'Woman' for 'Christ' as the centre and touchstone of their belief system. Pamela Dickey Young suggests that in putting 'woman' in the centre of their beliefs some Catholic feminists theologians are copying a past error of their Church; Christ is, and must be, the centre of Christianity, but at times the Roman Catholic Church has appeared to place itself and its own teachings in that central position. In the same fashion these theologians are putting 'women' rather than 'Christ' in the centre of their faith.

Feminist theology is not limited to white Europeans and North Americans. Black American feminists, who call themselves 'womanists' as they feel white feminism has failed to take account of their experiences, are also involved. There are also women in Asia, Africa and Latin America wrestling with these issues.

Inclusive Language

Christian feminism has also been responsible for developing new liturgies using inclusive language; these include basic changes like

285

'brothers and sisters' instead of 'brothers', and more radical changes, including addressing God as both Father and Mother. Many Christians see this as a justifiable reflection of the way the Bible uses metaphors of both fatherly and motherly love to describe God but for traditionalists it is an affront. Some feminists on the other hand feel it doesn't go far enough and wish to replace 'God the Father' with 'God the Mother'. A few modern translations of Scripture, like the New Revised Standard Version, no longer translate the Hebrew and Greek words for 'man' and 'brother' with their English equivalents when the context indicates that they are being used as generic terms that apply to both genders.

Biblical Feminism

There are many Christian men and women who do not like simplistic answers, whether from feminists or anti-feminists, but are concerned about the issues raised by the women's movement. They are anxious to free the church of patriarchal attitudes and assumptions without losing the essential elements of the Christian faith. They have been called biblical feminists. The new insights provided by scholars have encouraged them to challenge patriarchal attitudes in their churches, to support the use of inclusive language and the introduction of women into church leadership. If the mainstream Church is to continue to change in response to new attitudes to women then it will be this group of insiders, not those who have rejected the church, who will help it adapt.

This chapter has looked at the new challenges feminism has brought to the church, challenges some have eagerly and some gingerly embraced, while others have totally rejected them.

27 ORDAINING WOMEN

For many centuries churches had kept women in subservient positions reserving leadership for men.   This chapter will look at how women were eventually allowed to take a more prominent role in some mainstream churches.

Throughout history most men, educated and uneducated, have believed women to be inferior; the church's attitude has always been a reflection of the attitude of secular society. In fact women were given more value within the church, where their spiritual equality was recognised, than they were in a secular world that treated them as second-class citizens who couldn't be trusted with responsibility even for themselves and their own property.   The twentieth century brought revolutionary changes in the way women were regarded in western society and these changes in attitude were slowly reflected in socially conservative churches.

Nineteenth century beginnings.

As previous chapters have shown a number of women were preaching and teaching holiness in the nineteenth century but they did not lead churches and most had an itinerant ministry.   The few women who were ordained were seen as exceptions, whose role did not imply a more general change in women's status.   The experience women had acquired campaigning in the abolition and temperance movements and the example of missionaries had given them confidence.   But most gifted Victorian women either accepted their lot or sought a task in the secular world, even if what they really desired was a role within the church. Florence Nightingale is an example; she wrote of the Church "I would have given her my head, my hand, my heart. She would not have them. She did not know what to do with them. She told me to go back and do my crochet in my mother's drawing room." In time she found a wider sphere for her organising talents in the secular world.

A few individuals refused to be deterred by opposition and persevered in their desire to serve the church. The first woman to be ordained was Antoinette Brown (1825 - 1921) in the United States. She succeeded in completing a theology course despite strong opposition, from other women as well as men; although it was 28 years before she was awarded the degree she had earned. She was offered a pulpit in New York but instead accepted the invitation to be minister in a small Congregational church in a small town. In 1853, shortly after her arrival there, she was consecrated. Her pastorate was not a success; her reluctance to preach hell fire sermons was unpopular with influential members of her congregation. She was dismissed, apparently at her own request, after one year. She returned to New York and married a few years later. Her views became more liberal and she joined the Unitarian Church. After bringing up her family she wished to return to the pastorate, this time as a Unitarian. In 1878, the year she was finally granted the theology degree she had earned over twenty five years earlier, she made it known she was available but apparently didn't find any openings. There were no churches that wanted a middle-aged woman as minister. Eventually, in her seventies, she founded a Unitarian Church in another small town and was minister there for twenty years until her death.

In the following decades a few non-conformist denominations ordained women, but these women had to face opposition before and after their appointment. In one case the State Legislature in Massachusetts had to rule on the validity of a marriage as an unsuccessful attempt was made to declare a wedding ceremony invalid because the officiating minister was a woman.

Nineteenth century nuns

During the nineteenth century many new female religious orders were founded. Most were Roman Catholic but the Anglican and Episcopalian Churches in England and America and the Lutheran Church in Germany also started religious orders of nuns and Lutheran deaconesses. In Catholic communities teaching and nursing nuns became an essential part of Catholic life. However, the ecclesiastic authorities were still determined to control nuns; although they did at last recognise the impossibility of demanding all nuns were cloistered. When Canon Law was revised in 1917 it legislated for the daily life of nuns in great detail. Nuns were forbidden to nurse babies and maternity cases, and to teach in co-educational schools. Even more damaging were efforts to micro-manage their relationships so as to discourage 'particular friendships' and limit all contact with men. This distorted relationships within communities and made it almost impossible for a nun to work in co-operation with any man, even a priest. Nuns were not freed from these restrictions until the Second Vatican Council (1962 –65).

In 1862 the Anglican (Episcopalian) Church agreed to appoint women as deaconesses but not to ordain them. It would be over a hundred years before women deacons in the Anglican Communion were ordained.   Towards the end of the century a number of other denominations also allowed women deacons.   Methodist churches licensed a few women to preach but did not allow women to speak at the conferences where decisions about this were debated.

Feminism and Women's Rights

For centuries women had been denied civil rights by secular society. The first widespread movement for women's rights developed from the 1870's and by the early twentieth century women had fought for, and won, the vote and access to higher education and the professions. After achieving the vote the women's movement ceased to be a major force in society; but individual women and groups continued their efforts to extend women's civil rights.   Only a few women openly claimed they had a call to the priesthood.   Maud Royden (1876 – 1956) was one.   She was a gifted preacher and teacher who remained a loyal Anglican all her life, except for one year when she accepted employment as a preacher at the non-conformist City Temple in London.   In 1917 she saw her friend Constance Coltman consecrated as the first female congregational minister but she felt that she should remain an Anglican.   Despite her loyalty the Church of England gave her little encouragement or support and she was sometimes banned from speaking on church premises.   She finally settled on working in a mission in London that operated only during the week.

In the twentieth century the revolutionary idea of gender equality, unheard of in any earlier society, gradually took root in the west. In time this idea infiltrated the churches.   Women's groups and a number of theologians advocated a more liberal attitude to ordaining women.   In the mid twentieth century a steady trickle of denominations changed their rules to allow women to be ministers and preachers. Until 1970 these changes seem to have come more from a desire to recognise gender equality than from a desire for women ministers or pressure from women who wished to be ministers. The number of women in the pastorate remained low and they were usually confined to small, often rural, congregations.

One factor that influenced the question of women's ordination was the ecumenical movement, which grew in importance during the twentieth century and led to a number of formal attempts to achieve unity by merger. Some efforts were successful, like the creation of the United Reformed Church. This new denomination accepted women ministers, following the Congregational Church, one of its constituent parts. In other cases the desire for unity was a delaying factor. The Methodist conference accepted that there were no theological objections to ordaining women ministers in 1939 but did not ordain women until 1974, a year after the Church of England had turned down a scheme for union. In a similar way those Anglicans who longed for a closer link with Rome saw the prospect of the ordination of women as destroying their hopes. Pope John Paul II encouraged this attitude in a letter he wrote to the Anglican Communion in 1988, stating that the ordination of women would be an insuperable block to any hope of future unity.

Most denominations that accept the ordination of women are ones that regard their ministers as preachers and pastors. Churches who regard their leaders as priests find it more difficult to accept ordained women. Those who see vicars as representing mankind to God may come to accept that a woman can take this role. But Roman Catholics and Anglo Catholics, who also see priests as representing God to their congregations, generally feel that, since Scripture and tradition portray God as masculine, only a man can represent God. The other major group that resists recognising women's abilities in leadership are conservative evangelicals, who regard the Bible as the inerrant source of all authority and are reluctant to consider non-traditional interpretations of the text. For them, as for many Roman Catholics, this attitude is part of a more general resistance to modern liberalism.

Women priests in the Anglican Church

Exceptional circumstances led to the first ordination of a woman in the Anglican Church. South China during the Second World War was a difficult time and place for the church. Large numbers of refugees were leaving Japanese occupied China for Portuguese Macao and among the refugees were 150 Christians, who needed someone to minister to them. Clergy were in short supply and Bishop R.O. Hall, of Hong Kong, found only one available candidate who had the theological training and pastoral gifts required. Li Tim-Oi (1907–1992) was a deacon. She had trained for four years in theology and worked briefly in a Church in Kowloon before she was sent to Macao. For several years a Chinese Bishop made the long journey to consecrate the bread and wine for her congregation, but after the fall of Hong Kong this became impossible; so he gave her permission to administer communion herself during the emergency. Bishop Hall, who was an Anglo-Catholic, ratified this decision but felt uncomfortable with the arrangement and spent a day alone in prayer to consider his options. He came to an unexpected conclusion; "If I could reach her physically I should ordain her priest rather than give her permission (to celebrate Communion), as this seems to me more contrary to the tradition and meaning of the ordained ministry than to ordain a woman". He considered it more irregular to have a layperson administer communion than to ordain a woman. Li Tim-Oi travelled to meet him in occupied China and he ordained her in 1944. He felt that his situation was similar to that of St Peter who, after baptising Cornelius, the first Gentile Christian, said "If God gave them the same gift (the Holy Spirit) as he gave us… who was I to think that I could oppose God" (Acts11:17). Bishop Hall knew he would be heavily criticised but considered obedience to the Holy Spirit more important than obedience to church tradition. His action originated from concern to meet a spiritual need rather than any belief in gender equality. "Her work has been remarkably successful. My judgement is that it is only exceptional women who can do this kind of work but we are going to have such exceptional women in China and such exceptional need." Events in China were to prove him right.

Although the church locally supported Bishop Hall's decision the Anglican hierarchy, in both China and in England, did not. At the end of the war Li Tim-Oi was persuaded to give up her licence as a priest in order to protect Bishop Hall from the consequences of his action. Bishop Hall regretted this and both he and Li Tim-Oi believed that giving up her licence did not change the fact she was ordained in God's eyes. She continued to serve God and the Anglican Church for the rest of her life.

Li Tim-Oi stayed in China after Mao came to power despite constant suspicion from the authorities. During the Cultural Revolution she was banished to the countryside for 're-education' and found herself caring for a different kind of flock when she was put in charge of chickens. In 1971 Li Tim-Oi left China to join relatives in Canada.

Hall's successor as Bishop of Hong Kong had asked the Anglican Communion to allow him to ordain women and in 1971 an Anglican Consultative Council gave Provinces the freedom to choose to do so. The first two women priests were ordained in Hong Kong and twenty seven years after her ordination Li Tim-Oi's vocation was finally recognised.   She continued to work as a priest in Canada until her death at the age of eighty-five.   Forty years after her ordination Li Tim-Oi was honoured at a service in Westminster Abbey, where a tribute from the Archbishop of Canterbury was read out.   Li Tim-Oi was not only honoured but also much loved and her memory is kept alive by a Foundation in her name which gives training grants to Anglican women in the developing world.   They call themselves 'The Daughters of Li Tim-Oi'.

The Feminist movement bought many changes in society and religious life.   Although there were relatively few active feminists within churches the movement gave women increased confidence.   The 1970's saw an increase in the numbers of women undertaking theological training and expressing a belief that they were called to be ministers or priests.   Increasingly it was women who felt they had a call to ministry who led the campaign for women's ordination and, unlike an earlier generation, they banded together to press their case. The Anglican Church was reluctant to consider it but from the 1970's on they had to cope with determined, and increasingly vocal, deaconesses who were prepared to push for women's ordination.

The Episcopalians in the USA officially agreed to ordain women in 1976; although three retired Bishops had jumped the gun and ordained several women priests in 1974.   Scotland was the first Anglican province in the British Isles to ordain women. The Church of England was reluctant to embrace change; despite an increasing number of theologically trained deaconesses, who felt thwarted in their call to the priesthood. Archbishop Runcie expressed support for women priests but felt Church unity was more important and at times voted against them. The opponents of women's ordination organised themselves into an alliance of disparate groups, united in their opposition to female priests. Those for and against were not divided by gender, just as many men supported the idea of women priests, there were women who sincerely believed it was wrong. In 1986 a group calling themselves Women Against the Ordination of Women was formed. The most prominent opponent was Graham Leonard, the Bishop of London, who threatened that the issue would divide the Church and drive clergy to either form a breakaway church or to turn to Roman Catholicism.

Motions in Synod to allow women priests were supported by a majority of bishops and laymen but rejected by the House of Clergy. For many this felt like a personal rejection and was very hurtful. When the motion was defeated in 1978 the best known of the deaconesses, Una Kroll, called from the public gallery "We asked for bread and you gave us a stone." Anglican women felt increasingly hurt and betrayed by this rejection of what they had to offer. In 1979 the Movement for the Ordination of Women was started and, unlike its predecessors, it was prepared to stage quiet but public demonstrations. Monica Furlong, one of the founders expressed the dilemma of those seeking to introduce change "The most frightening aspect of it was discovering how angry we were – it felt disturbing and unchristian". Journalists regarded the issue as news and gave the

MOW, and their opponents, considerable publicity.   Synod was not used to being front-page news.   In a society where gender equality was accepted in theory, though not necessarily in practice, the issue was a public embarrassment to many in the Church.

In 1981 a sop was given to the women when it was agreed they could be ordained as deacons.   Opponents hoped this would satisfy them and started talking of a permanent order of deacons, challenging the long-standing Anglican tradition of ordaining deacons as priests after a year.   But the issue did not go away and in 1992, a Measure to ordain of women was passed by General Synod having achieved the necessary two-thirds majority in all Houses, Bishops, Clergy and Laity.   In order not to divide the church special arrangements were made for opponents of women priests to be managed by 'flying bishops'.   About two hundred clergy did leave and joined the Roman Catholics, some taking their congregations with them.   Pope John Paul II welcomed them and agreed to waive the celibacy rule, so Anglican priests who were already married could be accepted as Roman Catholic priests without leaving their wives.   This decision undermined the Papacy's commitment to clerical celibacy but underlined its opposition to women priests.   The decision not to insist on the whole Church of England accepting women priests has left a continuing legacy.   Anglican churches with an Anglo-catholic or a 'Reform' theology continue to oppose women's ministry.   It is one of several issues on which there are deeply held divergences of opinion within the Anglican Communion.   At times it seems as if strongly held opinions will split the Anglican Church, as has already happened in the United States.

The first women priests in England were ordained in 1994. Reactions varied between different dioceses; only a few were unwelcoming. There are now women priests in parishes across the British Isles and they are very well accepted, except in the minority of churches who oppose them on principle. A television comedy, the Vicar of Dibley, has helped make women vicars more familiar, especially among those who never normally attend church. Women priests may still have to face opposition but they have settled into their role with enthusiasm. Susan Boys, a Canon of Christchurch in Oxford and a rural Dean, expressed this clearly; "Politics is horrible, difficult and painful but reality is great". This issue remains a source of pain for many people. For centuries the pain was felt by women who felt frustrated and rejected; now it is felt by those men and women who see their Church changing in ways they find hard to accept.

A survey in 2005 found that twenty five per cent of stipendiary clergy were female and that of these eight per cent were in more senior positions. These figures do not include the many non-stipendiary women curates who do invaluable work without receiving a salary. Women already hold some positions of authority, as Archdeacons, Canons and lecturers and women bishops have already been appointed in North America, New Zealand, Canada, Polynesia, and Scotland. In 2009 the appointment of women Bishops was agreed in principle by the Church of England, without the special provisions arranged for those who disagree when women were first ordained. When this was passed by Synod Pope Benedict XVI made it clear he would welcome those who felt they should leave the Anglican Church and would make special provision for them. A number of clergy, many already retired, have taken him up on this.

Women vicars have not revolutionised the church, nor have any of the dire predictions of the dangers of women in leadership come true. More women than men are coming forward for ordination – in time the clergy may become one of the professions where women predominate. Although, as in other professions with a preponderance of women, it is likely that men will continue to hold a majority of senior posts.

Churches where 'leadership is male'

There are still a number of churches that will not consider ordaining women. The Roman Catholic Church refuses to discuss the matter and several recent Popes have used their authority to condemn the idea; in 1994-5 the refusal to ordain women became dogma. Many conservative evangelical churches also insist that male authority must be sacrosanct. One characteristic all these churches have in common is religious conservatism and a strong rejection of the liberal ideas, and morals, of modern western society. Their opposition to women in authority has gained strength from a more general rejection of secular liberalism, which has become part of their religious identity.

As so often in the history of women, actual practice often differs from theory. As Chaves pointed out, in his study of conflicts over ordaining women in the USA, a denomination's official line on women ministers may be only loosely linked to its practice. In denominations that have accepted them, women ministers do not necessarily find themselves equal to their male counterparts. A study of Presbyterians in San Francisco found that "Women clergy do not have the choices, the mobility, the positions or the pay of their male counterparts". This is likely to be equally true in other denominations and other countries. Again it is a reflection of a secular world, which pays lip service to gender equality but where for many equal opportunities, and equal pay, remains a distant hope. This discrepancy between theory and practice is also present in churches that reject the ordination of women. Chaves pointed out that in the 1990s twenty five percent of Catholic theological students were female and, after excluding priests, eighty percent of those employed by the Roman Catholic Church were women. In 1983 Canon Law made provision for laymen and women to carry out tasks normally regarded as priestly: "When the needs of the church require and ministers are not available lay people, even though they are not lectors or acolytes, can supply certain of their functions, that is, exercise the ministry of the word, preside over liturgical prayers, confer baptism and distribute Holy Communion, in accordance with the provisions of the law." (Canon 203.3) This allows nuns to pastor many congregations who are without priests, undertaking most of the tasks that would normally be performed by a priest. As so often in history women are doing the work but are not given the authority or status that a man doing the same work would have.

The majority of feminist theology now comes from a Roman Catholic base, as they follow the example of the liberation theologians of Latin America. Opposition is less vocal among Protestants, possibly because individuals who find their own church frustrates their desire to serve can move to another more easily. For many Protestant churches this is now a historical issue rather than a burning concern. The avalanche of religious books published on the subject of women in the 1980s has become a trickle. Among Catholics feminism is still a live issue and a number of individuals and groups are campaigning for the ordination of women. A majority of Cardinals now come from the developing world, especially Africa and Latin America, and it is not clear what effect this will have. It is possible they will overturn the Church's long commitment to compulsory celibacy but seems less likely that they will challenge the even older tradition of a male priesthood.

At the beginning of the twenty first century a majority of mainstream denominations in the western world accept women in at least some leadership roles. Many Anglican parishes are now served by a female vicar and are happy with this situation. Women have more freedom to take part, and even lead, in many churches. Even half a century ago women would have felt this was beyond their wildest dream.

28. CONCLUSION

I started by asking how a religion founded by one valued women had become a patriarchal organization that devalued them?   In this book I have tried to trace this process.   In late medieval times, when the Church was at the height of its secular power, women were valued less, and restricted more, than at any other time in European history. Since that time churches have slowly developed a more positive view of women and have begun to value them and their work.   However, much of the worldwide church remains patriarchal, although this attitude is usually a reflection of the views of the society in which the church is placed.

A disabled church?

It has been said that a church which limits its women is disabled, unable to function properly, like a stroke victim crippled by paralysis down one side.   Churches that expect women to be passive and subservient are more rigid and static.   It is when the church has been a vital and growing entity that it has allowed women to be more involved.   The early church, which fully involved women in spreading the Gospel, grew astoundingly fast; as its growth slowed it began to impose more limits on women.   Faced with the pagan tribes that overwhelmed the Western Roman Empire men and women worked together and converted them to Christianity.   In contrast the male dominated mediaeval church resorted to violent action, often encouraging the torturing or killing of non-Christians and heretics. Over the past two centuries the church worldwide has grown, mirroring the growth of the early church, and again women have been fully involved in the process. A negative attitude to women and a failure to attract outsiders into the Christian faith are both symptoms of a church that has lost touch with its roots.

St Paul told Christians that they were interdependent, that the church was a body which must value all its members, since all are essential to its functioning. There have always been Christians who remembered this. It is important not to forget that almost all the women whose lives have been recounted in this book received support or encouragement from men as well as from their fellow women, and discouragement from women as well as men. There have been always been men who recognised the need to challenge patriarchal attitudes and many men who were not prepared to concede the need for general change, still encouraged individual women to express their faith and follow their calling. Male priests, ministers and Christian teachers have all encouraged the spiritual growth and practical service of women. The achievements of almost all the married women in this book were made possible by the support they were given by their husbands; just as the achievements of many men have depended on the support and help given by their wives.

Two churches

It is no wonder that Christians sometimes think in terms of two churches. One is the institutional church, Catholic, Orthodox or Protestant; the other is the informal living church of individuals from all churches who seek to follow the guidance of the Holy Spirit as they understand it as they try to obey and serve God. The two churches overlap but are never identical. The institutional Church has historically kept women subordinate but in the informal spirit-led church, the limits put on women were often ignored. The Spirit led church is one where "There is no longer Jew or Greek, there is no longer slave nor free, there is no longer male and female". Unexpected individuals are often prominent in this informal church; the most unlikely people have been called to tackle great tasks. This has been true from the beginning; the twelve Apostles, working men from an obscure province, were an unlikely group to be chosen to establish a worldwide church that would last two thousand years.

It has never been as simple as those in established churches being of the world and those outside the mainstream being of the Spirit. As Jesus said, "The wind blows where it chooses, and you hear the sound of it, but you do not know where it comes from or where it goes. So it is with everyone who is born of the Spirit." (John 3: 8.) Some of the women whose lives we have considered were loyal daughters of the Church, even if they were crossing the boundaries it had set them; others were on the fringes or were considered heretics.

Women on the margins

The debate about women priests in the Anglican (Episcopalian) Church highlighted the pain felt by women prevented from following a call to the priesthood. Many women in the Roman Catholic Church are still struggling to accept the pain of being denied the right to follow what they regard as their vocation. Over the centuries women have been hurt by restrictions that limited their service to God and their neighbours. Even more devastating has been the effect on women whose self-esteem has been damaged because they accepted the valuation put on their gender by their Church's teachings.

Modern churches are more aware of women and the need to consider their views.   But many organisations and informal groups set up by women for women, have disbanded, or now include men, and with them some of the mutual group support women have always given each other has disappeared.   Western churches often gear their teaching and activities to families; ignoring the fact that a large minority of most congregations are not based in a conventional family.   The majority of these, the unmarried, divorced, separated or widowed, are women.   Even today many churches do not offer single women the support or the teaching, they need.

Women as religious innovators

Opponents of women in leadership appear to fear that women will take over from men and try to dominate their activities.   History shows that the reverse is true.   Women were often innovators in religious practice.   Over and over again practices and organisations started by women have been taken over by men.   Advocates of male only leadership also claim it is necessary because women are more gullible.   Research has shown that gullibility is linked not to gender but to lack of education and experience.   Women are only more gullible if they are deprived of opportunities to learn and think, as almost all St Paul's female contemporaries were.   Nor are women more likely than men to stray from orthodoxy.   Men, not women, founded the majority of the Cults which have attracted people out of mainstream Christianity.

Women in leadership

Christ taught that a true leader is a servant to his people. Women may find it easier to adapt to this concept of leadership as service. They have always been at the forefront of the church's practical and pastoral care both for its members and of the poor and sick. Throughout church history women have fulfilled leadership functions for other women. They have shared their faith with women, taught both women and children and taken responsibility for their spiritual and practical care. At times they have taught men or counselled them as spiritual directors.

One pattern that comes over clearly is that when any new religious initiative began, when there were too few workers for the many tasks which needed doing, women were welcomed and allowed to undertake responsibilities that would normally be restricted to men. Later, when an organisation was established and men were available, women's involvement in those activities was limited or forbidden. This pattern appears again and again throughout church history.

Invisible women

Throughout history women have been disregarded, as if they were invisible. They have struggled against restrictions imposed by a patriarchal system and coped with criticism based solely on their gender, which occasionally spilt over into hatred. This disregard of women extended into the study of history, which has often been a study of solely male actions and experiences. Many exceptional women, and women's groups, were neglected and almost forgotten until, very recently, scholars started to rediscover them. We need to celebrate their lives and rejoice at all they contributed to Christianity and to the world.

The Apocrypha says: "Let us now sing the praises of famous men, our ancestors in their generations." (Ecclesiasticus 44: 1.) It is right to remember the many men whose faith has enriched and sometimes transformed the church. But we should also celebrate the lives of the many exceptional Christian women who have also contributed so much.

SOURCES AND FURTHER READING

Introduction

C.S.Lewis, On Reading Old Books 1944.   Republished in First and Second Things, Collins, 1985

1. Jesus, Paul and Women

The New Testament, 1st century

The Gospel of Mary, 2nd Century (This can be found on Peter Kirby's website, www. earlychristianwritings.com which is a useful source of original material)

Richard and Catherine Kroeger, I suffer Not a Woman, Baker, 1992

Alvera Mickelsen, Women, Authority and the Bible, Inter Varsity Press, 1986

2. The world where Christianity was born

The Old Testament

James B Hurley, Man and Woman in Biblical Perspective, Inter Varsity Press, 1981

Xenophon, Economics, 5th century BC.

Sophocles, Antigone, 5th Century BC.

Ben Witherington III, Women and Genesis of Christianity, Cambridge University Press, 1990

3. Women in an Underground Church

The Didache, (available on www. earlychristianwritings.com) 1st century?

Aaron Milavec, Apprenticeship in the Way of Wisdom within the apocalyptic-orientated Didache communities 50 – 70 CE, published on the internet, 2002

Deborah Rose Gaier, Paper delivered to the Society of Biblical Literature in 1996. (No longer available on the internet)

Ruth Tucker and Walter Liefeld, Daughters of the Church, Zondervan, 1986

Eusebius, A History of the Church, 4th Century

D S Potter and D J Mattingly Ed., Notes on Life, Death and Entertainment in the Roman Empire, University of Michigan Press, 1999.

Arthur Frederick Ide, Woman as Priest, Bishop and Laity in the Early Church to 440 AD, Ide House, 1984

Karen Jo Torjesen, When Women were Priests, Harper, 1993

Gospel of Philip (available on www. earlychristianwritings.com) 2nd/3rd century

ww.markroberts.com.htmfiles/resources/jesusmarried reviews the evidence on Jesus' alleged marriage.

4. "Punishment attaches to the mere name "

FF Bruce, The Spreading Flame, Paternoster, 1958.

Henry Chadwick, The Early Church, Penguin, 1967

Jean Comby, How to Read church History, SCM Press, 1985

Eusebius, The History of the Church, 4th Century

J Stevenson, The New Eusebius, SPCK, 1987

5. "By chastity men and women can become as the angels"

St Athanasius, Life of St Anthony, 4th Century

F F Bruce, The Spreading Flame, Paternoster, 1958.

Henry Chadwick, The Early Church, Penguin, 1967

Gillian Cloke, This Female Man of God, Routledge, 1995

Jean Comby, How to Read Church History, SCM Press, 1985

Helen Wadell, The Desert Fathers, Constable 1936

The Desert Fathers: Sayings of the Early Christian Monks, translated by Benedicta Ward, Penguin Classics, 2003

Pseudo Athanasius, Life of the Blessed and Holy Syncletica.

St Jerome, Against Jovinian and Against Helvidius, 4th –5th Century (available on www.newadvent.org/fathers)

Robert Markus, essay in The Oxford History of Christianity', Oxford University Press, 1990.

Garry Wills, St Augustine, Weidenfeld and Nicolson, 1999

6. Theologians, Philosophers and Women

Henry Chadwick, The Early Church, (revised edition) Penguin books, 1993

Clement of Alexandria, Paedagogus, Book 1, (available on www.earlychristianwritings.com), 2nd Century

Eusebius, History of the Church, 4th Century.

Origen, Commentaries, (some of these are available on www.earlychristianwritings.com), 3rd Century

J Stevenson (Revised by W H C Frend), A New Eusibius, SPCK, 1987

Tertullian, To His Wife II, 8, 6-8, 2nd – 3rd Century (quoted in Jean Comby, How to Read Church History, SCM Press, 1985)

7. The Authority of the Clergy

St Ignatius, Letter to the Smyrnaeans, (In Early Christian Writings, translated by Maxwell Staniforth, Penguin, 1968), 2nd Century

FF Bruce, the Spreading Flame, Paternoster Press, 1958

Henry Chadwick, The Early Church (revised edition), Penguin books, 1993

Tertullian, 'On the Soul' 9. (quoted in A New Eusibius) 2nd – 3rd Centuries

J Stevenson (revised by WHC Frend) A New Eusebius, SPCK, 1987)

Eusebius, History of the Church, 4th Century

Peter Brown, Body and Society – Men, Women and Sexual Renunciation in the Early Church, Faber and Faber, 1989

Didascalia Apostolorum, (available on www. Earlychristianwritings .com), 3rd century.

8. Church and State

Theodosian Code quoted in Jean Comby, How to Read Church History, SCM Press, 1985

Valerie Abrahamsen essay in The Oxford History of Christianity, Ed. John McManners, Oxford, 1996

J N Hillgarth, Ed., Christianity and Paganism 350 – 750, University of Pennsylvania Press. 1986

9. "Who so surpassed her sex."

Robert Markus and Valerie Abrahamsen in The Oxford History of Christianity, Oxford University Press, 1990.

Peter Brown, Body and Society - Men, Women and Sexual Renunciation in the Early Church, Faber and Faber, 1988.

Palladius, Lausiac History, 420.

St Jerome, Letters, (available on www.newadvent.org/fathers) 4th –5th Century.

St John Chrysostom, letters to Olympias, 5th Century (www.newadvent.org/fathers)

Gregory of Nyssa, Life of Macrina, 4th Century (available on www.newadvent.org/fathers)

Patricia Ranft, Women and Spiritual Equality in the Church, Macmillan, 2000

10. The Fall and Rise of Rome

FF Bruce, The 'Spreading Flame, Paternoster,1958.

RW Southern, Western Society and the Church in the Middle Ages, Pelican, 1970

Barbara Mitchell, Anglo-Saxon Double Monasteries, History Today Vol. 45 Issue 10.

11. The Church and the Barbarians

FF Bruce, The 'Spreading Flame, Paternoster, 1958

Patricia Ranft, Women & the Religious Life in Pre-modern Europe, Macmillan 1996

Rudolf, Life of St Leoba, 836 AD (available on www.Fordham. edu/halsal/basis/leoba)

12. Reforming Monks and Popes

FF Bruce, The 'Spreading Flame, Paternoster,1958.

RW Southern, Western Society and the Church in the Middle Ages, Pelican, 1970

Patricia Ranft, Women and the Religious Life in Pre-modern Europe, Macmillan, 1996

Vivian Green, A New History of Christianity, Sutton 1996

13. A Triumph for Misogyny

Anne Llewellyn Barstow, Married Priests and the Reforming Papacy: the Eleventh Century Debates, The Edwin Mellen Press 1982.

Ruth Tucker and Walter Liefeld, Daughters of the Church, Zondervan 1987

Leigh Churchchill, The age of Knights, and Friars, Popes and Reformers, Authentic Media 2004.

Vivian Green, A New History of Christianity, Sutton 1996

14. Gifted Nuns and New Religious Houses

Anne Llewellyn Barstow, Married Priests and the Reforming Papacy: the Eleventh Century Debates, The Edwin Mellen Press 1982.

Ruth Tucker and Walter Liefeld, Daughters of the Church, Zondervan 1987

Leigh Churchchill, The age of Knights, and Friars, Popes and Reformers, Authentic Media 2004

Vivian Green, A New History of Christianity, Sutton 1996

Fiona Maddocks, Hildegard of Bingen the Woman of Her Age, Headline 2001

Gottfried and Theoderic, Life of the Holy Hildegard. Between 1180 and 1190

Patricia Ranft, Women and the Religious Life in Pre-modern Europe, Macmillan 1996

R W Southern, Western Society and the Church in the Middle Ages' Penguin 1970

15. Powerful Men and Confined Women

RW Southern, Western Society and the Church in the Middle Ages, Penguin, 1970.

Vivian Green, A New History of Christianity, Sutton 1996

Mary T Malone, Women and Christianity, Columbia 2001

Dyan Elliot, Proving Woman: Female Spirituality and Inquisitorial Culture in the Late Middle Ages, Princeton University Press 2004

Leigh Churchill, The Age of Knights and Friars, Popes and Reformers, Authentic Media 2004

16. Mystics Outside the Cloister

RW Southern, Western Society and the Church in the Middle Ages, Penguin 1970.

Mary T Malone, Women and Christianity, Columbia 2001

Julian of Norwich, Revelation of Divine Love

The Book of Margery Kempe, 14 century, translated by B A Windeatt, Penguin books 1985

17. Heretics and Outsiders

RW Southern, Western Society and the Church in the Middle Ages, Penguin 1970

Ruth Tucker and Walter Liefeld, Daughters of the Church, Zondervan 1987

Malcolm Lambert, The Cathars, Blackwell Publishing 1998

Emmanuel Le Roy Ladurie, Montaillou, translated by Barbara Bray, Penguin 1980

Heinrich Kramer and Jacob Sprenger, Malleus Maleficarum, 1487

Leigh Churchill, The Age of Knights and Friars, Popes and Reformers, Authentic Media 2004

Margaret Aston, Lollards and Reformers: Images and Liturgy in late medieval religion, Hambledon Press 1984

Shannon McSheffry, 'Gender and Heresy: Women and Men in Lollard Communities 1420 - 1530, University of Pennsylvania Press 1995

Chaucer, The Canterbury Tales, translated by Nevill Coghill, Penguin books.

18. Women in the Reformation

Erasmus of Rotterdam, Colloquies 1519

Walter Lazareth, Luther on the Christian Home, Muhlerberg Press, 1960

Jane Dempsey Douglass, Women, Freedom and Calvin, Westminster Press, 1985

Ruth Tucker and Walter Liefeld, Daughters of the Church, Zondervan, 1987

The Examinations of Anne Askew, 1546

The Book of Martyrs by John Foxe, 1559 (English version 1563)

Patrick Collinson, essay in The Oxford History of Christianity, Ed. John McManners, Oxford, 1996

19. The Counter Reformation

St Teresa of Avila – My life 1562-5; The Way of Perfection. 1565

Shirley Du Boulay, Teresa of Avila, Hodder and Stoughton, 1991

Mary T Malone, Women and Christianity Vol. 3, Columba Press, 2003

Patricia Ranft, Women and Spiritual Equality in Christian Tradition, St Martins Press, 1998

20. Women in Protestant Sects

Bonnelyn Young Kunze, Margaret Fell and the rise of Quakerism, Macmillan, 1994

Isabel Ross, Margaret Fell, Mother of Quakerism, William Sessions Book Trust, 1984

Ruth Tucker and Walter Liefeld, Daughters of the Church, Zondervan, 1987

Mary T Malone, Women and Christianity Vol. 3, Columba Press, 2003

CP Claser, Anabaptists – A Social History, Cornell University Press, 1972

Aston Ed., Crisis in Europe 1500-1660 (Essay by Keith Thomas) Routledge and Kegan Paul, 1965

21. The Fires of Revival

Susanna Wesley Complete Writings, Ed. Charles Wallace, Oxford University Press, 1997

Paul Wesley Chilcote, John Wesley and Women Preachers of Early Methodism, Metuchan American Library Association, 1991.

Earl Kent Brown, Women of Mr Wesley's Methodism, Lewiston E Mellen Press, 1983

Alexander Allen, Jonathan Edwards: The First Critical Biography, 1889 (Republished by Yale 2007)

Jonathan Edwards, Sermons and Discourses

22. Abolitionists and Feminists

Anne Stott, Hannah More, the First Victorian, Oxford University Press, 2003

Women Romantic Poets 1785-1832 Selected by Jennifer Breen, JM Dent and Sons, 1992.   (This anthology includes three of Hannah More's poems.)

John Pollock, Wilberforce, Kingsway, 1977

Mary T Malone, Women and Christianity Vol. 3, Columba Press, 2003

23. Evangelical Faith and Social Action

Nancy Boyd, Josephine Butler, Octavia Hill and Florence Nightingale: Three Women Who Changed Their World, Macmillan, 1982

Roy Hattersley, Blood and Fire: William and Catherine Booth and Their Salvation Army, Little Brown and Company, 1999

R Tucker and W Liefeld Daughters of the Church, Zondervan, 1989

Mary T Malone, Women and Christianity Vol. 3, Columba, 2003

24. To the Ends of the Earth

Ruth Tucker, Guardians of the Great Commission, Zondervan, 1988

Mary T Malone, Women and Christianity Vol. 3, Columba, 2003

JC Pollock, Hudson Taylor and Maria, McGraw Hill, 1962

W P Livingstone, Mary Slessor of Calabar, Hodder and Stoughton, 1917

Irwin T Hyatt, Our Ordered Lives Confess: Three Nineteenth Century American Missionaries in East Shantung, Harvard University Press, 1976

Lottie Moon, Selected letters, available on ibm.org/main/give/page. asp?storyI=5524

Phyllis Thompson, Capturing Voices (Count it all Joy in the USA) Hodder and Stoughton, 1978

Helen Roseveare, Give Me This Mountain, Inter-Varsity Press,1966

25. Women in Non-western Churches

John and Ellen Webster, The Church and Women in the Third World, Westminster Press, 1985

Ruth Tucker and Walter Liefeld, Daughters of the Church, Zondervan, 1986

Mercy Oduyoye & Musimbi Kanyoro, The Will to Arise: Women, Tradition and the Church in Africa, Orbis books, 1992

Alan Hunter and Kim-Kwong Chan, Protestantism in Contemporary China, Cambridge University Press, 1993

Daniel Bays, Ed. Christianity in China from the Eighteenth Century to the Present, Stanford University Press, 1996

26. Woman's Place or Woman's Liberation?

Mary Daly, The Church and the Second Sex, Harper Colphon, 1975
Rosemary Ruether Radford, Women and Redemption, SCM Press, 1998
Elaine Storky, What's Right with Feminism, SPCK, 1985
Pamela Dicky Young, Feminist Theology/Christian Theology, Ausberg Fortress, 1980

27. Ordaining Women

Mark Chaves, Ordaining Women, Harvard University Press, 1997.
Monica Furlong, A Dangerous Delight, Women and Power in the Church, SCM Press, 1991
Miranda Threlfall-Holmes. Furlong Survey, 2007

28. Conclusion

Kristin Aune, Single Women: a Challenge to the Church, Paternoster Press, 2002

	1st Century
Powers	Augustus, Emperor 27 BC-14 AD
	Tiberius, Emperor 14-37AD
	Nero, Emperor 54-68
	Domitian, Emperor 81-96
Events	c5 BC Birth of Christ
	c25-28 AD Christ's ministry, death and resurrection
	Apostolic Church
	c64 St Peter and St Paul martyred
	Most of New Testament written
People	The Apostles,
	Mary Mother of Jesus,
	Mary Magdalene
	Phoebe, Priscilla, Junias, Lydia
	Ignatius, St c35-107
	2nd Century
Powers	Marcus Aurelius, Emperor 161-180
Events	Christianity illegal
	Intermittent persecution and martyrdoms
People	Tertullian c155-c225
	Blandina d. 177
	Clement of Alexandria d. c215

	3rd Century
Powers	Diocletian , Emperor 245-313
Events	Church leaders and ordinary Christians martyred
People	Perpetua, St d. 202
	Origen c185-253
	Cyprian, St c200-258
	4th century
Powers	Constantine , Emperor c280-337
	Julian the Apostate , Emperor 361-363
Events	313 Christianity decreed to be a legal religion.
	Eusibius writes the first history of Christianity
	337 Emperor Constantine baptised.
	361 Julian tried to reintroduce paganism
	363 Christianity reinstated by Julian's successor
People	Marcella 325-410
	Macrina 330-379
	Jerome, St c340-420
	Paula 347-404
	Augustine of Hippo, St 354-430
	Olympias 361-408
	5th Century
Powers	Theodosius II , Emperor 415-450
Events	410 Rome Sacked by Goths
	Start of Anglo Saxon immigration into England

People	Patrick, St c385-461
	Pulcheria, St 399-453
	Bridget, St c451-525
	6th Century
Powers	Pope Gregory the Great 590-604
Events	Foundations laid for Papal power
	Augustine sent to England to convert the Anglo-Saxons
People	Augustine of Canterbury, St d. 604
	7th Century
Powers	Mohammed born c570-632
Events	Rise of Islam
People	Hilda of Whitby 614-680
	8th Century
Powers	Charlemagne 768-814
Events	718 Boniface commissioned to convert the heathen in Northern Europe
People	Bede c673-735
	Boniface, St c675-754
	Leoba 710-780
	9th Century
Powers	Alfred the Great, King of Wessex, 871-900
Events	From 800 Vikings invaded British Isles, and other parts of Europe, and soon began to settle.

	10th Century
	10th Century
Events	910 First reformed monastery founded at Cluny
	High point of Muslim culture, especially in Spain
	11th Century
Powers	Holy Roman Emperor Henry III 1039-1056
	William the Conqueror 1066-87
	Pope Gregory VII 1073-85
	Pope Urban II 1088-99
Events	First European settlers in America under Leif Ericsson
	1046 Reforming Pope appointed
	1054 Great Schism between Rome and Orthodox Churches
	1074 Clerical celibacy imposed
	1096-99 First Crusade
	12th Century
Powers	Henry II 1154-89, Ruler of England and Aquitaine
Events	Universities founded in Paris and Oxford
	Beguine movement started
People	Heloise 1098-1164
	Hildegard of Bingen 1098-1179
	13th Century
Powers	Pope Gregory IX 1227-41

Events	1203 Fourth Crusade sacked Constantinople
People	Clare of Assisi, St 1194-1253
	Elizabeth of Hungary, St 1207-31
	Peter de Valdes b.1218
	Thomas Aquinas, St 1225-74
	14th Century
Powers	Pope Urban IV 1378-89
Events	1304 Papacy moves to Avignon
	1378 Return of Papacy to Rome and election of a French anti-pope leads to the Western Schism
People	Marguerite de Porete d.1310
	Brigitta of Sweden, St 1303-73
	John Wycliffe 1320-84
	Catherine of Siena, St c1347-80
	15th Century
Powers	Pope Innocent VIII 1484-92
Events	1417 Western Schism ends
	1448 Printing press invented
	1453 Fall of Constantinople to a Muslim Army
	1487 Manual on witchcraft published
People	Julian of Norwich c1342-1416
	Margery Kempe b. 1373

	16th Century
Powers	Henry VIII, King of England 1509-47
	Charles V, Holy Roman Emperor and King of Spain 1516-1556
	Mary I, Queen of England 1553-58
	Phillip II, King of Spain 1556-98
	Elizabeth I, Queen of England 1558-1603
Events	1517 Luther posts 95 Theses on a church door starting the Reformation
	1534 England breaks with the Pope
	1545 Council of Trent and start of Counter Reformation
	Elizabeth establishes inclusive church in England but RC priests and collaborators persecuted
People	Martin Luther 1483-1546
	Anne Askew 1521-46
	Teresa of Avila, St 1514-82
	Margaret Clitherow, St 1556-86
	17th Century
Powers	James I (& VI) King of Britain1603-25
	Gustavus Adolphus, King of Sweden 1611-1632
Events	1611 King James Bible published
	1618-48 Thirty years War devastates Germany
	1620 Mayflower sails to America
	1643-49 English Civil War

People	Mary Ward 1585-1645
	Louise de Marillac 1591-1660
	Anne Hutchinson 1591-1643
	Mary Dyer 1611-60
	Margaret Fell 1614-1702
	Susanna Wesley 1670-1742
	18th Century
Powers	George III, King of Britain 1760-1820
	President George Washington 1789-97
Events	1738 John Wesley starts Methodist movement
	1776-89 American War of Independence
	1789 French Revolution
	1793 William Carey sets out for India
People	Sarah Edwards 1710-58
	Hannah More 1745-1833
	Mary Wollstonecraft 1759-97
	19th Century
Powers	Napoleon Bonaparte 1804-15
	Victoria Queen of Britain 1837-1901
	Pope Pius IX 1846-1878
	Abraham Lincoln 1861-1865
Events	1805 First order of missionary nuns founded
	1807 Abolition of Slave Trade in UK
	1833 Abolition of Slavery in UK and its overseas

	possessions
	1861-1865 American Civil War
	1864 Pope attacks modern ideas, in 'Syllabus of Errors'
	1878 Salvation Army founded
	Campaigns for women's rights to vote and to academic education in Western countries
People	Ann-Marie Javouhey 1779-1851
	Sojourner Truth c1790-1883
	Sarah Grimke 1792-1873 Angelina Grimke 1805-79
	Phoebe Palmer 1807-74
	Antoinette Brown 1825-1921
	Josephine Butler 1828-1906
	Catherine Booth 1829-90
	Octavia Hill 1838-1912
	Charlotte Moon 1840-1912
	Bernadette Soubirous, St 1844-79
	Mary Slessor 1848-1915
	Pandita Ramabai 1858-1922
	Therese of Lisieux, St 1873-1897
	20th Century
Powers	President Franklin D Roosevelt 1932-45
	Fuhrer Adolf Hitler 1934-45
	Chairman Mao Ze-dong 1949-76
	Pope John Paul II 1978-2005

Events	1914-1918 World War I
	1917 Russian Revolution
	1939-1945 World War II
	1949 Communists take power in China
	1976 Episcopalian women ordained in US
	1989 First Episcopalian woman bishop in USA
	1992 Church of England agree to Women priests
People	Maude Royden 1876-1956
	Mildred Cable 1878-1952
	Joy Ridderhof 1903-84
	Li Tim Oi 1907-1992
	Helen Roseveare b 1925
	21st Century
Powers	Pope Benedict XVI 2005-
Events	Increasing use of indiscriminate violence by militant Islamists provokes violent Western response
	2006 First woman Archbishop in USA
	2009 Church of England agree to Women bishops

ACKNOWLEDGEMENTS

I would like to thank all the people who helped me with this book. My sister, Christine Hogg, patiently read several drafts; without her encouragement it might never have got this far. Andrew Criddle, Jonathan Ingleby, Jen Lovering, Olive Rogers and Barbara Ward kindly read all or part of the manuscript, corrected errors and suggested improvements. Any remaining errors are my responsibility. I would like to thank the Rev. Canon Christopher Hall for talking to me about his Father, Bishop R. O. Hall and Li Tim-Oi and, Rev. Canon Susan Boyes for giving me an insider's view of the ordination of women in the Anglican Church. Finally I would like to thank the staff of the libraries I used in researching this book: Bristol City Library, Bristol University Library and Trinity College Library, Bristol.

INDEX